Using Computers
in Archaeology

Using Computers in Archaeology

A Practical Guide

Shannon P. McPherron
University of North Carolina at Greensboro

Harold L. Dibble
University of Pennsylvania

McGraw-Hill
Mayfield

Boston   Burr Ridge, IL   Dubuque, IA   Madison, WI   New York
San Francisco   St. Louis   Bangkok   Bogotá   Caracas   Kuala Lumpur
Lisbon   London   Madrid   Mexico City   Milan   Montreal   New Delhi
Santiago   Seoul   Singapore   Sydney   Taipei   Toronto

McGraw-Hill Higher Education

A Division of The McGraw-Hill Companies

Library of Congress Cataloging-in-Publication Data

McPherron, Shannon P.
  Using computers in archaeology : a practical guide / Shannon P. McPherron,
  Harold L. Dibble.
    p. cm.
  Includes index.
  ISBN 0-7674-1735-6
  1. Archaeology—Data processing. I. Dibble, Harold Lewis. II. Title.

CC80.4 .M37 2001
930.1′0285—dc21   2001054643

1 2 3 4 5 6 7 8 9 0 DOC/DOC 0 9 8 7 6 5 4 3 2 1

Sponsoring editor, Phil Butcher; *production editor,* Jennifer Mills; *manuscript editor,* Tom Briggs; *design manager* and *cover designer,* Susan Breitbard; *text designer,* Glenda King; *art manager,* Robin Mouat; *illustrators,* J&J Waller, Cristin Yancey; *manufacturing manager,* Pam Augspurger. This text was set in 10/13 Janson by Thompson Type and printed on 50# Williamsburg Offset by R. R. Donnelley & Sons.

www.mhhe.com

To our respective parents

Contents

Preface

When we mentioned to colleagues that we were writing a textbook on computer applications in archaeology, some of them immediately replied, "What? Are you crazy? It will be out of date before it hits the shelves." The computer industry, which produces both software (programs) and hardware (the machines themselves), does indeed move so fast that it hardly seems worth even trying to learn the "latest"—by the time you learn it, it is out of date. John Dvorak, a commentator on the computer industry and host of a radio show dedicated to the topic, used to close each week's show with "Remember, tune in next week, when everything you learned today will be obsolete."

While we acknowledge the fast pace of change in this field, we believe that there are certain fundamentals in how technology is used in archaeology that have changed very little in decades. Yes, we use different computers today: They are faster than ever before, hold more data than ever before, and connect to an increasing number of specialized devices. Software changes rapidly as well, with regard to its sophistication, complexity, and, in most cases, ease of use. Nevertheless, we still use our total station in exactly the same way to survey, map, and piece provenience artifacts in our Paleolithic sites. We continue to put our data into databases, and while the specific database software changes, the basic considerations in organizing the data and tracking down and eliminating errors remain the same. We still make the same kinds of maps, analyze our measurements and observations, and produce monographic site reports when we are done. But we can work faster now, and often we can accomplish with a single click of a mouse what used to take several complicated steps. Like everything else technological, from cars to airplanes to vacuum cleaners, things get more complicated and easier to work with at the same time. Certain fundamentals, however, remain the same.

Thus, we have tried to write a textbook that focuses on the basic principles that all archaeologists face when trying to apply information technologies to their work. Of course, we realize as well that the future of information technologies will bring us capabilities that we cannot yet imagine or even perceive a need for. We would be foolish, therefore, to think that even a book on funda-mentals would last forever.

The subtitle of this book is *A Practical Guide*, and we should define what we mean by "practical." Let's begin, though, by discussing what we do *not* mean. We know that some people would really like to have a book that offers practical advice on which computer is best for the field, or what brands of electronic calipers are available, or even which button to press to send data from a total station to a computer. We try to avoid that kind of practical information, how-ever, for the reason just given: The technology changes too rapidly, and this type of book would be obsolete not just before it hit the shelves but even before we could finish writing it. Moreover, there are many resources already available for that kind of information, from product reviews to manuals.

Perhaps more obviously, as the word "practical" suggests, we do not cover highly specialized applications that would be of limited use for most archaeolo-gists. Exciting new developments occur virtually every day, but not all of them will find their way into standard archaeological work. Sometimes they require too much of an investment in training or equipment; other times they ultimately turn out to be more flash than substance. From our point of view, it is almost impossible to write a textbook that keeps up with such developments. What we do offer, however, is a series of Web-based descriptions of current projects that utilize such new technologies. These descriptions, written by the developers of those projects themselves, will continue to change and grow in the future. By being published on the Web, these examples of exciting new applications can stay current.

Okay, enough on what we do *not* mean by "practical." What do we mean, then? First, we mean things that are useful to a large number of archaeological applications. All archaeologists deal with data of some sort, which means a dis-cussion of database concepts is highly relevant. All field archaeologists are con-cerned with mapping and point proveniencing. We all have to be concerned with images of our finds or of our excavations, and we are all expected to report our results. So, these are among the topics that we cover. For each of these topics, we present and discuss what we believe are the fundamental concepts necessary to develop an effective and efficient application based on computer technology.

The level of detail and specificity will vary. Some of the concepts are in themselves rather abstract (e.g., how data are stored in a computer) or theoreti-cal (e.g., how to build efficient relations among database tables), and some are extremely down-to-earth (e.g., how to construct a permanent datum on a site). We present just enough of the theory so that you, the reader, can actually design and manage an application yourself. Just as you do not have to be a mechanic to learn how to operate a car, you do not have to understand everything about a computer to use it effectively. We tell you only what you need to know to get by in a variety of situations. Along the way we pass on some of the practical tricks that we have learned by doing this kind of work for many years.

For some readers, the topics covered in this book will seem intimidating at first glance. Computers, and especially numbers, provoke a certain level of anxiety in some archaeologists. Some students have even said that the reason they went into archaeology in the first place was because they were not good enough with numbers to pursue a "real science." Keep in mind, however, that we are not trying to make "quant(itative) jocks" out of anyone, and we do not even touch on statistical analysis. Our concern here is with how to use computers in archaeological applications. It is true that computers use numbers, and occasionally we do have to cover a little of the mathematical basis of what is happening. In fact, however, what is usually involved is more logic than math, and when we deal with a mathematical problem, we walk you through it with plenty of examples.

There is sometimes a layer of mystique surrounding many computer applications, a mystique made worse by technical jargon. We all know someone who can spew forth computer acronyms and buzzwords. Fortunately, we do not like computer technobabble any more than you do, and we do not like it when it is used to make something that is relatively simple appear to be much more complex. While we define clearly some of the more important terms used in computing, we also avoid jargon where possible. By demystifying what is involved in using computers, we can provide you with a better understanding of the options that are readily available to you. Also, there are many books, textbooks and otherwise, that cover in much more detail some of the topics addressed here.

For the most part this book is organized according to the logical steps involved in carrying out a standard archaeological field project. As every archaeology student learns, these steps include development of a research design, survey and/or excavation, analysis, and presentation. Our focus here is on particular aspects of these steps.

Chapter 1 introduces the fundamentals of databases, one of the most basic and far-reaching aspects of computer applications. As we said, all archaeologists deal with data, but not all of them know how to deal with it effectively and efficiently. Today's database programs are very powerful and can handle enormous quantities of data. But data storage is not the goal; rather, the goal is to be able to work with the data easily and quickly. To do this requires careful consideration of how you will design the database. This is always the first step of any successful project.

Chapter 2 is the first of several chapters dealing with the basics of using computers and computer-assisted instruments in fieldwork. In this chapter we discuss basic equipment used to collect field data, which include both point provenience data and topographic data. Our focus is on two of the more common types of equipment: total stations and geographic positioning systems. Chapter 3 presents many of the issues that are involved in actually setting up a site or survey area. This is followed by a discussion in Chapter 4 of how to make site maps and in Chapter 5 of how to point provenience artifacts during excavation.

Once you have excavated, you have to analyze and photograph your objects. Chapter 6 returns to the subject of database design and then discusses how to integrate electronic instrumentation into your analysis project. Chapter 7 examines some of the issues involved in acquiring and storing bit-mapped digital images of artifacts or other subjects.

In Chapter 8 we present an example, focused on database organization, that brings all of these concepts together.

Chapter 9, on Geographic Information Systems (GIS), focuses on one way of integrating various kinds of data, including field provenience data, analytical (or laboratory) data, and images. A GIS is an important new application in many different disciplines, but it is particularly well suited to archaeological work.

In Chapter 10 we address some of the prospects and problems in publishing archaeological reports in digital format, which includes media such as CDs and the Internet. This is an area in which things are changing rapidly, and few standards have emerged. The ability to publish not only text but also, and perhaps more importantly, data electronically will likely change how archaeology is done.

Finally, Chapter 11 is a guide to getting ready for a field project. There are a number of practical considerations to be addressed when taking computer equipment in the field. Among other topics, we discuss backup strategies and ways to power your computers and electronic devices.

ACKNOWLEDGMENTS

Over the years, we have profited greatly from the comments, criticisms, insights, and suggestions made by students and colleagues who have attempted to use our computer systems, at our own and other archaeological sites, to solve various archaeological problems. Your help has always been greatly appreciated. With regard to this book, we would like to thank Jan Beatty for her support and encouragement. Special thanks go as well to Jen Mills and the McGraw-Hill staff for putting this book together. We would also like to thank Marie Soressi, Daphne Katranides, John Rick, Dana Jensen, and the anonymous reviewers for their helpful comments and edits, and Don Seigrist (ESSCO) and Topcon Corporation for their help over the years with the total station equipment.

1 The Fundamentals of Data and Databases

Data can be many different things to different people and to different research needs. Data can also be of several different formats or structures. In the early days of archaeological computing, almost all data were converted into numeric format, primarily because of memory limitations of the machines and analytical limitations of the software. A stone tool described as a "single side-scraper," for instance, would be converted to a type number 9 and stored that way. But things have changed quite a bit, and computers now can handle many different, and sometimes very specialized, data formats. The trick is not how to get different data formats into the computer; rather, it is how to integrate data of different formats so that they interact seamlessly. For most applications this is the function of the database.

Many applications can be used to store data. Examples of specific database software include Access, Paradox, and Oracle. But these are by no means the only software that can store and manipulate data. Depending on the application, data can also be stored in various spreadsheet programs (e.g., Excel, Quattro Pro, Lotus), in word processor or simple text files, or as files in themselves, as is often the case when storing images. In fact, most archaeological projects use all of these.

We do not claim that there is only one right way to handle archaeological data. The most important criterion for choosing one program over another, or one database design over another, is its effectiveness in getting the job done. This, of course, has to be balanced against the level of expertise of the people running the project and the resources available.

To understand the practical aspects of archaeological databasing, it is important to understand the structure of database design and the individual components of a database. As in all disciplines, archaeology included, the principles of database design are constantly being revised and refined. Here we present basic database principles, employing the most commonly used terminology.

1

RECORDS, FIELDS, AND VALUES

To understand basic database design, it is perhaps easiest to start with spreadsheets. Almost everyone has worked with these kinds of programs, so the fundamental concepts should be relatively clear. A spreadsheet is, in a sense, much like the standard archaeological grid system used to identify excavation units, with rows going across (usually identified with numbers) and columns going down (usually identified with letters). The intersection of a specific row and a specific column is a *cell*. In a spreadsheet used as a database, each row represents a *record*, each column represents a *field*, and each cell contains *values*.

Records

Let's talk about each of those concepts for a moment, beginning with what constitutes a record. Most often a record will represent an object, so that each object in the collection is represented in the database by only one record, and each record reflects only one object. We can call this a one-to-one relationship between the objects and records, and we can think of the objects as being individual artifacts.

As an example, let's set up a simple spreadsheet database for a collection of stone tools (see Table 1.1). Each artifact will be represented by a record (or row) in the spreadsheet, and for each artifact we want to record a number of observations. Each of these observations will be a separate field, and each field will be represented by a specific column. In this example we have five records of five artifacts and four fields.

A one-to-one relationship between objects and records is easy to understand, but it is not always appropriate. There are also one-to-many and many-to-one relationships. In a one-to-many relationship between objects and records, each object may be represented by more than one database record. This can be desirable under certain circumstances—for example, when recording the provenience of objects. Assume that we are point proveniencing within a global Cartesian system of X (from west to east), Y (from south to north), and Z (depth below datum). For each object we recover, we want to record the number of the object (its ID) and its X, Y, and Z coordinates. If we were to take one provenience measure for each object, the result would be a simple one-to-one relationship like the one shown in Table 1.2.

We may, however, want to record several points on an object, as a way of recording either the orientation of the object (by proveniencing both ends of it) or the overall outline of the object as it was found in the ground. In this case, we would have more than one set of X, Y, and Z coordinates for a single object, as shown in Table 1.3. In this case artifact 1 is recorded with two points, and artifact 2 is recorded with three. Thus, we have a one-to-many relationship

TABLE 1.1	A one-to-one database		
ID	Type	Length	Weight
1	Scraper	58.2	65
3	Point	46.3	35
4	Flake	64.7	77
6	Core	57.0	65
8	Scraper	65.0	49

TABLE 1.2   One provenience measure per object

ID	X	Y	Z
1	12.544	14.232	−5.42
2	13.543	14.475	−5.50
3	12.751	13.875	−5.34
4	12.780	14.003	−5.65

TABLE 1.3   Multiple provenience measurements per object (one-to-many relationship)

ID	X	Y	Z
1	12.544	14.232	−5.42
1	12.553	14.235	−5.47
2	12.751	13.875	−5.34
2	12.760	14.853	−5.39
2	12.761	14.845	−5.38

TABLE 1.4   Measurement table (one-to-many relationship)

ID	Edge Location	Retouch Type	Length
1	Right	Scraper	2.47
2	Left	Scraper	3.42
2	Distal	Notch	1.53
3	Right	Bifacial	6.61
3	Left	Denticulate	4.14

between objects and records, and it is not an object that constitutes each record but rather the provenience points themselves.

Another example of a one-to-many relationship might occur if we were interested in making observations on each of the retouched edges of stone tools (see Table 1.4). Some stone tools are retouched on only one edge, others on two, and perhaps others on three or more. Suppose we want to record the location of the retouch, the type of retouch, and the length along the edge that the retouch includes. The table might look like that shown in Table 1.4, with each retouched edge constituting a record. In this example, artifact 1 has only one retouched edge, and thus one record in the table. Artifacts 2 and 3, however, have two retouched edges each, and thus are represented by two records each.

The opposite, a many-to-one relationship, occurs frequently as well, especially when objects are aggregated during excavation. A common example of this is when artifacts are collected in spits or lots, in which case they share both provenience and identifier. Let's assume that an excavation has a meter-square grid system and that each square is divided into four quadrants, designated A, B, C, and D. The excavation strategy is to dig one quadrant at a time down 5 centimeters; then all of the recovered artifacts from each 5-centimeter level of each

TABLE 1.5   Small flakes collected in lots (many-to-one relationship)

Square	Quad	Depth	Number of Flakes	Weight
A16	A	–5.50	32	123
A16	B	–5.50	16	102
A16	C	–5.50	43	132
A16	D	–5.50	20	86

quadrant are bagged together; later, the contents of the bag are counted and weighed. Table 1.5 shows what the resulting table might look like, with each spit or lot treated as a single record even though each contains several objects.

As you can see, there is no reason to insist on there being a one-to-one relationship between objects and database records. Later in this chapter (and in subsequent chapters), we will discuss some of the situations in which each of these different kinds of structures may be more or less appropriate and some of the limitations of each. Before we do that, let's turn our attention to the fields that we can define and the values that they will contain.

Fields

In an analytical database fields are often thought of as variables, or observations, and there are certain issues involved with how to represent them in a computer database. First, the values entered in the fields of a single row must all correspond to observations of a particular record. So, in our example, the X of 12.544, the Y of 14.232, and the Z of –5.42 refer to those respective coordinates of artifact 1 (see Table 1.6, part A). If we somehow lose the "physical" correspondence between the rows and columns, then the integrity of the database will be lost as well. This is easy to do accidentally in a spreadsheet. Suppose you want to sort your data by depth (Z), so you select that column and tell the program to sort in ascending order. What this table is telling us now is that artifact 1 has an X of 12.544, a Y of 14.232, and a Z of –5.34, which is wrong (see Table 1.6, part B). If you sort only that one column, the other columns will remain unchanged, and you will destroy the relationship between the Z field and the other fields in the table. To do it correctly, you should sort the entire table by the Z field, which will result in part C in Table 1.6, in which the correspondence between the rows and columns remains intact. This example illustrates the fragile nature of the relationship between fields and records.

One topic relating to database fields that we should touch on briefly has to do with the names you give your fields. What's most important is that the names be unique; otherwise, you will not be able to differentiate them. They should also be descriptive and interpretable; that is, it should be clear from the name

TABLE 1.6   Results of different sorting operations

	A. Original Table				B. Sorting by Z Column Only				C. Correctly Sorted		
ID	X	Y	Z	ID	X	Y	Z	ID	X	Y	Z
1	12.544	14.232	−5.42	1	12.544	14.232	−5.34	3	12.751	13.875	−5.34
2	13.543	14.475	−5.50	2	13.543	14.475	−5.42	1	12.544	14.232	−5.42
3	12.751	13.875	−5.34	3	12.751	13.875	−5.50	2	13.543	14.475	−5.50
4	12.780	14.003	−5.65	4	12.780	14.003	−5.65	4	12.780	14.003	−5.65

itself what kinds of data are contained in the field. In other words, you should avoid names like VAR1, VAR2, and VAR3, which are essentially meaningless. This will not only help you to keep things straight but also help others who may access and use your published or archived database.

In the past almost all computer applications imposed strict limits on the size of the field names, as a way of conserving computer memory. This is becoming much less of a problem, and field names now can—and should be—as large as necessary. At the same time, however, you should try to avoid including spaces in a field name (a minor consideration), and you should definitely avoid any characters (e.g., # and %) other than letters and numbers. Some software packages have a problem with spaces and do not allow you to use special characters; thus, you may have difficulty moving your data from one program to another. One common special character that is frequently used to preserve readability is the underscore character (e.g., EDGE_LENGTH).

Values

Turning our attention to the values contained in the fields, the most important consideration involves the format they will take. Again, a few years ago virtually everything entered into a computer database was numeric in format. This was fine for entering measurements or other metric data, but for qualitative types of observations, it meant that people had to rely on cumbersome code lists to translate nonmetric observations into numeric codes. As we will explain in a moment, converting data to numeric format has the primary advantage of economy of space (in terms of computer memory), but it is inherently clumsy for interpretive purposes and can lead to errors. When you are dealing with large databases, space may still be one consideration, but almost never should it dictate the format of your data.

There are several different data formats that can be used in databasing. The primary ones are numeric, character (text or string), date, and Boolean. We will discuss each of these in turn in terms of how a computer works with them. But

TABLE 1.7   The relationship between base 2 and base 10 values

Number of Bits	Binary (Base 2)	Decimal (Base 10)
1	0	0
1	1	1
2	10	2
2	11	3
3	100	4
3	101	5
3	110	6
3	111	7
4	1000	8
5	10000	16
6	100000	32
7	1000000	64
8 (1 byte)	10000000	128
8 (1 byte)	11111111	255
16 (2 bytes)	1111111111111111	65,536
24 (3 bytes)	111111111111111111111111	16,777,216
32 (4 bytes)	11111111111111111111111111111111	4,294,967,296

first we have to provide some background in terms of how a computer actually stores information.

As members of the "Digital Age," we all understand that computers basically view the world in terms of numbers. In fact, however, computers really rely on only two numbers: 0 and 1. These two numbers represent the smallest meaningful unit of computer space, the *bit*, which originally stood for Binary InTeger. Because a bit can only have the value of 0 or 1, a computer represents larger numbers by stringing several bits together. A string of 8 bits is a computer *byte*, which represents a number in base 2, or binary, rather than the base 10, or decimal that is most familiar to us.

How many bits are strung together determines the maximum absolute value of the number that can be represented. As shown in Table 1.7, one bit alone can have a maximum value of 1, and an 8-bit byte can have a maximum value of 255. To get even higher numbers, it is necessary to string together several bytes.

Based on this logic, computers try to store data as efficiently as possible based on the requirements of the values to be represented. If we are only concerned with Boolean, or binary, values such as presence/absence, yes/no, or true/false, then we only require one bit of storage for each value. If we require a maximum

TABLE 1.8   Storage requirements for different numeric data formats

Number Format	Numeric Range	Maximum Decimal Places	Storage Size
Bit (Boolean)	0, 1	None	1 bit
Byte	0 to 255	None	1 byte
Integer	–32,768 to +32,767	None	2 bytes
Long integer	–2,147,483,648 to +2,147,483,647	None	4 bytes
Single precision (real numbers)	–3.402823 E38* to +3.402823 E38*	7	4 bytes
Double precision (real numbers)	–1.79769313486231 E308* to +1.79769313486231 E308*	15	8 bytes

*Note that the E notation in single and double precision numbers is scientific notation. It means that the number before the E has to be multiplied by 10 to the power of the number after the E. Thus, 3.4 E2 means 3.4 × 10^2 or 3.4 × 100 or 340.

of 256 values, including 0, then we need 8 bits or 1 byte, and so forth. Other considerations are whether decimal representation (i.e., real numbers as opposed to integers) is needed and, if so, at what precision (i.e., how many significant decimal places are required); and whether the values can be both positive and negative. The common formats are summarized in Table 1.8, along with their storage requirements. For most numeric fields used in archaeology, integer or long integer formats are appropriate for nondecimal numbers, and the single precision format is good for measurements requiring decimal representation.

Using these storage size requirements for each number format, it is relatively straightforward to calculate the rough size of a database (ignoring other information that may be stored with the file). Let's use one of the tables in which we stored ID, X, Y, and Z as an example. Assume that we will require space for more than 255 but less than 32,000 artifact numbers (so ID can be stored as an integer) and that the X, Y, and Z coordinates should be stored as single precision numbers (because they require decimals). The ID field requires 2 bytes per record, and the three coordinates require 4 bytes each, for a total of 14 bytes per record. Assuming that we have 20,000 records, this results in a file of approximately 280,000 bytes.

To put this value in perspective, a *kilobyte* (K), is 1024 bytes. Thus 280,000 bytes is a little over 273K. A standard 3.5" floppy disk stores approximately 1440K, so this database would easily fit on a floppy disk. A *megabyte* (mb) is 1024K (or 1024 × 1024 bytes), and a standard compact disc (CD) holds 650 megabytes. A *gigabyte* is 1024 mb (or 1024 × 1024 × 1024 bytes). Today's hard disks are typically measured in gigabytes, though probably by the time you read this book some will be measured in *terabytes* (1024 × 1024 × 1024 × 1024 bytes). In any case, the point is that, when it comes to basic numeric databases, size is no longer an issue.

Clearly we can be very inefficient with our storage. Suppose we are dealing with binary data and store it as a double precision field. Our resulting database will be 63 times bigger (1 bit versus 8 bytes × 8 bits) than necessary, making it both wasteful and perhaps a little slower under extreme conditions. At the same time, with computers being what they are today, it is not a good idea to be too miserly either. If we initially define ID as a long integer, we add 2 bytes per record, but we do not have to worry about the 32,767 record limit imposed by using standard integer format.

What about character data? How can a computer recognize and store character data when it is limited to 1s and 0s? The answer is that it has to translate characters into numeric values. This is done according to a conversion standard called ASCII (pronounced AS-kee, and short for American Standard Code of Information Interchange), where 1 byte is required to store a single character. One 8-bit byte, of course, can hold up to 255 values greater than 0, which means that standard ASCII conversion has a maximum of 255 different characters that can be represented. (The accompanying box lists the relevant ASCII characters.) So, when you type an "A" at the computer keyboard, the computer remembers this by storing the number 65 (though in binary format, of course).

This means that when you are storing text, the value requires as many bytes as there are individual characters in your text, which can be very wasteful. This is the reason numeric codes were used for so long. A value of 1, which stands for "SCRAPER", 2 for "POINT", 3 for "DENTICULATE", and so forth would require only 1 byte of storage for the numeric code, versus 7 bytes for the word "SCRAPER", 5 bytes for "POINT" and 11 bytes for "DENTICU-LATE". Even so, given the size of today's storage devices, this is no longer such an important concern, and there are many important benefits of using character values when they are appropriate. Just as field names should be descriptive and readily interpretable, so should the values you put in the fields. There are some other considerations that we will deal with a little later.

Notice, by the way, that text values are normally represented as surrounded by quotation marks. These quotation marks are not actually saved in the computer; rather, the use of quotation marks sometimes serves to explicitly identify to the computer that a value is a string of characters. Some programs will also accept apostrophes for the same purpose. Note, too, that because computers look at text as simply a *string* of single characters, text values are also called strings. Thus, character variables and string variables are the same thing and are different from numeric variables.

ASCII CHARACTER SET

ASCII	Character	ASCII	Character	ASCII	Character	ASCII	Character	ASCII	Character
32	[space]	71	G	110	n	181	µ	220	Ü
33	!	72	H	111	o	182	¶	221	Ý
34	"	73	I	112	p	183	·	222	þ
35	#	74	J	113	q	184	,	223	ß
36	$	75	K	114	r	185	¹	224	À
37	%	76	L	115	s	186	º	225	Á
38	&	77	M	116	t	187	»	226	Â
39	'	78	N	117	U	188	¼	227	Ã
40	(	79	O	118	v	189	½	228	Ä
41	)	80	P	119	w	190	¾	229	Å
42	*	81	Q	120	x	191	¿	230	Æ
43	+	82	R	121	y	192	À	231	Ç
44	,	83	S	122	z	193	Á	232	È
45	-	84	T	123	{	194	Â	233	É
46	.	85	U	124	|	195	Ã	234	Ê
47	/	86	V	125	}	196	Ä	235	Ë
48	0	87	W	126	~	197	Å	236	Ì
49	1	88	X	127	·	198	Æ	237	Í
50	2	89	Y	160	[space]	199	Ç	238	Î
51	3	90	Z	161	¡	200	È	239	Ï
52	4	91	[	162	¢	201	É	240	Ð
53	5	92	\	163	£	202	Ê	241	Ñ
54	6	93	]	164	¤	203	Ë	242	Ò
55	7	94	^	165	¥	204	Ì	243	Ó
56	8	95	_	166	¦	205	Í	244	Ô
57	9	96	`	167	§	206	Î	245	Õ
58	:	97	a	168	¨	207	Ï	246	Ö
59	;	98	b	169	©	208	Ð	247	÷
60	<	99	c	170	ª	209	Ñ	248	Ø
61	=	100	d	171	«	210	Ò	249	Ù
62	>	101	e	172	¬	211	Ó	250	Ú
63	?	102	f	173		212	Ô	251	Û
64	@	103	g	174	®	213	Õ	252	Ü
65	A	104	h	175	¯	214	Ö	253	Ý
66	B	105	i	176	°	215	×	254	þ
67	C	106	j	177	±	216	Ø	255	Ÿ
68	D	107	k	178	²	217	Ù		
69	E	108	l	179	³	218	Ú		
70	F	109	m	180	´	219	Û		

Note: ASCII codes 1–31, and 128–159 are normally reserved for uses other than printable characters.

Some special characters in the ASCII set deserve comment. First, note that a space is a real character and requires 1 byte. Also note that the numbers 0–9 each have ASCII representations. It is important to think of these not as numbers, but as character representations. Thus, the character string "13,147.25" requires 9 bytes of storage (including the comma and decimal point), whereas the same thing stored as a single precision number requires 4 bytes. Also, numbers that are represented as characters cannot be manipulated like ordinary numbers. For example, the computer cannot add "1" and "2" and get "3". What it can do is concatenate (or string together) "1" and "2" and get "12", which is very different in terms of both the nature of the operation and the result.

One consideration with character fields has to do with their length, or with how many characters can be held in the field. Most database programs distinguish between normal character fields (often called text fields), which can hold a maximum of 255 characters, and memo fields, which can hold a much greater number of characters—often an unlimited number, in fact. The other distinction between these two types of character fields is that actual maximum length of text fields is defined by the user when the database is defined, and all records will have that much length available; they are referred to as fixed-length fields. Memo fields, in contrast, are variable-length fields, which means that the length of the field can be different for different records. By their very nature, memo fields are rather clumsy to work with, and we will not deal with them further.

Defining the proper length of text fields is important because you cannot enter more characters than the maximum that is defined for a specific field. But bear in mind that each record in the table will automatically have that much space set aside for the field, whether it is used or not. Since each *potential* character is a byte, this can result in a lot of wasted space. Thus, in the example using the words "POINT", "DENTICULATE", and "SCRAPER", the database field that stores these values will have to be as long as the longest value. So, whereas "DENTICULATE" will exactly fit in an 11-character field, "POINT" will have 6 extra or wasted characters or bytes. There is little you can do about this except to try to define the lengths of your text fields so that you can keep your values understandable and discrete but, at the same time, as small as possible.

There is another data format that can be of considerable use: the date or date/time format. Most modern computer systems store dates as a positive integer representing the number of days since some arbitrary starting point (such as January 1, 1900) or as a negative integer for dates earlier than that. Time is stored as the decimal part of the field. Date alone can be stored as a long integer (4 bytes), though date and time together usually require 8 bytes (double precision). In a date/time format, December 25, 2000, 2:35 P.M. is actually stored as 36885.6077740741.

Storing dates in this fashion is much preferable to storing them as a character variable (e.g., as "12/25/2000") since the special date format can be manipulated in many ways, including accurate sorting. Most computer systems also let you automatically change the way dates are presented if they are stored in the date format. So, for example, you do not need to change your database if you decide to print dates as "2000/12/25" or "December 25, 2000" instead of "12/25/2000". If you store your dates as text, changing the way they are displayed is much harder to do.

Finally, you should consider using a special value to indicate missing data. Almost all programs recognize that the absence of anything in a field (what is called a null value) represents missing data. Depending on how you handle data entry, however, you may or may not be able to enter null values (keeping in mind that neither a space nor a 0 is "nothing" to a computer). This means that you will have to decide what to use to represent missing data. We will discuss this further in Chapter 6.

DATA MANIPULATION

It should be clear, then, that in designing a database it is important to define the type, or format, of every field. While we have presented the definition of different formats in terms of their storage requirements, you must take into account other considerations as well, such as the ability to manipulate the values appropriately and to present them in understandable ways.

The ability to manipulate your data is obviously important. However, because different data formats can be manipulated in only certain ways, you must be careful to initially define your data so that the manipulations you require are possible. We will focus on two kinds of data manipulations: manipulating fields and sorting data. As we will discuss later, these manipulations are useful not only for transforming your data but also for searching, or querying, and for presenting them.

Manipulating Field Values

There are two basic ways of manipulating fields: through the use of operators and functions. *Operators* are special signs that make (usually) simple changes. *Functions* are more like formulas that often process several inputs to provide a result, and they can be quite powerful and complex, depending on the software you are using. We will present the various operators and functions according to the data formats we have already discussed, since operators and functions vary by data format. Note that when you are working with a database you do not usually change the values contained in a field. Rather, you either put the result of your manipulation into a new field or output the manipulation in database search or report. The main reason for not replacing or changing the values of a field, at least initially, is that if you do it incorrectly it can be difficult or impossible to undo. Suppose you have a field called "color" with the values "blue", "red", or "yellow" in each field. You intend to change all "red" to "blue" but accidentally change all "yellow" to "blue". You now have no way to know which "blue" values need to be converted back to "yellow". So, it is always best to place the results in a new field, which can be compared side by side with the old field. Once you are satisfied that the new field contains the results you want, you can delete the old field and rename the new field as the old field.

Numeric Fields   The basic operators that can be used with numeric fields reflect all of the various arithmetic operations with which you are already familiar: addition (+), subtraction (–), multiplication (*), division (/), raising to a power (^), and so forth. The basic concept is exactly like algebra. For example, if Field1 and Field2 are two fields containing numeric values, we can do the following:

Field3 = Field1 + Field2—add the two values.

Field3 = Field1 – Field2—subtract the value of Field2 from the value of Field1.

Field3 = Field1 * Field2—multiply the two values.

Field3 = Field1 / Field2—divide the value of Field1 by the value of Field2.

Field3 = Field1^2—square the value of Field1.

We could then compute a value for a new field, AREA, by multiplying the values found in the LENGTH and WIDTH fields:

AREA = LENGTH * WIDTH

Notice too that we can perform these arithmetic operations not just with the values contained in fields but with any numeric parameters, or *constants*. For example, to convert a value recorded in inches to one expressed in centimeters, we would do the following:

LENGTH_CMS = LENGTH_INS * 2.54

Such algebraic *expressions* (or formulas or equations) can be very complex, of course, with the combined use of several different operators. In this case, it is important to bear in mind that there is an inherent priority to certain operations: exponentials are calculated first, followed by division and multiplication, and finally addition and subtraction. So, in the expression

Field3 = 3 + 4 / 2^2

the result is 4. This is because the first operation performed is to square 2 (resulting in 4), which is then divided into 4 (giving 1), which is then added to 3. It is possible to get around this inherent order through the use of parentheses, in that any expression enclosed within parentheses is computed before other operations take place. Thus, in the expression

Field3 = ((3 + 4) / 2)^2

the result is 12.25. The first operation performed is the addition of 3 and 4 (resulting in 7); next this is divided by 2, and then the result is squared. Adjusting the innermost set of parentheses slightly yields a different answer, as in

Field3 = (3 + (4 / 2))^2

which results in the value of 25.

Obviously you have to be very careful with these kinds of complex operations, and it is always a good idea to check a few answers by hand to be sure that you are getting the results you intend. Note as well that a common mistake when entering complex formulas with parentheses is to leave off one of the matching pairs of parentheses. Obviously, for every open parenthesis, or "(", there must be a corresponding closed parenthesis, or ")". So, if the computer gives you an error message, first count the number of open and closed parentheses in your formula.

Functions are similar to operators, but whereas operators combine values to produce a new value, functions typically transform or act on a given value. They also have a different format, with the function name followed by a set of parentheses containing the numeric argument (or value) to be acted upon by the function. If there is more than one argument, they are separated by commas. Most applications contain literally hundreds of possible functions, and unfortunately the names of the functions do vary among different applications. The square root function, for instance, is sometimes written as SQRT and other times as SQR. Thus, you should consult the documentation for your own application.

Commonly used arithmetic functions include the following:

Field3 = SQRT(Field2)—the resulting value is the square root of the value in Field2.

Field3 = ABS(Field1 – Field2)—first, the value of Field2 is subtracted from the value in Field1; then the absolute value is returned.

Field3 = INT(Field1 / Field2)—first, the value of Field1 is divided by the value of Field2; then the integer portion of the result is returned.

Field3 = RAND()—this returns a random number between 0 and 1. To get a random number within a specified range, you can use the formula: Number = Int((upperbound – lowerbound + 1) * RAND() + lowerbound). For instance, to get a random number between 65 and 90, do this:

Number = Int((90 – 65 + 1) * RAND() + 65).

There is also a large class of trigonometric functions. As you will see in the chapters that follow, these can be useful in dealing with coordinate data—for example, in determining the orientation of objects or rotating a grid. These include COS( ), SIN( ), and ATAN( ), which return the cosine, sine, and arctangent of the given argument. When using trigonometric functions, it is important to keep in mind that most programs require that the arguments be in radians rather than degrees; likewise, results that are angles will be expressed as radians.

Finally you can convert a numeric value into a character value with the STR( ) function (STR is short for STRing, which, as we mentioned, is "computerese" for text variables). For example,

Field3 = STR(19.27)

returns the character value of "19.27". Alternatively a string with a number value can be converted to a true numeric value with the VAL( ) function. For example,

Field3=VAL("19.27")

returns the numeric value of "19.27".

You can combine functions in one expression just as we combined operators previously. For instance, suppose you want to take the square root of the difference of two numbers. Sometimes the difference of two numbers is negative, and most computer systems do not permit you to take the square root of a negative number. To avoid this possibility, you can take the absolute value of the difference before you take the square root. This function looks like this:

Field3 = SQRT(ABS(Field2 – Field1))

Character or Text Fields   Typically only one operator is available for working with character values: the concatenation operator (+ or &). Concatenation combines two character values by simply joining one to the other. For example, "Mousterian" & "biface" results in the string "Mousterianbiface". Notice that if we want to format that better, we can do the following:

"Mousterian" & " " & "biface"

which results in "Mousterian biface".

In contrast, there are many useful character functions. Common ones include the following:

Field3=LEN(field1)—returns the length (i.e., the number of characters) of the character argument: LEN("biface") = 6.

Field3=LEFT(field1, # of characters)—returns the leftmost number of characters specified: LEFT("biface", 3) = "bif".

Field3=RIGHT(field1, # of characters)—returns the rightmost number of characters specified: RIGHT("biface", 3) = "ace".

Field3=MID(field1, starting character, # of characters)—returns the number of characters specified beginning with the starting character specified: MID("biface", 2, 3) = "ifa". You can also omit the "# of characters" argument to return all of the rightmost characters beginning with the starting character specified: MID("biface", 3) = "face".

Field3=INSTR(field1, starting point of the search, value to be found)—returns the number of the character of field1 where the value to be found begins. The starting point of the search can be omitted. For example, INSTR("biface", "face") returns the numeric value of 3. If the value to be found does not occur in the searched value, then INSTR returns 0.

Field3=UCASE(field1) or LCASE(field1)—changes all of the characters in the value to uppercase or lowercase, respectively.

Field3=TRIM(field1)—removes leading or trailing spaces from the value.

Field3=SPACE(number of spaces)—returns a string containing the number of space characters specified: SPACE(5) = "   ".

Field3=CHR(number between 32 and 255)—returns the character represented by the ASCII code number (see the ASCII chart).

Here, too, you can, and will probably want to, combine functions. Take the INSTR example with "biface" and "face". Depending on your software, INSTR might not find the word "face" in the word "biface" if "face" is spelled "Face" with a capital F. We call this a "case-sensitive" function, and most string functions are case sensitive. As a result, the LCASE and UCASE functions are a good way to standardize the case before making any comparisons. You might want to simply use LCASE and UCASE to replace all values in a particular field:

Field2=UCASE(field2)

Or, you can standardize the case as needed by combining functions:

Field3=INSTR(LCASE("Biface"), LCASE("Face"))

We will see more of this when we consider how to correct field values to make them sort properly.

Date/Time Fields   Depending on the software being used, you may have a number of possibilities for manipulating date/time fields, especially when retrieving the individual components of YEAR, DAY, MONTH, HOUR, MINUTE, SECOND. Assuming that Field1 contains the value of "1/5/00 12:53:27" (i.e., January 5, 2000, 53 minutes and 27 seconds past noon), the following functions will be returned:

Field3=YEAR(Field1) = 2000

Field3=MONTH(Field1) = 1

Field3=DAY(Field1) = 5

Field3=WEEKDAY(Field1) = 4 (i.e., the fourth day of the week, where Sunday is the first day)

Field3=HOUR(Field1) = 12

Sorting Data

When you enter data into a database, it is stored in the order you enter it. Most often, the order in which you enter it is probably not the order in which you will want to look at it. Changing the order means sorting the data—at different times and in different ways. You are especially likely to sort according to the values in a particular field or a combination of fields when presenting your data (e.g., in an appendix to an archaeological report). When you are dealing with properly formatted numeric or date/time fields, this usually poses no problem, and we won't worry about it here. Numeric and date/time fields sort as you would expect them to. However, character fields can be very difficult to sort correctly, depending on how carefully you have defined your values and what the limitations of your particular software application are. Without some planning, it is easy to get unintended and unexpected sorts with character fields.

By and large, the sorting of character fields is based on the ASCII values for the characters. That is, a space character is considered "smaller" than character numbers; then come uppercase and then lowercase letters, with all sorts of special characters in between and accented characters at the end (see the ASCII values box). Also bear in mind that sorting takes place from left to right, character by character, in the string. These two rules for sorting, while perfectly logical, can lead to unexpected results. In Table 1.9, for example, all four text fields are sorted in ascending order according to these rules, but the results are not very satisfying.

Note that the first two fields could have been sorted correctly if the fields had been defined correctly in the first place, as numeric and date/time, respectively. However, because they are defined as strings for illustrative purposes, the sort order is not appropriate. Assuming that their definition as text fields is necessary, let's look at what can be done to correct the sort order for each of the columns.

For Field1, where numeric values are stored as characters, the best solution is to "pad" the front of the values with leading spaces. Assuming that there are a

TABLE 1.9   Sorting issues with string values[*]

Field1	Field2	Field3	Field4
1	1/1/00	Type1	Biface
10	11/5/95	Type10	Denticulate
100	12/11/97	Type2	Point
2	2/2/99	Type27	Scraper
20	2/27/97	Type3	BIFACE
200	3/5/95	Type33	DENTICULATE
3	4/6/98	Type4	POINT
30	5/10/00	Type45	SCRAPER

[*]The order shown here is how the records would be sorted without special modifications to the values.

maximum of five digits to be represented in this field (which could be "numbers" from "1" to "99999"), you can accomplish this using the following set of functions that put the result back into the same field:

Field1=RIGHT(SPACE (5) & Field1, 5)

Field1
1
2
3
10
20
30
100
200

This expression first concatenates five space characters to the front of each value in Field1. Thus, the original value of "1" would be changed to "*****1", where each * represents a space. This results in a value that is six characters long. Using the RIGHT function, we then take the rightmost five characters, giving a result of "****1". If we do this to the value of "100", the result is "**100", and starting with a value of "99999", we get back the same value. Since space characters sort before numeric characters, the resulting values will sort as we expect them to in numeric order, as shown here.

Field2
1995/03/05
1997/02/27
1998/04/06
1999/02/02
1999/12/11
2000/01/01
2000/01/05
2000/05/10

For Field2, a date field stored as characters, the situation is more difficult to deal with. In fact, the best solution to this problem would be to redefine the character format as YYYY/MM/DD—that is, to use four digits for the year (otherwise, years after 1999 would sort lower than preceding years—this is the so-called Y2K problem that, thanks to efforts by computer programmers around the world, was not much of a problem after all), two digits for the month, and two for the day. In this format, the first date in the table would have been written as "2000/01/01", the second as "1995/11/05", and so on. We will leave it to you to try to write a series of expressions that will reformat these dates correctly as shown here.

For Field3, the problem can be fixed using a solution similar to that used for Field1, by padding the trailing numeric portion of the value with either spaces or zeros. Assuming that the values range from TYPE1 to TYPE99, we could do the following:

Field3=LEFT(Field3, 4) & RIGHT("0" & MID(Field3, 5), 2)

Field3
Type01
Type02
Type03
Type04
Type10
Type27
Type33
Type45

Here, using the LEFT function separates the character's "TYPE" from the rest of the value. The MID function then separates the characters following "TYPE" (i.e., "1" or "27"). To the latter we concatenate a leading "0", and then take the rightmost two characters of the result. Then we concatenate this to the characters "TYPE", resulting in "TYPE01" or "TYPE27". Alternatively, since the first part is always the word "TYPE" we could just write:

Field3="TYPE" & RIGHT("0" & MID(Field3, 5), 2)

The accompanying table shows the results.

Field4
BIFACE
BIFACE
DENTICULATE
DENTICULATE
POINT
POINT
SCRAPER
SCRAPER

Field4 is the easiest to fix, by making all of the values either uppercase or lowercase with either the UCASE or LCASE function, as here:

Field4=UCASE(Field4)

Note, however, that more programs are able to deal automatically with uppercase and lowercase issues, so making these kinds of adjustments is becoming less necessary. You can also easily standardize to proper case (e.g., "Biface" rather than "biface") with the following function:

Field4 =UCASE(LEFT(Field4, 1)) & LCASE(MID(Field4, 2))

The accompanying table shows the results.

We hope that these examples have also made clear that taking the time to learn some basic functions can save huge amounts of time later. We know lots of people who have spent hours and hours editing their databases to standardize fields by hand when a few well-placed and well-written functions would have done the same task quite literally in minutes. Obviously it is always best to enter the data correctly in the first place, and we will discuss this further in succeeding chapters. But there will always be mistakes that need to be corrected using the kinds of techniques that we have outlined here.

TABLES

One concept that is fundamental to good database design is that of the *table*, which is a collection of records that all have the same fields. It is important to emphasize that every record in a table must have the same fields, but it is not necessarily the case that each record will have an actual value for each field. In other words, some fields in some records might be null. Also, different tables can store different kinds of information regarding the same objects, and some objects may be represented in some tables but not in others. For many database applications the terms "database" and "table" are synonymous, and each table (or database) is stored in a separate file. This was especially true in the past. In other applications, and more commonly today, a single database file can contain multiple tables.

Of course, storing all of your data in a single table is the easiest and most straightforward approach, and it can be an efficient one under certain circumstances. This is called a *flat-file database*. Flat-file databases are most appropriate, for example, when there is always a one-to-one relationship between objects and records and when most of the fields contain data for most of the records. If the data are more complex than this, then it is necessary to consider a multiple-table or *relational database* design.

Consider, for example, the situation that arises when an archaeological field project recovers several different classes of material—perhaps stone tools, bones, and ceramics. Each of these classes of objects obviously has different kinds of analytical fields that would be relevant to it alone. Let's say we set up a single table to hold all of the data, in which case it will look something like Table 1.10. Now, while this may not look too bad, keep in mind that such a database will likely contain several stone-tool-related fields, several others for ceramics, and several more for bones. That in itself would result in a lot of empty fields and, therefore, wasted space. Let's make the situation even worse by including multiple point provenience information, as shown in Table 1.11. At this point, not only do we have a file that is mostly blank space, but we are also duplicating values where there is more than one record per object. This is not merely a waste of space. It also makes working with the data very difficult.

A much better organization creates four separate tables: one each for stone tools, bones, and ceramics, and another for storing the provenience information for all three data classes. Such an organization is shown in Tables 1.12–1.15.

In this organization the stone tool, ceramic, and bone tables do not have anything in common, and there is no wasted space (other than missing values). But the provenience data table contains data that are relevant to each of the other three tables. What we have lost, therefore, is the physical association between the rows (records) and columns (fields) that were central to the integration of different fields to the same object. To correct this problem we need to define *relations* between the provenience data table and the other tables so

TABLE 1.10   A table design containing several blank fields

ID	Dataclass	Stone Tool Type	Ceramic Type	Taxon
1	Stone	Scraper		
2	Stone	Point		
3	Ceramic		Crudware	
4	Fauna			Canis lupus
5	Stone	Core		

TABLE 1.11   A one-to-many table design with several blank fields

ID	X	Y	Z	Dataclass	Stone Tool Type	Ceramic Type	Taxon
1	12.544	14.232	−5.42	Stone	Scraper		
1	12.553	14.235	−5.47	Stone	Scraper		
2	12.751	13.875	−5.34	Stone	Point		
2	12.760	14.853	−5.39	Stone	Point		
2	12.761	14.845	−5.38	Stone	Point		
3	12.635	14.66	−5.40	Ceramic		Crudware	
3	12.693	14.68	−5.41	Ceramic		Crudware	
4	12.555	14.79	−5.38	Bone			Canis
5	12.742	14.33	−5.60	Stone	Core		
5	12.831	14.43	−5.55	Stone	Core		

that the data can be combined. This notion of designing different tables and integrating them through relations is what defines a relational database.

The primary requirement in defining relations among tables is that each of the tables to be related share a common field that uniquely identifies the object, record, or case to which the various observations and values in different tables refer. In this example, we can use the ID field for this purpose, since ID is unique for each object. Thus, for example, by using a relation between the provenience and stone tool tables based on ID, we can combine the X, Y, and Z data for artifact 1 with the proper stone tool type, length, and weight values for that same object.

Although the definition of relations among tables is the responsibility of the user at the time the database is designed, relational databases assume the task of combining fields almost seamlessly. Results can be obtained almost as quickly as with a single-table design, but with a much more efficient organiza-

TABLE 1.12 A single table for provenience data

ID	X	Y	Z
1	12.544	14.232	−5.42
1	12.553	14.235	−5.47
2	12.751	13.875	−5.34
2	12.760	14.853	−5.39
2	12.761	14.845	−5.38
3	12.635	14.66	−5.40
3	12.693	14.68	−5.41
4	12.555	14.79	−5.38
5	12.742	14.33	−5.60
5	12.831	14.43	−5.55

TABLE 1.13 A single table for stone tool data

ID	Stone Tool Type	Length	Weight
1	Scraper	58.2	65
2	Point	46.3	35
5	Core	64.7	77
8	Scraper	57.0	65
9	Flake	65.0	49

TABLE 1.14 A single table for ceramic data

ID	Ceramic Type	Vessel Form	Sherd Type
3	Crudware	Jar	Rim
7	PP B/W	Bowl	Body
10	Crudware	Jar	Body
11	PP Poly	Plate	Body
15	PP Poly	Bowl	Rim

TABLE 1.15 A single table for bone data

ID	Taxon	Bone	Side
4	Canis	Rib	Left
6	Bos	Femur	Right
12	Equus	Mandible	
13	Pan	Frontal	
14	Bos	Rib	

tion overall. The only information that is repeated is in those fields on which the relation is built (in this case, ID).

We will return to the subject of relations later, but for now it is worthwhile to stress again the importance of unique identifiers. Since we, as archaeologists, are usually dealing with artifacts, the most common thing to do is to make the artifact ID number the basis for most relations between tables. This requires, however, that we take the utmost care to assign each and every artifact a unique ID number, and that there is no ambiguity between the number associated with the object and the one in the database. Although artifact ID numbers have been around for a long time, they have sometimes been viewed as a rather trivial aspect of archaeological recording. In any computerized project, however, these numbers play a central role, and so you must pay a great deal of attention to them. We will take up this issue in greater detail in Chapter 6.

INDEXES

Earlier in this chapter we discussed some issues in sorting data, especially regarding the way character values are treated. The better way to handle the ordering of records is with indexes. An *index* is essentially a key to a table—in fact, indexes are sometimes called keys—and one that is automatically maintained by the database program. Indexes provide an important means of ordering your view of the data without having to physically sort the individual records. Indexes also serve as the backbone for powerful and extremely fast searches and provide fundamental support for relations among tables. Thus, they are central to effective and efficient databasing. Recall that many different kinds of programs can fulfill certain database functions, but only an actual database program can work with indexes.

In some ways indexes are like tables, though you would never view or work directly with an index yourself (it is maintained by the database program). One point to remember is that there is a strict correspondence between an index and a table, in that a particular index can only be used on a particular table (although a table may have several indexes). Typically indexes contain as many records as the table with which they are associated. They can be stored in the same file as the table or in different files. However, the purpose of an index is not to store data, but rather to provide a key to the cases contained in the table itself. That key is based on the index being a kind of list of the records (actually a list of "pointers" to the records), sorted according to one or more fields contained in the table.

Indexes are often described initially in terms of their ability to order, or sort, the underlying table, and so we will begin this discussion with that function. Let's start with one of the tables we presented earlier in this chapter, though with the record number shown in the leftmost column (see Table 1.16).

This table is physically sorted by ID, and we could immediately produce a report, or listing, ordered in this way. However, if we wanted to produce a report ordered by TYPE, or LENGTH or WEIGHT, we would first have to sort the data according to the values of that field. Depending on the size of the table, each of those sorts could take some time, since all of the records and their fields have to be shifted around. Let's imagine, however, a series of smaller tables, the indexes, that contain the values of only one field and the corresponding record numbers that refer back (or point) to the record numbers of the original table. If these smaller indexes remain sorted (which involves much less work and is actually done automatically by the database program itself), we can utilize the relation between the record numbers in the index and the record numbers in the table to produce a report based on whatever order we choose.

TABLE 1.16   A simple table containing stone tool data

Record Number	ID	Type	Length	Weight
1	1	Scraper	58.2	65
2	3	Point	46.3	35
3	4	Flake	64.7	77
4	6	Core	57.0	65
5	8	Scraper	65.0	49

TABLE 1.17   Four indexes related to the separate fields shown in Table 1.16

Index 1: ID		Index 2: Type		Index 3: Length		Index 4: Weight	
Original Record Number	ID	Original Record Number	Type	Original Record Number	Length	Original Record Number	Weight
1	1	4	Core	2	46.3	2	35
2	3	3	Flake	4	57.0	5	49
3	4	2	Point	1	58.2	1	65
4	6	1	Scraper	3	64.7	4	65
5	8	5	Scraper	5	65.0	3	77

For example, imagine four sorted indexes, as shown in Table 1.17. Let's say we want to produce the report sorted by the TYPE field. Instead of sorting the original table by this field, the program simply goes to the type index and, starting at the top, gets the original table record number (or pointer) of the first record in the list (4), goes to the table itself to record number 4, gets the values from the fields, and prints them. Then it gets the second record number in the index (3), uses this to position itself directly on the third record in the table, gets the values, and prints them. And so on, until all of the records are printed. The same would work for the indexes built on LENGTH, WEIGHT, and ID.

There are quite a few advantages to this approach. As we have already said, it is much easier to keep an index sorted (since the amount of data is limited) than it is to keep sorting the original table. In fact, database programs use very efficient and automatic procedures to keep indexes sorted even as new cases are being added to the tables. Even better, and at little cost in terms of storage, we can keep multiple indexes associated with the table. This allows us to change the order of the table virtually instantly merely by using a different index. This multiple view provided by indexes simply cannot be matched by any application

TABLE 1.18   A simple table with two indexes

Table			Index 1: ID		Index 2: Type	
Record Number	ID	Type	Original Record Number	ID	Original Record Number	Type
1	3	Flake	7	1	4	Core
2	6	Flake	1	3	5	Core
3	11	Flake	4	4	10	Core
4	4	Core	2	6	13	Core
5	7	Core	5	7	7	Flake
6	9	Scraper	6	9	1	Flake
7	1	Flake	10	10	2	Flake
8	17	Scraper	3	11	3	Flake
9	22	Flake	8	17	9	Flake
10	10	Core	9	22	6	Scraper
11	31	Scraper	12	24	8	Scraper
12	24	Scraper	11	31	12	Scraper
13	36	Core	14	34	11	Scraper
14	34	Scraper	13	36	14	Scraper

that does not use indexes. Also, indexes can be based on multiple fields at the same time; that is, the values of two or more fields can be joined together in creating the index. And, finally, it is usually possible to create indexes in either ascending or descending order.

Because an index is kept in sorted order, it is also useful for searching the table, whether we are looking for a particular record or groups of records that all have the same value for a given field. We will demonstrate this with a different table that is not sorted in any particular order with two indexes: one for ID and one for TYPE (see Table 1.18).

To find a particular ID in the original table without the use of an index, the program must search every record in the table until it finds the ID we are looking for. To find ID 24, for example, the program has to read 12 records until it reaches it. On average, of course, it is necessary to read half the file, though this can take a long time if the file is large. By using the ID index, however, we can find the record quickly.

Here is one way in which a very fast search can be performed on an index. Because the index is sorted, when a particular record in the index is read, we have some idea of where to keep searching for the value we are looking for. If that value is greater than the value that's contained in the current record, then we know that the record must be farther along in the table. If the value we are looking for is less than the value that is contained in the current record, then we know that it must be back toward the top of the table. This process is rather like looking for a particular person's number in a phone book. We open the pages, look to see where we are, and then know whether to turn back the pages or move forward based on the natural order of the alphabet. We can actually increase the efficiency even more, however, by halving the distance, up or down, in the area to be searched.

To find a particular value in an index, the program starts at the middle of the index and compares the value of that record against the value we are looking for. If the current value is less, then it goes to the record that is halfway between the one we were at and the end of the file, and makes the comparison again. If this current value is less, the program again halves the difference between the current position and where we just were, and makes the comparison at that location. And so forth. When we try this ourselves on the ID index in Table 1.18, we go initially to the halfway position, which has an ID of 10. This is less than the 24 we are looking for, which means we have to look farther down toward the end of the file. Halving the distance from where we are currently (the midpoint) and the end of the file takes us immediately to the record containing ID 24—the one we are looking for. We see that it corresponds to record number 12 in the table, which means that the twelfth record in the table is the one we want.

This simple search procedure is called a binary search. Although it is not as efficient as the procedures used in most database applications, it is easy to understand, and it demonstrates the efficacy of indexing. For the small table here, the difference between reading through the entire table and using a binary search is not significant. However, to search for a particular item out of a list of 1 million items requires only a maximum of 20 "reads," versus the 500,000 on average that it takes to search the same file sequentially (from start to finish). This method provides virtually instant access to any specific record, regardless of the size of the file.

We can find all of the cases that have the same value just as quickly. All we have to do is find any one case that has the value we are looking for, using the same binary search procedure. Then, because we know that all of the cases with the same value are together, we can read forward from there until the values change and thus quickly find the last case that contains the searched value. Returning to our initial case, we can then read backward until the values change again, which gives us the first case. While we are doing this, of course, we also keep track of the record numbers that are matches. In this way we will quickly find all of the matching records, and with a minimum of "wasted" reads. Notice, however, that if a field is not indexed, we have to read literally every record in the table to see if the value matches the one we are looking for.

Why not build indexes on every field in a table? Usually there is no reason to do this since we would seldom need to produce sorted lists on the basis of every field or to find particular values for every field. Moreover, each index does take up space and requires some maintenance on the part of the program.

Indexes also provide the means for building relations between tables, since the field common to two tables, which serves as the basis for the relation, should be indexed as well. When we are accessing the data from one table, we can use the index of the common field with the second table to go immediately to the corresponding record in the second table. This enables us to pull together data from several fields almost as quickly as if the fields all existed in the same table. It should be emphasized again that this requires that every record have a unique identifier that can serve as a *primary key* or *master index* for the table.

We began this chapter by saying that there are a number of ways to store data, from text files to spreadsheets to actual database programs. While all of these can work, there are clear advantages to using an application that has been designed to work both effectively and efficiently with the data you have. As your data become more complex and/or the database becomes larger in terms of the number of records stored, the advantages of a relational database quickly become apparent, especially in terms of storage requirements and speed of access.

SEARCHING A DATABASE

The discussion on how to use indexes to find specific records in a database leads us to the topic of how to search a database. In this section we will concern ourselves not with how the program does the actual searching, but with how to tell it which cases you want to find. For the moment we will also not emphasize the specific syntax that you would use, as this can vary considerably among programs. In computer jargon the process of searching a database is called querying, and a particular search, which often can be saved and reused, is called a *query*.

In using a database we do not typically ask the database program to find a value anywhere in the table (as you might search for a word in a word processing program). Rather, what we look for are values that exist in a certain field or group of fields. There are always three elements that form a search query: the field(s) in which to look, the value(s) that we specify to compare with (or the search criteria), and a comparison operator to specify how the comparison is to be made. The more common comparison operators are equals (=), is greater than (>), is less than (<), is greater than or equal to (>=), is less than or equal to (<=), and is not equal to (<>). The basic structure of a query is FIELDNAME operator VALUE, as in, for example,

    TYPE = "CORE"

which will look for all cases in which the TYPE field contains the value "CORE", or

TYPE <>"CORE"

which will find all of the cases in which the TYPE field contains anything else. Notice, of course, that the character values are enclosed by quotes; numeric values are not (e.g., LENGTH > 0).

There are two other search operators that are important, namely, AND and OR. Both allow you to search more than one field at a time, and the OR operator allows you to specify multiple criteria for the same field. AND specifies the intersection of the named criteria, and OR the union. You might remember this concept from Venn diagrams in high school.

When we use the AND operator, we are saying that two or more conditions must be met in order to select a particular record. For example, if we ask the computer to find all of the records in which

TYPE = "CORE" AND LEVEL = "SURFACE"

we will find only records corresponding to cores found in the surface level; all other cores from other levels will be excluded. In contrast, if we ask the computer to find cases in which

TYPE = "CORE" OR LEVEL = "SURFACE"

we will get all the cores (regardless of level) and, in addition, everything (including but not limited to cores) from the surface level (although the cores from the surface level will not be duplicated). The OR operator can also be used to specify multiple criteria for the same field, as in

TYPE = "CORE" OR TYPE = "FLAKE" OR TYPE = "SCRAPER"

in which case records having any of these values will be found. Of course, you cannot specify multiple criteria from the same field with the AND operator, since a field can have only one value. There can be no such record, for example, that would satisfy the expression

TYPE = "CORE" AND TYPE = "FLAKE"

since a record would have either the value "CORE" or the value "FLAKE" (or something else), but not both values at the same time.

The <, >, >=, and <= comparison operators are relatively straightforward, though there are some small issues to keep in mind. First, the difference between the < (less than) and <= (less than or equal to) operators (and between the > and >= operators) is only that with the latter the specified criterion value will be considered a match. Thus, if we look for cases in which ID < 8, we will get records with IDs 1–7; asking for ID <= 8 will give us IDs 1–8. Second, when we use the < or > operators with character fields, all of the preceding discussion concerning sorting applies. Thus, < and > make their comparisons based on the ASCII sequence values and on one character at a time, left to right.

The <> (not equal to) operator can also be a little tricky if used in conjunction with AND or OR. For example, suppose we want to search the TYPE field for records that are neither cores nor flakes. It might be tempting to ask for it this way:

TYPE <> "CORE" OR TYPE <> "FLAKE"

but this would give us *all* records, including both cores and flakes! This is because flakes will satisfy the condition of not being equal to "CORE", and cores will satisfy the condition of not being equal to "FLAKE". The proper way to ask for no cores or flakes is

TYPE <> "CORE" AND TYPE <> "FLAKE"

Finally, be aware that you can search on the basis of virtually any kind of expression including operators and functions, rather than specific values. For example, we can ask for all records in which length is greater than width using a comparison operator such as

LENGTH > WIDTH

We can also do any kind of manipulations, such as records in which the length is more than twice the width, using

LENGTH > 2 * WIDTH

or types that begin with the letters "BIF" using

LEFT(TYPE, 3) = "BIF"

These functions or manipulations do not, of course, change any of the values in the underlying data, but rather affect only the comparisons when doing the search.

Note, too, that you can use parentheses in your queries. Suppose you want only cores and flakes from both levels 1A and 1B. Your query will look like this:

(TYPE="CORE" OR TYPE="FLAKE") AND (LEVEL="1A" OR LEVEL="1B")

Without the parentheses this query would not only be hard to read but also give the wrong results. Just as multiplication and division are evaluated before addition and subtraction in expressions without parentheses, AND is evaluated before OR. So, the query would be evaluated as if the parentheses were as follows:

TYPE="CORE" OR (TYPE="FLAKE" AND LEVEL="1A") OR LEVEL="1B"

This would give all cores, flakes from Level 1A only, and all artifacts from Level 1B.

SUMMARY

Databases are at the core of almost any application of computing technology to archaeology. The database design has an impact on what kinds of things you can do with the data stored in it and how easy it is to do them.

Deciding what fields will be in the database, what format they will take, and how they will be organized into tables are the basic steps. We cannot help you with what fields need to go into the database, but we have outlined a number of different formats they can take. Storage space used to be a large consideration in selecting among field formats, and it can still lead to certain problems if the number of records is relatively large. A more important consideration, however, is whether the field can be manipulated in the ways that you need. Storing numbers as characters often does take up more room, but the more important issues have to do with how they can be sorted and transformed.

Designing an efficient database involves consideration of not only the format of the fields but also the structure of the tables and the way they can be related to each other. Although the idea of dividing your fields into several tables may seem complicated at first, it is actually much simpler to use related tables than it is to store everything in the same table. The most important point to remember is that these relations require that you have unique identifiers for each object, so that the data from one table are properly linked to the corresponding records in another table.

2 Mapping Equipment

Now that we have some basic database skills, it is time to start collecting data. Of course, archaeologists collect data both in the field and in the laboratory; we will cover the field in the next four chapters, and the lab in Chapters 6–9. Our focus on field data collection is presented primarily from the perspective of mapping and point proveniencing (giving an exact location to excavated artifacts). This is because all field data have one theme in common, namely, they are associated with a location on the ground. Clearly the basis of all archaeological analysis is context—that is, where an object was found. How we describe or record that location can vary, however, from a local arbitrary grid of X, Y, and Z coordinates to a world coordinate grid like latitude/longitude. It can be quite difficult to compare archaeological data when the find locations are at different scales, but this is an issue involving geographic information systems, which are discussed in Chapter 9.

In this chapter we discuss the kinds of equipment needed to record data in the field, focusing on the principles behind total stations and global positioning systems (GPS). This equipment is used to record the location of sites and features within sites, topics covered in the three following chapters.

TOTAL STATIONS

One of the most basic pieces of equipment for doing archaeological fieldwork is a total station. A *total station* is a survey instrument that allows archaeologists to record accurately and quickly the three-dimensional location (X, Y, Z) of a point of interest by measuring the vertical angle, horizontal angle, and distance from the instrument to that point. Actually a total station is the latest incarnation of a basic piece of equipment called a *theodolite*, which records a horizontal and a vertical angle between the theodolite itself and the point where it is looking. But while theodolites are good at recording angles, they are not able to record the distance. Over the years archaeologists have developed a number of methods to do this. The most basic, and one of the most popular, is to simply stretch a tape from the theodolite to the measured point. This is a variant of something called tape-and-compass mapping, and while it is very simple to implement, it is also highly problematic. Obviously, for example, it can be difficult to stretch a tape to get an accurate measure of distance across irregular topography and through thick vegetation.

Total stations are theodolites that solve the distance problem by incorporating an *electronic distance meter*, or EDM (see Figure 2.1). An EDM uses an infrared laser to measure distances. The laser is beamed from the EDM to the measurement point where it is then reflected back to the EDM by a set of specially arranged mirrors known as a *prism* (see Figure 2.2). By measuring the length of time it takes the light to travel to the prism and back, the instrument can then calculate the actual distance. Once it measures the distance, the horizontal angle, and the vertical angle, the total station calculates and instantly returns the X, Y, and Z coordinates of the measured point (see Figure 2.3). These XYZ coordinates can be stored in the memory of the total station or transferred to an external data collector where they are stored until the end of the day or mapping session. At this time they are transferred to a larger computer and organized with other coordinates to make maps.

While many archaeologists still use standard theodolites, we will consider only total stations since they offer the most potential for computerized data collection. Indeed, the only reason not to use a total station is the expense. While costs have dropped over the years, total stations are still, and probably always will be, expensive. In our own work, over the years, however, we have found that a total station pays for itself quite quickly in the speed with which it collects points and the drastic reduction in the number of errors. Thus, many archaeologists are switching to total stations as quickly as budgetary constraints allow.

The Cartesian Grid System

Now let's take a look at the trigonometry behind measuring points with a total station. A total station works within the same kind of XYZ grid that archaeologists are already familiar with—what we call a *site grid*. Trigonometrically this is basically a Cartesian coordinate system in three dimensions, where X and Y represent axes along the ground and Z represents depth (see Figure 2.4, page 34).

Grids can be defined in any scale (meters or feet), and they can represent virtually any numeric range. In other words, while the theoretical origin of every grid is the XYZ point (0, 0, 0), a given site can be located anywhere in the grid even if it is hundreds of kilometers from the origin. Remember, however, that the theodolite part of a total station works with angles. We mentioned earlier that there are two types of angles: horizontal and vertical (see Figure 2.5, page 34). Horizontal angles form a circle in the XY plane that describes which way

FIGURE 2.1 A total station

the total station is looking—left or right. Vertical angles also form a circle (though more often a semicircle) that describes how far above or below the horizontal plane the total station is looking. As shown in Figure 2.6, in the Cartesian XY (horizontal) grid of the total station, the positive Y-axis is equal to an angle of 0 degrees. Angles then increase in a clockwise fashion. Thus, the positive X-axis corresponds to an angle of 90 degrees, the negative Y-axis corresponds to 180 degrees, and the negative X-axis corresponds to 270 degrees. A point somewhere in the positive X and positive Y direction will therefore have an angle between 0 and 90 degrees. Obviously this principle holds true no matter where you are standing: if you look in a direction parallel to the Y-axis, this angle will be 0 degrees as well.

FIGURE 2.2 The prism shown here is attached to a small nail and held over the end of an artifact.

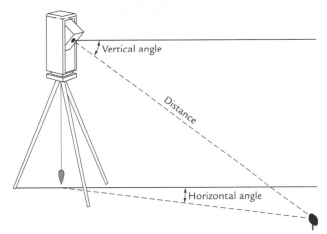

FIGURE 2.3 Measurement of two angles (vertical and horizontal) and distance

This is all fine in the ideal world of Cartesian coordinate systems, but in the real world there is a very definite problem in defining the 0 (positive Y) direction. When a total station is first powered on, for example, it automatically sets the 0 horizontal angle as the direction where the instrument is facing, which means that the total station's horizontal angle of 0 degrees might be different from the site grid's angle of 0 degrees. The site grid, for instance, might be pointed toward magnetic north and the total station's grid pointed in some random direction depending on where the instrument was pointed when it was powered on. The first step in using a total station is thus to align its 0 angle with that of the site grid. This process, called *station initialization*, will be covered in Chapter 3.

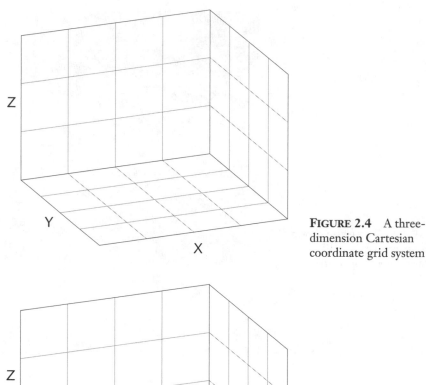

FIGURE 2.4   A three-dimension Cartesian coordinate grid system

FIGURE 2.5   Horizontal and vertical angles

Theoretically vertical angles also range from 0 to 360 degrees, but in practice they are much more limited since it is impossible to record points below the instrument's field of vision. Unlike the horizontal angle, which must be set each time the total station is installed, the vertical angle remains constant and does not need to be set each time. That is the good news. The bad news is that there are several standards for initially setting vertical angles.

One way is to set a vertical angle of 0 degrees at the zenith (the angle straight above the machine). In this case the horizontal angle looking directly in front of

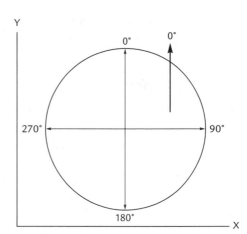

FIGURE 2.6   Grid compass headings for the horizontal angle

the total station becomes 90 degrees, and in general, angles increase as the direction the instrument is looking moves from above to below. Another way to set the vertical angle is to define 0 as the horizontal position. In this case, looking straight above the machine is 90 degrees, and angles increase from below to above. In both of these systems, the vertical angle ranges from 0 to 360 degrees. A third system breaks the 360-degree range into two 180-degree ranges from –90 to 90, with 0 degrees at the horizontal position. While intuitively this may be easier than the other two systems to visualize and use, there is a subtle problem: there is no way to distinguish between looking forward and looking backward. In other words, when the eyepiece is flipped 180 degrees to look in the opposite direction without turning the instrument in the horizontal (i.e., left or right), the computer has no way of differentiating these measurements. Measurements taken directly in front of and directly behind the instrument will return the same results. While it may seem unlikely that someone would rotate the eyepiece 180 degrees in the vertical rather than turn the instrument 180 degrees in the horizontal to view a point behind the instrument, we once had a student who did exactly that. The resulting errors confounded us for some time until we carefully watched this student at work with the instrument and discovered the problem.

Obviously, confusing these three systems will have adverse effects on the measurements. Some survey programs may expect one measurement system or the other. Fortunately all total stations can be set to either system, so refer to the manual and make sure you set the instrument appropriately. Once set, the instrument will remember the setting, and you will not have to do it again.

One thing to notice about the vertical angle is that no matter how 0 is defined it still represents a nonarbitrary setting. In other words, there is a real horizontal (what is level) and a real vertical (what is plumb). This is very different from the rotation of the horizontal angle, where there is no such thing as a "real" 0 setting.

Measuring Angles

Angles can be expressed in different ways. The traditional way is to divide each degree into 60 minutes and, in turn, to divide each minute into 60 seconds, for a total of 3600 seconds to a degree. A typical degree/minute/second (DMS) angle measurement, for instance, might read 235 24' 30", which translates to 235 degrees, 24 minutes, and 30 seconds. Note how minutes and seconds are marked with single and double prime marks, respectively, although in some systems these can be separated with periods (e.g., 235.24.30). In fact, it is also common to express fractions of degrees as decimals rather than in terms of minutes and seconds. The angle 235 24' 30" expressed in decimal degrees is equal to 235.4083. The formula to compute this is as follows:

Decimal Degrees = Degrees + (Minutes / 60) + (Seconds / 3600)

Sometimes angles are expressed in decimal minutes or decimal seconds based on exactly the same logic. Decimal seconds extend the precision of the angle beyond what is possible with only the standard degrees, minutes, and seconds. In other words, with only degrees, minutes, and seconds there is no way to distinguish an angle of 235 24' 30" and an angle just beyond this but not yet at 235 24' 31". But we can describe the angle halfway between the two in decimal seconds as 234 24' 30.5". Different mapping programs will have different requirements, so you need to be aware of this issue and be prepared to convert one format to another.

Going in the other direction—that is, converting decimal degrees to degrees, minutes, and seconds—is a bit more difficult. First, calculate the minutes by taking the decimal portion of the decimal degrees, multiply by 60, and keep the integer portion. Next, calculate the seconds by doing the same thing to the decimal portion of the above calculation. Let's see how this works, using the decimal angle measurement of 235.4083.

First, get the decimal portion of the angle by using the integer function:

DECPORT=(ANGLE – INT(ANGLE))

or

=(235.4083 – INT(235.4083))
=(235.4083 – 235)
=.4083

To find the minutes, multiply this by 60 and drop trailing digits to the right of the decimal:

    MINUTES=INT(DECPORT * 60)

or

    =INT(.4083 * 60)

    =INT(24.498)

    =24

Likewise, to find the seconds, multiply the decimal portion of minutes:

    SECONDS=INT(((DECPORT * 60) - MINUTES) * 60)

or

    -INT(((.4083*60) - 24) * 60)

    =INT(((24.498) - 24) * 60)

    =INT((.498) * 60)

    =INT(29.88)

    =29

Because of rounding errors, this is 1 second different from the angle we started with (235 24' 30"). The INT function does not round to the nearest integer, but rather simply removes the decimal portion. To correct this, we can add .5 before we use the INT function. Thus, the formula should read

    SECONDS=INT(((DECPORT * 60) - MINUTES) * 60 + .5)

Note that working with angles expressed in DMS is much more difficult than if they are stored as decimal representations of degrees. This is true with respect to any calculations that must be done on the angles (e.g., adding or subtracting angles) and with respect to how they are stored in the database. DMS angles must be stored as text values, whereas decimal angles can be stored as single precision numbers.

A third way of expressing angles is in terms of *radians* rather than degrees. There are 2 * pi (pi = approximately 3.141593) radians in a circle, which means that there is approximately 0.017453292 radian in a degree. The reason it is important to know about radians is that you will use them when working with trigonometric functions, such as finding the sine or cosine of an angle. For example, you will have to use these functions when you want to find the angle defined by two points or when you have to rotate a grid.

To convert an angle in degrees to radians, first make sure that the angle is expressed in decimal form, and then multiply this value by 0.017453292. Thus,

Angle in Radians = Angle in Decimal Degrees * 0.017453292

or

=235.4083 * 0.017453292
=4.10864980

You can then use this value to find, for example, the sine or cosine of the angle:

Sine of Angle = SIN (Angle in Radians)
Cosine of Angle = COS (Angle in Radians)

To convert an angle in radians to degrees, multiply it by 57.2958 (the number of degrees in a circle divided by the number of radians in a circle):

Angle in Decimal Degrees = Angle in Radians * 57.2958

or

=4.10864980 * 57.2958
=235.4084

Here again we have a rounding error. This time, however, it has to do with the precision with which we have represented the numbers. If you are looking for a more precise representation of π (pi), one that matches the precision of your computer's software, you can use this formula:

PI = 4 * ATAN(1)

where ATAN is a function that returns the arctangent. This formula gives you a better way to express the radians-to-degrees conversion factor. Rather than using the number 57.2958, you can substitute this formula:

Angle in Decimal Degrees = Angle in Radians * (360/(2 * (4*ATAN(1)))

or this simplified version:

Angle in Decimal Degrees = Angle in Radians * (45 / ATAN(1))

Similarly the conversion factor for degrees to radians becomes

Angle in Radians = Angle in Decimal Degrees * ((2 * 4 * ATAN(1)) / 360)

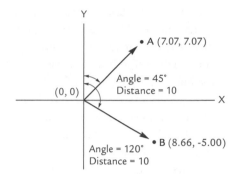

FIGURE 2.7 Calculating XY coordinates based on distance and horizontal angle

or, simplified:

Angle in Radians = Angle in Decimal Degrees * (ATAN(1) / 45)

The Relationship Between Angles and XYZ Points

The XYZ grid and the angles used by the total station are related in that the grid has an orientation that is measured by angles. Given that, as we have just learned, vertical angles are fixed relative to the horizontal plane and never adjusted, let us concentrate only on horizontal angles in the XY plane, which are the most important in aligning the total station's internal grid to the site grid. The problem here becomes determining the X and Y coordinates of a point given the horizontal angle and the distance measure. This will take you back to your days in Trig 101.

Let's look first at Point A in Figure 2.7. Imagine that the total station is set on the origin, or with X and Y coordinates of 0, 0, and the 0 horizontal angle is set to be parallel to the increasing Y-axis. We turn the total station to Point A and read an angle of 45 degrees and a distance between the instrument and the point of 10 meters. The X and Y coordinates of the point are defined as

X = Distance * Sine (Horizontal Angle)

Y = Distance * Cosine (Horizontal Angle)

Since both the sine and cosine of 45 degrees are 0.707, multiplying 0.707 by the distance of 10 gives us the X and Y coordinates of the point as 7.07. For Point B, the angle we read is 120, which has a sine of 0.866 and a cosine of –0.5. Multiplying these by the distance of 10 gives us an X coordinate of 8.66 and a Y coordinate of –5.00. We would compute the Z coordinate of a point exactly the same, except that we would use the cosine of the vertical instead of the horizontal angle.

In the real world complications can arise that we have to consider, assuming that the total station is making its measurements relative to itself. In other words, when a total station is initially powered on, it will set a 0 horizontal angle to be the direction in which it is pointed, and it will also consider its X, Y, and Z coordinates to be 0, 0, and 0. This point (0, 0, 0) is actually located in the exact center of the instrument itself. Remember, however, that when we set up the total station over a datum, its X, Y, and Z coordinates are probably not going to be 0, 0, and 0. In addition, the height of the instrument itself above the datum must be taken into account. Finally we must also correct for the fact that the prism itself will probably be mounted on a pole, and so the elevation to the prism will not represent the elevation of the actual point we are interested in.

Basically, to correct for this, we add the values of X, Y, and Z as calculated relative to the center of the total station to the X, Y, and Z of the datum. For Z we must also add the height of the instrument above the datum and then subtract the height of the prism pole (really, the distance from the center of the prism to the ground). Here are the formulas:

Real X = Measured X (relative to Instrument's Center) + Datum X

Real Y = Measured Y (relative to Instrument's Center) + Datum Y

Real Z = Measured Z (relative to Instrument's Center) + Datum Z +
        Instrument Height – Prism Pole Height

Precision in Recording Angles

Total stations vary a great deal in the precision with which they record angles. (See the accompanying box for a discussion of considerations in selecting a total station.) The least expensive total stations typically have a precision of 10 seconds. This means that the horizontal angle will always end in a multiple of 10 (i.e., the last digit will always be a 0). So, for example, if the actual angle measurement is 243 43' 14", the angle actually recorded will be 243 43' 10". Slightly more expensive machines have 5-second accuracy, and the most expensive machines have 1-second accuracy or better.

You might think that it is always better to have a machine that is precise to 1 second rather than one that is precise to 10 seconds. However, there is a considerable difference in price between these two extremes and not much difference in terms of the accuracy of the results as required for most archaeological fieldwork. This is because the error represented by these different levels of precision is greater as the distance of the measurement increases. At small distances the error is small; at larger distances the error becomes larger.

To understand what this means, let us consider an actual measurement. As Table 2.1 shows, 5-second accuracy produces no significant errors for distances

SELECTING A TOTAL STATION

The basic issues when selecting a total station are accuracy, speed, and the interface to a data collector or PC. All of these variables directly affect price. Fortunately the demands of archaeological survey are such that the lowest-grade survey equipment is typically more than sufficient for most applications.

When considering accuracy, basically you need to consider the resolution of the horizontal angle measurement (whether the angle is measured to the nearest second, 5 seconds, or 10 seconds). We have found that 5-second machines are more than adequate for most archaeological applications.

Speed is less of an issue today than it has been in the past. Most new instruments take a measurement in a matter of seconds. Some of the older models, however, require as long as 15 seconds. While this may not seem like a lot, it quickly becomes a factor when you are trying to record hundreds of topographic points in a day or to point provenience artifacts as fast as a large crew can excavate them.

If you plan on working in an area that is either often wet or susceptible to wind-blown particles (e.g., a desert environment), you might consider getting a waterproof instrument, which has extra seals on the exposed joints and buttons. Of course, it will cost a little more, but it might be worth it under some circumstances.

As for the interface to the data collector or PC, this is one of the more important features that you will want to investigate. If you find PC software that you like, make sure it is compatible with the total station. If you decide to use a data collector made to work specifically with your total station, be sure to use the software first to ensure that (1) it will do what you need, (2) it is easy to use, and (3) it is easy to connect with your PC and the software that will eventually store and work with the recorded points. With most total stations you can also elect not to purchase a data collector and store the points directly in the memory of the instrument. For some applications this might be sufficient, but the extra features of the data collector or PC software, particularly for station installation, will likely make it worth the extra cost (see the box on storing data in the field).

that would typically be used for point proveniencing artifacts from excavation units and very small errors for distances that would be used for most topographic survey and mapping projects. Even the 10-second machines are acceptable for most applications, and the 1- and 2-second machines provide more accuracy than most applications require.

In our experience we have found that 5- and even 10-second precision is more than sufficient for nearly all archaeological applications. For point proveniencing of artifacts or features, for example, the distance between the instrument and the objects will be small, and therefore the error itself will be small. For larger-scale survey and mapping applications, the larger errors will usually

STORING DATA IN THE FIELD

The connection to a computer or data collector is probably the single most important factor separating models today, and it is where a lot of the cost lies. The main advantages of data collectors are (1) they are built to withstand all sorts of inclement field conditions, (2) they come with built-in software specifically designed for survey, and (3) they come with some support.

The main disadvantages to data collectors (see photo) lay primarily in their nonstandard operating system and hardware, which means that they cannot run other kinds of software. Also, the survey software built into the data collectors might be too complicated for the nonprofessional. Likewise, these programs are not always flexible enough to record the kinds of data that archaeologists require. These are exactly the advantages of using a personal computer to operate the total station. A personal computer gives you the flexibility to use different programs—although there are very few programs for archaeological survey. Personal computers are also typically a lot less expensive than data collectors.

The main disadvantage to personal computers is their lack of portability. Laptop computers, even the lightest and smallest of them, are still too bulky to carry across the landscape while doing topographic surveys. Moreover, laptops require a solid surface to rest on, have a number of moving parts that can fail when they are moved too much, and have too many openings that are vulnerable to wind-blown dirt and sand. We have also found that laptop screens are very difficult to read in the sun and can be damaged by constant direct sunlight. Thus, laptops are probably best only in circumstances in which a permanent station exists to accommodate their frailties. In contrast, some of the smaller, handheld computers have solid-state memory and no hard disks and are perfect for surveys. Since personal computers are typically so much less expensive, you may be able to purchase two. We strongly recommend that you have duplicates of every piece of equipment—computer, cable, and so on—that you possibly can.

Either way, be sure to protect the keyboard with something because keyboards are the first to fail both in the field and in the laboratory. Many companies make products that fit over the keyboards of various models. If you cannot locate one for your model, then cut a piece of clear plastic from a heavy-duty artifact bag and tape it to your keyboard.

not affect any behavioral interpretations. Furthermore, increased precision is not without a price. For example, 1-second machines are extremely expensive and far more difficult to operate, and they require greater attention to detail than most archaeologists can or are willing to invest.

TABLE 2.1   A comparison of measurements taken over varying
distances and with varying horizontal angle precision.*

	1 Second	2 Seconds	5 Seconds	10 Seconds
10 Meters	0.00	0.00	0.00	0.00
50 Meters	0.00	0.00	0.10	0.20
100 Meters	0.00	0.10	0.20	0.50
1000 Meters	0.50	1.00	2.40	4.80
5000 Meters	2.50	4.80	12.2	24.10

*The middle row shows the distance error (in centimeters) associated with various angle errors while measuring a point 100 meters away. With a given angle error the measurement error increases with distance, and with a given distance the measurement error increases with angle errors.

Atmospheric, Earth Curvature, and Refraction Corrections

As you now know, calculating the XYZ coordinate of a point requires a vertical angle, a horizontal angle, and a distance. We have discussed the properties of angles, but there are factors that affect distances as well.

Most total stations use an infrared laser to measure the distance between the instrument and the prism. However, although the speed of light is a constant in a vacuum, it varies with atmospheric conditions such as temperature and pressure (height above sea level), and this in turn will affect distance measurements. Thus, total stations have a correction factor that can be set to reflect the current atmospheric conditions. This correction factor is then used to adjust the distance measurement to provide a more accurate result. Fortunately, while it is important to understand this concept, for most archaeological applications it can be ignored. To understand why, take a look at the following examples.

Suppose you set up your total station at sea level on an extremely cold day in January. According to the atmospheric correction chart shown in Figure 2.8, at a temperature of –20 degrees Celsius, the correction factor should be about –38. Next, you measure a point that is exactly 100 meters away. According to the formula below, which represents how the correction factor (Ka) is used to correct distance measurements, the instrument will perceive that point to be 100.0038 meters away.

Distance = Measured Distance $* (1 + Ka * 10^{-6})$

or

Distance = $100.0038 * (1 + -38 * 10^{-6})$

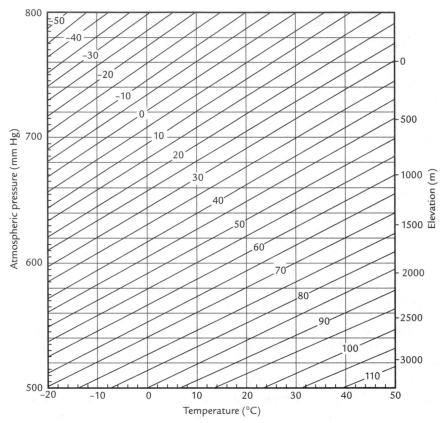

FIGURE 2.8   Atmospheric correction chart

If the atmosphere correction factor is not set to −38 and the default value of 0 is used instead, then the machine will return 100.0038 as the measured distance for a point 100 meters away. In other words, for a measurement of 100 meters, there is nearly a 4-millimeter error.

Now consider the opposite extreme: the same site and the same point on a really hot day in July when the temperature reaches a scorching 48 degrees Celsius. The atmospheric correction factor is now 25; thus, the instrument will perceive a point 100 meters away as only 99.9975 meters. Again, if the atmospheric correction factor is not set, the machine will return 99.9975 (rounded to the nearest millimeter), for an error of 0.0025 meter or 2.5 millimeters. Thus, under the most extreme conditions, the combined error on a 100-meter measurement is only 6.5 millimeters, and under normal conditions it will be much less.

Since it is difficult to imagine many situations in archaeology in which such precision is required over such a long distance, the default atmospheric setting is usually sufficient. Alternatively, if you do set the correction factor, use an average-temperature and average-pressure day. Be sure to consult the manual that comes with the total station. If from day to day the atmospheric pressure constant varies less than ±5 from your setting and if the distance measurements are less than 100 meters, there is probably no need to bother resetting the constant, especially since this small error is going to be overwhelmed by other factors.

Most total stations can also correct for the curvature of the earth and the refractive effect the atmosphere has on the normally straight path of the infrared laser. As with atmospheric correction, or perhaps even more so in this case, these calculations provide a level of accuracy that is not needed in archaeological applications, and so you can safely ignore them. If, on the other hand, you are trying to make sure that two ends of a tunnel carved under the English Channel from England to France exactly meet, then you should consider applying these corrections.

PRISMS, POLES, AND TRIPODS

Prisms

As you will recall, prisms are what reflect the total station's laser back to the instrument so a measurement can be recorded. They consist of three mirrors arranged like the corner of a box, with each mirror perpendicular to the other two, so that, regardless of where they are pointed, they reflect light back in the precise direction from which it came. This is extremely important for a total station. It means that the person holding the prism does not have to point it directly at the total station (which would clearly be impossible anyway), but rather needs only to point it in the general direction. Bicycle reflectors work on the same principal and can, in fact, sometimes be used with a total station. This basic configuration is also how scientists measured the distance to the moon: astronauts left behind a large prism that earth-based lasers can find and bounce a laser off of.

There are several issues to consider when thinking about prisms. First, the size of the prism, in conjunction with the strength and sensitivity of the total station, determines the longest distance that can be recorded. The problem is that the laser energy diminishes as the distance increases. Thus, at very long distances not enough of the laser's original energy is reflected back to the machine to make an accurate measurement. With a larger prism, more energy is caught and reflected back to the total station. Large prisms, however, are expensive and cumbersome. Likewise, more expensive machines can generally take a more distant measurement with a given prism (see Table 2.2). However, once you reach the limit for a particular machine, the only way to take measurements from farther away is to use either a larger prism or a set of prisms. Thus, the typical solution is to arrange a set of prisms in a geometric fashion symmetrically around the

TABLE 2.2   Distances measured with different brands of total stations and different numbers of prisms.*

	1 Prism	3 Prisms
Sokkia Set-5	800–900 meters	1000–1200 meters
Topcon GTS-212	900–1000 meters	1200–1400 meters

*When considering a total station, it is important to consult its relevant statistics. A less expensive total station will require larger or more prisms to take more distant measurements.

point to be measured (see Figure 2.9). Special brackets known as triple mounts can be purchased from the prism manufacturer to help you accomplish this.

The second important issue with prisms is related to the mounts. The prism offset refers to the fact that the point in the center of the prism that marks the farthest point for the laser beam before it is reflected back to the total station may be offset from the physical center of the prism or from where it is mounted into a bracket (see Figure 2.10). Thus, all prism mounts are marked with a prism offset. Sometimes they are designed to have an offset of 0, meaning that no adjustments are necessary. More likely, however, the prism will have an offset of 25 to 30 millimeters. This means that, unless a correction is made at the total station or data collector, all measurements will be off by as much as 3 centimeters. Since this error is systematic, it will quickly add to unacceptable levels of error. Note as well that the error will affect all three dimensions—X, Y, and Z—and it will affect them differently depending on both the vertical and the horizontal angle.

Since prism offsets are a normal aspect of surveys, most total stations and data collection programs allow you to specify the offset so that all distance measurements can be corrected. Thus, if the prism offset is –30 millimeters, a distance measurement of 23.040 meters becomes 23.070 meters. In other words, a negative prism offset means that the center of the prism is too far forward or too close to the total station, so that the true distance is that much longer. For example, a prism offset of +30 millimeters would mean that 30 millimeters need to be subtracted from each measurement. Whether this correction is done by the total station or the data collector depends on a number of factors. On the one hand, having the total station do it means that the measurements on the station's display are correct. This might be important if you are using the total station without a data collector. On the other hand, if you have multiple prisms with multiple offsets, this value will have to be adjusted each time you switch prisms. A sophisticated data collector program will offer programmable prism definitions. Thus, each recorded point can be associated with a particular prism and correspondingly adjusted. Of course, it is always best to keep things as simple as possible and to use only one prism offset.

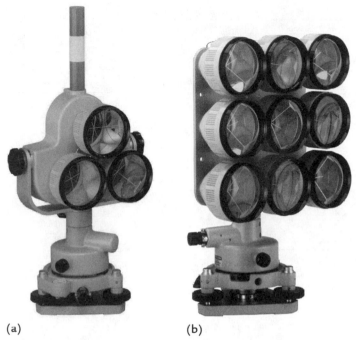

(a)   (b)

FIGURE 2.9   (a) A triple-prism set and (b) a nine-prism set. A larger prism can be made by combining several small prisms. These arrangements allow longer measurements to be made with a particular total station.

Prism Poles

Most prisms are purchased in a combination of the prism itself and a mounting bracket, to which the prism is attached. This mounting bracket can then be screwed onto a pole, which is either of fixed length or adjustable. When measuring an object or point on the ground, you place the tip of the pole on the object and aim the total station at the exact center of the prism. As we have already discussed, this means that you must know the exact height of the pole—from its tip to the center of the prism— in order to correctly adjust the Z measurement.

The type of pole needed depends on the type of survey. For topographic surveys, adjustable-height poles are best. You will need flexibility in the height to shoot under or over branches, over dense foliage, into deep ravines, and so on. The amount of height depends on the local circumstances and your specific needs. Be aware as well that the use of adjustable poles can lead to errors. When the pole person changes the pole's height, it is extremely important that he or she communicate this fact to the total station operator so that it can be noted in the data collector. Otherwise, every subsequent point will have an elevation error. For instance, if the pole is lowered from 5 to 2 meters without the operator's

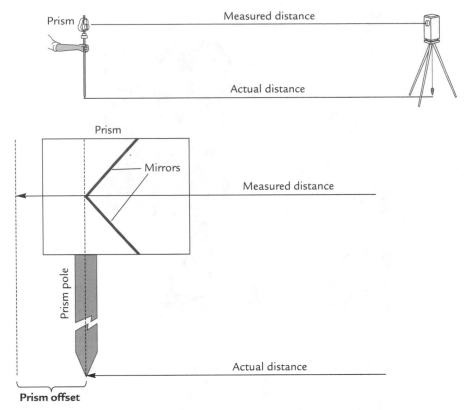

FIGURE 2.10   There is usually a difference between what the total station measures as the distance to the prism and the actual distance to the prism. The difference between the two is called the prism offset, and it can vary from one prism to another and from one prism mount to another.

knowledge, then all of the points will appear on the map 3 meters too low. If the error is noted quickly, then the erroneous points can be identified and corrected. But if the error goes undetected for a long period or if more pole height changes are made in the interim, then it can be very hard to make corrections. Thus, even with adjustable poles, you should select a height that works and stay with it for as long as possible.

There are several things to keep in mind when you use prisms with poles. As we just discussed, the physical back of the prism is not necessarily the point at which the incoming laser beam is reflected back to the total station. So, when you mount the prism on the pole, it is important that you center the pole on the optical center of the prism; otherwise, there will be a constant error as the prism

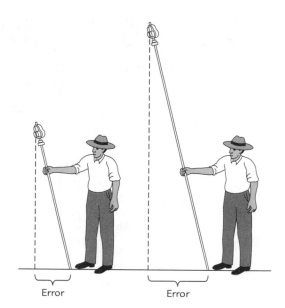

FIGURE 2.11   Tilting prism poles. For the same degree of tilt, the resulting error increases with higher poles.

is turned. The mounts that come with your prisms will, of course, be manufactured so that the pole is at this center point. However, if you build your own poles, you will have to center them as well.

In addition, it is important that, when you place the tip of the pole on the object, the pole itself remains absolutely vertical (or plumb). Any tilt to the pole will affect not only the Z but also the X and Y measurements, and the amount of error will be directly proportional to the height of the pole (see Figure 2.11). Most prism mounts incorporate a bubble level that indicates whether the prism pole is absolutely vertical. If there is no built-in bubble level, you can hold a separate pole level against the pole to make sure it's level.

The point proveniencing of artifacts generally requires a different set of poles from those used in topographic surveys. For point proveniencing the level of acceptable error is much lower, so smaller poles are recommended. In fact, under ideal conditions you can use a prism with its mount and no pole. This is because most mounts have a fitting that brings them to a point rather than attaching them to a pole. We have taken this a step further by making our own mounts using a small prism, a hose clamp, and a nail—what we refer to as "nail prisms" (see Figure 2.2). Their primary advantage is that they are very low to the ground, so that, even if they are not held absolutely vertical, the error will be quite small. The nail itself also provides a very fine, manageable point to place over an object to be recorded.

SETTING UP A TRIPOD

You will face three challenges in setting up a tripod over a datum. You have to make sure that (1) the mounting platform of the tripod is directly over the datum, (2) the platform is relatively level, and (3) the height of the station is suitable for the person who will be operating the instrument.

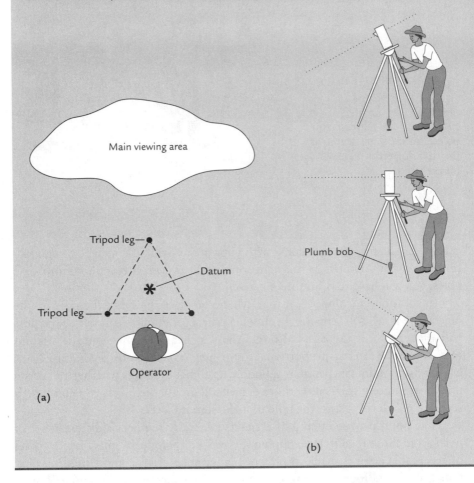

(a)

(b)

In making a mount, however, you must accurately measure the new height and offset. The easiest way to do this is with the total station and another prism with a known height and offset. First, mark a precise point on the floor and then measure it with the known prism. Next, use the new prism to measure the same point. You might think that the measured point will have the same coordinates, but it will not. To correct this, slide the bracket forward and backward or by

Here are the steps you should follow before you even place the instrument on the tripod:

1. Attach a plumb bob to the mounting platform and make sure that it is in the center of the hole on the platform.

2. With the legs retracted, position them in such a way that they are fairly well spread apart—the more spread they are, the more stable the tripod will be. Imagine the three feet as forming a triangle, as shown in (a). For the comfort of the operator, try to have the base of that triangle on the side where the operator will be standing. In other words, try to avoid a situation in which the operator must straddle one of the legs or in which the legs could be accidentally kicked.

3. Unlock the legs and extend them to the proper height, while at the same time making sure that the plumb remains over the datum. Keep in mind that the eyepiece of the instrument will be even higher than the tripod's mounting platform. There are other considerations when setting the height of the tripod, depending on how the main viewing area is situated vertically relative to the instrument. If you will be looking more or less level to the viewing area, then the eyepiece of the instrument should be at your eye level. However, if you will be looking mostly up, the instrument should be raised a bit; if you are looking mostly down, it should be lowered, as shown in (b).

4. Make final adjustments to put the plumb bob directly over the datum—the closer it is to the datum now, the easier it will be to center the instrument over it later. Make these adjustments by gently pushing one leg at a time farther into the ground. Try to avoid moving the legs themselves.

adjusting the prism offset in the total station or data collector until the X and Y coordinates are identical. Then note the difference in the Z, which will be the height of the new prism.

When defining a new datum or when initializing your station, it is very important that your measurements be as accurate as possible, since all subsequent measurements will be affected by errors introduced at these critical moments. At this stage we do two things to minimize the error. First, we always use the smallest pole possible. Second, we aim the total station at the very tip of the pole—in the horizontal angle—and then raise only the vertical angle to the center of the prism. This minimizes left-right errors in how the prism is being held, though it does not prevent front-back errors.

Tripods

Tripods come in two basic styles: wood and aluminum. Aluminum tripods are less expensive and much lighter, making them most useful when you have to do considerable hiking. The major drawback to aluminum tripods is that the metal will contract and expand as the temperature changes. When this happens, your instrument will be thrown out of level. For this reason wooden tripods are usually preferable.

You will encounter problems when you have to set up a tripod in mud or sand, namely, that the tripod will shift. If the setup is temporary, the best way to deal with this problem is to push the feet of the tripod into the ground as far as possible. If you are going to be using the total station for any length of time, however, another solution is to pound lengths of pipe into the ground and then set the tripod feet into those. Long pipes (even up to a meter or so) will provide stability and keep the tripod from shifting. (See the box on page 50 for tips on setting up a tripod.)

A total station does not have to be mounted on a tripod, and under some circumstances it is possible for and even recommended that you not use a tripod. At a cave site in France, for instance, the ceilings were so low that a normal tripod would not fit. After experimenting with a miniature tripod, the excavator eventually placed the total station on a board resting directly on the ground. The position of the total station could be controlled each day by simply tracing the outline of its base on the board. Verification datums were recorded after each setup and checked periodically throughout the day to ensure that the board had not moved.

At Fontéchevade, France, we built a cement pillar to support the total station (see Figure 2.12). At the top of the pillar, we mounted a metal plate fabricated at a local machine shop with a hole at the center and feet to be cemented in place. With this setup there was absolutely no chance that the "tripod" would shift from day to day or year to year. It also made it very easy to set up the total station each day. Because the site was relatively secure, we left the lower part of the total station, called the tribrach (see Figure 2.13), attached to the pillar. The operator then set the total station into the tribrach, set up the computer, and cabled the equipment together. We mounted a prism on the wall of the cave so

FIGURE 2.12 The cement
pillar at Fontéchevade

that the operator could initialize the station on his or her own, using a point
that would not move from day to day or year to year. Thus, we were able to
train excavators to set up the total station each morning in 10 minutes or less
and with accuracies of 1 millimeter or less in either the X, Y, or Z dimension.

Cement pillars, however, are not always possible, and you have to be a little
careful about building something so solid that you might not be able to remove
it easily when the time comes. We have found that pounding metal pipes into
the ground at the foot of each tripod leg makes it easier to set up the tripod each
day. If you can leave the tripod legs extended when packing up at the end of
each day or if you can mark where each leg is set, then you can simply set the
tripod into the pipes the next day and avoid the sometimes time-consuming
process of leveling the total station over a datum. As discussed previously, this
technique also works very well when you are setting up in water-soaked or otherwise soft and shifting ground.

FIGURE 2.13   A tribrach. The total station sits in a tribrach, which is detachable. It contains the leveling knobs, a level bubble, and sometimes an optical plummet. Prisms are available that mount in the tribrach so that their center is exactly where the total station's center would be.

THE GLOBAL POSITIONING SYSTEM

The *Global Positioning System*, or *GPS*, was designed by the U.S. military to give troops the ability to identify their location to within a few meters without giving away their position to an enemy. In other words, a GPS unit can passively receive signals but it does not broadcast a signal that others can detect. This system, which covers the entire world 24 hours a day, 7 days a week, consists of a ring of 24 satellites (21 operational satellites and 3 backups) that orbit the earth. These satellites are not in geostationary orbits, but rather orbit around the earth every 12 hours at an elevation of 20,200 kilometers. The constellation or arrangement of satellites was designed to provide four satellites over every location on the earth. Why four? Because four satellites are needed to take a GPS measurement.

How GPS Works

GPS positioning is based on the principle of triangulation. Each satellite sends a radio wave toward the earth with information about when the signal was sent and where the satellite was located at the moment it was sent. This is important because the satellites are constantly moving. A GPS receiver on the ground takes this signal and calculates how far it is away from that satellite by identifying how long it took for the signal to travel there. The principle is similar to the one we described for total stations. Since the signal travels at the speed of light, if we know how long it has been traveling, then it is easy to calculate how far it has traveled.

With a total station, however, we also have directional information: the horizontal and vertical angles. With the GPS signal there is no indication of direction. This means that, when the GPS receiver calculates that it is, say, 20,000 kilometers from the satellite, it only knows that it is somewhere on an imaginary sphere (or, actually, a hemisphere, since the signals cannot be received if the satellite is below the horizon) with a radius of 20,000 kilometers around that particular satellite. To solve this problem, we add another satellite (see Figure 2.14). The GPS receiver measures its distance from this second satellite. This, too, provides a solution that can be described as a hemisphere, but now we can look at the intersection of these two hemispheres. Unfortunately their intersection is a circle and not a point. Thus, with two GPS satellites a receiver can narrow its location down to a circle. But with *three* satellites the GPS receiver can triangulate its position to one of two points. Fortunately one of these two points will make no sense at all—it will be either deep within the earth's crust or far out in space. Thus, by first telling the GPS receiver approximately where it is, it is able to reject the point that makes no sense and keep the other.

If three satellites are required to triangulate, why does it take four of them to make a GPS measurement? Remember that this distance is calculated based on the time the signal takes to travel to the receiver. Thus, an accurate measure of time is critical. The GPS satellites each have four atomic clocks in them—two rubidium and two cesium—that are accurate to within billionths of a second per month. A lot of effort has gone into setting and updating the satellites' clocks, so we can assume that they are correct. But what about the clock in the GPS receiver? It is not an atomic clock, but rather more like a normal watch. Since it takes only about $1/15$ of a second for the signal to travel from the satellite to the receiver, the receiver's clock is not sufficiently precise to provide an accurate measurement of the travel time. Moreover, the GPS receiver's clock needs to be set to the satellite's clock. Rather than use one of the three satellites already being used to calculate the position, a fourth, and in effect independent, satellite is used to tell what time it is. In other words, calculating a location means solving an equation with four unknowns: X, Y, Z, and the time. Four unknowns require four known satellites.

What GPS Gives You

GPS receivers give you your location on earth. While that is easy to say and easy to conceptualize at one level, it turns out that specifying a location is a lot more difficult than you might imagine. Obviously the goal is to place yourself on a map, but as you probably know there are many different kinds of maps. The problem is that the world is more or less spherical, and putting it on a flat map means bending and stretching it in various ways, using what are called *projections*. We will address this topic further in Chapter 9 when we discuss GIS.

To further complicate matters, while the world is spherical, it is not perfectly spherical; it is a spheroid rather than a sphere. This makes it even more difficult to stretch a nice smooth grid over the surface of the earth. In recent

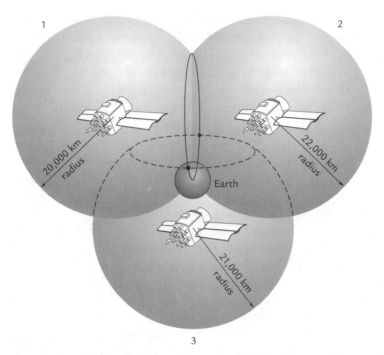

FIGURE 2.14   The spheres around each satellite represent the distance the signal traveled to reach the GPS unit; the intersection of these spheres represents the calculated position of the GPS. With three spheres, there are only two possible positions. By telling the GPS unit approximately where it is or by ignoring solutions that are off in space or deep within the earth, the GPS unit can eliminate the obviously incorrect solution. *Source:* Adapted from Gregory T. French, *Understanding the GPS: An Introduction to the Global Positioning System, What It Is and How It Works* (Bethesda, MD: GeoResearch, 1996).

centuries, as mapping techniques have progressed, so has the ability of cartographers to describe accurately the shape of the earth. This means that they have periodically made changes to the grid systems. So, coordinates for a site placed on a map printed in 1930 are not necessarily the same coordinates that would be used today. This does not mean that the site was not accurately mapped in the first place, but rather that the whole grid may have been shifted since the original map was drawn.

Partly in response to these kinds of issues, surveyors have divided the world into smaller grids. The idea is that the effects of projecting a portion of a sphere onto a two-dimensional surface are minimized if one considers a smaller area. There are two widely used systems in the United States based on grids. One of these, the *State Plane Coordinate System (SPCS)*, is based in feet and is used for surveys in individual states. Another, the *universal transverse Mercator (UTM)* system, divides the entire world into a series of grid cells, measured in meters. Other countries have their own local systems. Which system you use will likely depend on where you are and with whose data you want to be compatible.

You might be tempted to avoid some of this complexity by using latitude/longitude, which is truly a global grid designed to work across the entire earth. But latitude and longitude actually can be quite cumbersome to work with, and unless you are recording GPS coordinates across more than one SPCS or UTM grid, you will probably want to avoid them (for more about coordinate issues see Chapter 9).

Issues with GPS

Accuracy   Once you determine which coordinate system you will be using, your next concern is the accuracy of your GPS measurements. This is a very complicated subject, as a great number of variables affect accuracy. In addition, as already noted, the GPS was designed for the military, and until quite recently the military was concerned about allowing everyone else to have access to fast, accurate location information. Thus, two standards for location accuracy were developed: the *Standard Positioning Service (SPS)* and the *Precise Positioning Service (PPS)*. PPS originally was available only to the military, whereas SPS was available to anyone who had an inexpensive receiver. Now PPS is available to everyone.

Nevertheless, as Table 2.3 shows, even with PPS accuracy, GPS measurements contain a sizable error. The error is small enough that the GPS can be used to put a dot on a map to show the location of a site, and it is probably small enough that the location of the site as measured by the GPS could be used to guide you back to that site at a later time. This, of course, depends on the size of the site and how obvious it is on the landscape. The level of accuracy, however, is not sufficient to map features within a site or to measure the aerial extent of the site by walking around its perimeter.

Several different techniques can be used to increase the accuracy of a GPS measurement, and more expensive receivers apply more sophisticated techniques. The simplest technique is to increase the number of readings taken for a given point. If you assume that each reading will have a random error distributed around the actual correct reading, then you can take the average of a series of points to estimate the actual correct point. Thus, by increasing the amount of time you spend taking measurements, you increase the accuracy of the measurement as well. Actually GPS receivers do this automatically, though most of them take only a few seconds to average the measurements obtained in a few seconds. Nevertheless, with a single, civilian-grade GPS receiver, accuracy will be no greater than 10 to 30 meters.

TABLE 2.3   Accuracies for Precise Positioning Service (PPS) and Standard Positioning Service (SPS)

	PPS	SPS
Horizontal Accuracy	17.8 meters	100 meters
Vertical Accuracy	27.7 meters	156 meters
Time Accuracy	100 nanoseconds	167 nanoseconds

Source: Adapted from Gregory T. French, *Understanding the GPS: An Introduction to the Global Positioning System, What It Is and How It Works* (Bethesda, MD: GeoResearch, 1996).

Differential Correction   Currently the best way to get beyond this limitation in accuracy is by using a technique called *differential correction*, which requires two GPS receivers, a base station and a rover (see Figure 2.15). The base station receiver is installed over a known datum or benchmark. As this unit takes GPS measurements, it compares the calculated X, Y, and Z coordinates with the actual coordinates known for that point. The difference, or differential, between the GPS-measured coordinates and the known coordinates defines the error in GPS measurements at that moment in time in that part of the world. This error factor can then be used to adjust measurements taken at the same time with rover or mobile GPS units in the vicinity of the base station.

Depending on where you work, a base station might already be available. Currently a large portion of the United States is covered by very accurate base station data via a network operated by the federal government. Eventually the entire country will be covered under this network. If you are working outside the United States, you will have to do some research. Generally the odds are better if you are closer to waterways since GPS is critical to marine navigation. You can also create your own base station, but depending on what you want to do with it, this can be very expensive. Remember, too, that the accuracy of the base station is largely dependent on the accuracy of coordinates of the datum point on which it rests.

You can do the differential correction when you return from the field. The data are uploaded from the rover GPS receiver to a computer where they are combined with data from a base station receiver using special software. This is called postprocessing differential correction. Some base stations that may cover your area automatically post the differential correction files on the Internet so that they can be easily downloaded and processed. There is even a common format for sharing this kind of data, called RINEX, so that different brands of GPS can share the same base station data.

The important factors are that the base station measurements be taken at the exact same time as your GPS measurements and that the base station be

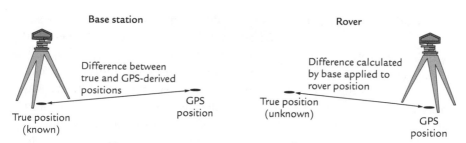

Base station   Rover

FIGURE 2.15   Differential correction works by measuring the error associated with a GPS measurement over a known point and then using this calculated error factor to correct measurements taken at the same moment by roving GPS units. *Source:* Adapted from Gregory T. French, *Understanding the GPS: An Introduction to the Global Positioning System, What It Is and How It Works* (Bethesda, MD: GeoResearch, 1996).

located near your study area. In other words, the base station must use the same set of satellites that you used for your GPS measurements. Fortunately for most survey applications, "nearby" means within 300 kilometers. The reason the time matters is that GPS errors constantly fluctuate with time as the satellites move across the sky.

The problem with this kind of postprocessing differential correction is that the more accurate readings are available only after you have come in from the field. Sometimes this does not matter. If you are mapping archaeological features like terraces or walls, for instance, it is probably sufficient to process the data after you do the fieldwork and before you make your map. But if you are trying to relocate a site or if you want to establish a series of datums with GPS coordinates, then it is nice to have the differentially corrected data instantly, or in real time, in the field. Fortunately some base stations (known as beacons) broadcast the error correction factors over radio waves. Thus, differential GPS units can receive this signal and use the data to differentially correct field measurements on the fly. You have only to do some background research before going into the field to make sure that a broadcasting base station is in the vicinity of your research area and that your equipment is compatible with their broadcast signal. Alternatively you can purchase a base station that has the ability to broadcast differential information, but this will be expensive.

With postprocessing differential correction, accuracies to within a few millimeters are possible. Though this section will likely have to be rewritten fairly soon because of advances in the field, real-time differential correction yields accuracies to within only 50 centimeters to 1 meter unless very expensive equipment is being used, in which case accuracy to within 2 to 3 centimeters is possible. In general, if base station data are available in your area, then postprocessing differential correction is a very effective way to get good data at a low cost.

Mask Angle   Another factor that affects GPS readings is the angle of the satellites above the horizon. The signal sent to the GPS receiver is affected by the same kinds of atmospheric factors that affect the distances recorded by a total station. Here, however, the effect is greater and cannot be ignored. The closer the satellite is to the horizon, the more atmosphere the signal has to travel through before it reaches the receiver. As the signal travels through the atmosphere, it is slightly refracted or bent. Some refraction can be corrected for automatically, but as the satellite gets closer to the horizon, this becomes more difficult. Thus, GPS receivers include something called a *mask angle*, which refers to the fact that satellites falling below this angle to the horizon will be masked or ignored (see Figure 2.16). Most sources suggest that the mask angle be set at between 15 and 20 degrees. This means that all satellites within 20 degrees of the horizon will be ignored for purposes of taking a GPS reading.

Dilution of Precision   The *dilution of precision (DOP)* is an expression of the error associated with a GPS measurement that results from the alignment or geometry of the satellites used to take the measurement. Given the triangulation technique described previously, how the satellites are distributed across the sky will affect the accuracies of the measurement (see Figure 2.17). With the minimum of four satellites, the best distribution is one satellite directly overhead and three others distributed evenly around the GPS receiver 20 degrees or so off the horizon (i.e., just above the mask angle). In the worst-case scenario all four satellites are tightly clustered in the same region of the sky.

How the satellites are arranged at any one time constantly varies since the satellites themselves are constantly on the move. As with the mask angle, now that the full suite of 21 operational satellites is in place (the other 3 satellites are backups), it is easier to obtain good satellite geometry.

While DOP is the general term used to express this type of error, you will sometimes see it divided into subcategories and expressed with various acronyms; these are listed in Table 2.4. All GPS receivers will calculate at least one of these DOP values. The lower the value, the better the measurement. While there are not hard-and-fast rules for when a DOP value can be considered acceptably low, Table 2.5 is a fair guide. A DOP of 2 or less is considered excellent, but values of between 4 and 5 are considered acceptable for most survey applications. A value of 6 is acceptable only when very coarse data are required or when the GPS receiver is being used to navigate to a location as opposed to measuring a specific location. Values greater than 6 are generally not considered acceptable.

Since DOP is based on the location of the satellites, and since the exact position of the satellites can be predicted in advance, most GPS receivers come with software that allows you to predict what kinds of DOP values you can expect for a given location over a given time. The logic may seem circular here because if you

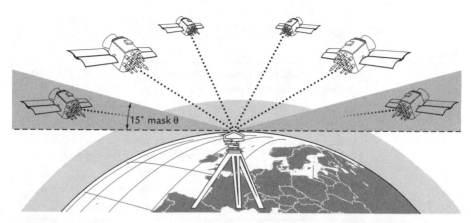

FIGURE 2.16 When a GPS satellite is too close to the horizon, its signal becomes unusable due mainly to atmospheric effects. The mask angle tells the GPS unit to ignore satellites that pass below the specified angle. *Source:* Adapted from Gregory T. French, *Understanding the GPS: An Introduction to the Global Positioning System, What It Is and How It Works* (Bethesda, MD: GeoResearch, 1996).

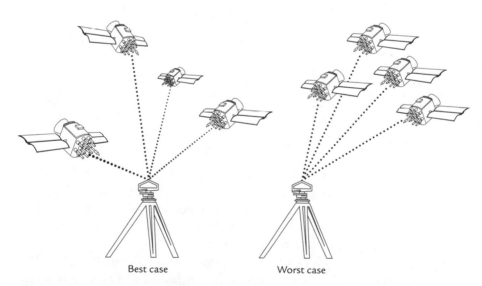

Best case   Worst case

FIGURE 2.17 How the satellites are distributed across the sky affects the measurement. In the worst-case scenario, the satellites are clustered tightly together. In the best-case scenario, one satellite directly overhead and three others are spread evenly throughout the rest of the sky. *Source:* Adapted from Gregory T. French, *Understanding the GPS: An Introduction to the Global Positioning System, What It Is and How It Works* (Bethesda, MD: GeoResearch, 1996).

TABLE 2.4   Subcategories of dilution of precision

Subcategory	Description
GDOP	(geometric dilution of precision) Represents an overall measure that includes the other measures
PDOP	(precision dilution of precision) Expresses the error in three dimensions (X, Y, and Z); the most commonly used measure
HDOP	(horizontal dilution of precision) Expresses the error only in the horizontal (X and Y); often preferable because of the larger errors typically associated with Z
VDOP	(vertical dilution of precision) Expresses the error in the elevation (Z)
TDOP	(time dilution of precision) Expresses the error in the measure of time

Source: Adapted from Gregory T. French, *Understanding the GPS: An Introduction to the Global Positioning System, What It Is and How It Works* (Bethesda, MD: GeoResearch, 1996).

TABLE 2.5   Interpretation of DOP values

Quality	DOP
Very good	1–3
Good	4–5
Fair	6
Suspect	> 6

Source: Adapted from Gregory T. French, *Understanding the GPS: An Introduction to the Global Positioning System, What It Is and How It Works* (Bethesda, MD: GeoResearch, 1996).

know your location then you will not need to take a GPS reading in the first place. But these programs require only a rough or approximate location to predict DOP values. Depending on the type of survey work you are doing with your GPS receiver and whether you have flexibility in when locations are recorded, it might be worth consulting the DOP values in advance.

It might seem that with 21 satellites in place and a proper mask angle, DOP should not be an issue. There are, however, other factors that affect how much of the sky is available, and therefore the DOP of a GPS measurement. First, GPS units need a clear line of sight to the satellites. Large buildings, deep canyons, and steep cliffs make GPS readings difficult because they block a large portion of the sky. As you approach a steep cliff, for instance, over 50 percent of the sky may be removed from view. Under these conditions you may have no alternative but to accept a higher DOP. Second, water absorbs the satellite signal. As a result, GPS units do not work well under heavy vegetation because of the moisture in leaves and limbs. It is sometimes possible to overcome the foliage issue by mounting the GPS antenna on a pole that extends above the canopy. In some instances, because of these kinds of terrain-related factors, it may simply be impossible to take a GPS reading where it is needed. The solution to this problem leads us to a consideration of how total station mapping and GPS mapping work together.

GPS VS. TOTAL STATION MAPPING

As the accuracy of GPS increases and, in particular, as the ease of doing differential GPS increases, the question arises as to when to use GPS and when to use a total station to survey. There is no easy answer to this question, but here are some general guidelines. Clearly, without differential correction GPS units are limited to recording only the location of sites. With accuracy of between 10 and 30 meters, there is not much point in trying to record the locations of features within sites.

With differential correction, however, GPS can do more. If you have access to extremely sophisticated equipment, there is not much you cannot do with GPS. But for most users GPS is not the best choice for point proveniencing artifacts or staking out an excavation grid. Depending on your needs, GPS might be able to measure the dimensions and alignments of major surface features. Differentially corrected GPS is probably sufficient to map large features such as walls, roads, and trails that extend across the countryside. In these instances you can quickly create a very accurate map simply by walking along the wall or road or trail taking measurements along the way.

The best solution, however, is often to combine GPS and total station mapping. The former can be very effective for establishing a datum at a site, and the latter is fast and extremely accurate for mapping surface features. Imagine, for example, a project to survey thousands of acres of land and map the sites that are there. Once you discover a site, you can place a datum on it and record it by taking a long series of GPS measurements. Next, you can set up the total station over this datum. If real-time differential correction is available, then you can enter the global grid coordinates into the total station before surveying the site. Alternatively, you can simply give the datum some arbitrary coordinates for the site survey. Then, once you process the data back in the laboratory and calculate the coordinates of the datum, you can shift the survey points appropriately. Note, however, that while this will place the site in the global grid in terms of X and Y, you will still need to rotate the points as well because the site grid will not be oriented with the global grid used by GPS. The global grids are all oriented to true north. One possibility is to orient the site grid on magnetic north and then rotate the points to true north later. Alternatively, you can establish a base line with the GPS unit, though this is advisable only if differential correction is available.

SUMMARY

Total stations and GPS units are fast becoming essential tools for mapping archaeological features. If you glance through a surveyor's manual or some other book on the operation and use of these pieces of equipment, you will likely be quickly overwhelmed by their complexity and apparent lack of relevance to mapping archaeological sites. To really understand how they work and what their full potential is, you need a fairly high level of knowledge of mathematics and trigonometry. Fortunately, as we note in the following chapter, you do not have to be a professional surveyor to put them to good use in archaeology. Knowledge of a little trigonometry, however, is essential. In particular, you need to know how to work with angles and coordinates. As is clear from this chapter, angles come in many different formats, and you will likely need to be able to translate from one format to another. In the next chapter, you will also need to know how to add and subtract angles.

Much of what we have discussed may seem relevant only if you are about to purchase a total station and its associated equipment. We hope, however, that it also gave you some insights into how to get the most from equipment you may already have or that you understand its strengths and limitations a little better now.

3 Setting Up a Site

At first glance, archaeological survey (by which we mean mapping archaeological sites, features, and objects, and not the process of discovering these same things) may appear to be quite difficult and best left to specialists. As Chapter 2 demonstrates, it certainly requires some knowledge of trigonometry, and total stations do look a little intimidating at first. Anyone can learn the basics of archaeological survey, however. We know this because over the years we have trained dozens of students to do just that. In this chapter we will discuss how to use a total station to set up and survey an archaeological site.

The most difficult aspect of survey is initializing the total station. By this we mean, not the physical aspect of leveling the instrument on a tripod (which can be quite difficult at first, but which gets easier with practice; see the accompanying box for an explanation) but instead the more mathematical aspect of aligning the total station's internal grid with your site grid. This process can be confusing for the novice, although most total stations come with software that includes a number of features specifically designed to make station initialization easier.

Defining the Site Grid

As we discussed in Chapter 2, when the total station is leveled and turned on it instantly establishes a three-dimensional grid on a site. In doing so, the total station assumes that it is at the center or origin of this grid; that is, it assumes that its exact center is located at the point of 0, 0, and 0. These coordinates are referred to as the X, Y, and Z of the station, or as the *northing*, *easting*, and *elevation* (sometimes abbreviated as NEZ). Note that Y corresponds to the northing since it is standard practice to orient both maps and XY graphs with north, or the Y-axis, pointing toward the top.

When we say the center of the instrument, we really mean the exact center of the optics in the total station. Most total stations have a mark on the side that indicates where the center is located vertically. You will probably want to find

LEVELING THE TOTAL STATION

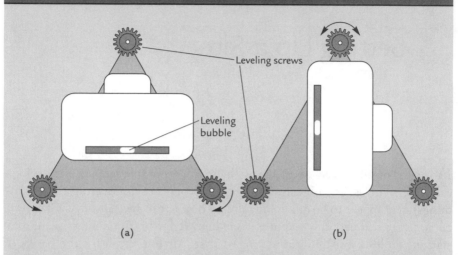

Leveling screws

Leveling bubble

(a)   (b)

There are two things you must do when mounting the total station: Make sure (1) that the instrument is directly over the datum and (2) that it is completely level. The following instructions are based on a total station with three leveling screws and a linear bubble level mounted on the instrument. Some instruments use electronic levels built into the instrument and accessible through a menu screen, but the principle is the same. If the instrument includes two levels, one for each orientation, then you do not need to turn it while leveling it. Simply align it with one pair of leveling screws and follow these directions without turning it.

1. To level the instrument, first turn it so that it is parallel to two of the leveling screws, as shown in part a of the accompanying figure. To level it in this orientation, turn the two leveling screws *simultaneously and in opposite directions*. Never adjust one of these screws without adjusting the other an equal amount and in the opposite direction. Once you level the instrument in this direction, turn it 90 degrees, as shown in part b of the figure, so that one of its sides is directly in line with the third leveling screw. Turn this screw—*without touching the other two screws*—until the instrument is level in this orientation. Repeat the procedure to make sure that the instrument is level in both orientations.

2. Once the instrument is level, use the optical or laser plumb built into the machine to move it directly over the datum. Be sure that the machine is completely level before you use the plumb, however. If you are using a plumb bob, leveling it first is not important. Note that you can move the instrument only a limited amount on the mounting platform. This is why it is important to center the tripod as closely as possible over the datum before you mount the instrument.

3. After you have the instrument over the datum, verify the level as outlined in step 1. Note that you may have to repeat steps 1 and 2 several times. Each time you will get closer to being over the datum and closer to being level.

this point on your instrument since it provides a means of measuring the height of the total station above a datum on the ground.

Remember that the Y-axis is set to whatever direction the total station is facing when it is first powered on. As discussed in the previous chapter, the horizontal angle, which ranges from 0 to 360 degrees, describes how the XY grid is oriented across the site. It is extremely important that the site grid be oriented in a consistent fashion with each setup. In other words, besides having a fixed XYZ origin, the grid must be fixed such that the northing (Y-axis) consistently faces in the same direction. There are a number of methods for achieving this, the most intuitive of which is to orient the grid to the north. Since north is 0 degrees on a compass, the simplest way to orient the total station is to point it north and set the horizontal angle to 0. In this way the horizontal angle read from the total station will correspond exactly to compass degrees, and the site grid will be aligned with north, meaning that the northing points (Y-axis) north. Note that the horizontal angle increases in a clockwise direction. As a result, the easting (X-axis) will have a horizontal angle of 90 degrees.

There are a number of advantages to having a site grid aligned with north. First, any XY maps that you produce will automatically be aligned on north, which eliminates the need to record the north angle. Second, this orientation is intuitively easy to understand and explain. Nevertheless, there are many reasons you might *not* want to do so. For instance, given the layout of your site, it may not be desirable to align your excavation units and site grid this way. Also, there are a number of subtle pitfalls in aligning a grid with north. In this regard, keep in mind that magnetic north is not the same as true north. The difference between the two varies around the earth in unpredictable ways and must be read from published maps or tables (see Figure 3.1). If you use magnetic north, it can be difficult to align the total station with it accurately if a compass is not built into the instrument; expensive optional equipment is often required, and under no circumstances would a handheld compass work. If you use true north, then finding it using astronomic sightings raises mathematical and meteorological difficulties. Actually, for most purposes, it is better to have your maps aligned with true north rather than magnetic north since most modern maps are aligned on true north and almost all geographic information systems (GIS) layers are aligned the same way.

The problems of finding north can lead to long-term consequences. We know of an archaeological site, which will remain nameless, where the surveyor decided to align the grid on true north using Polaris (the North Star). In principle this is quite simple. Once the sky is dark enough to see Polaris, the total station is set up over a datum and aimed at this star. The surveyor then sets the horizontal angle to 0. The problem in this case, however, was that the surveyor incorrectly identified Polaris. As a result the entire grid was off by several degrees for an entire season. Once the error was identified it was corrected, but

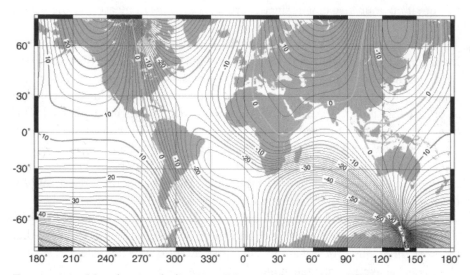

FIGURE 3.1   Map showing declinations (Mercator projection)—differences in angle between magnetic north and true north. The contour numbers on this map are declinations. So, for instance, a compass reading taken at the tip of Baja California will be 10 degrees off from true north.

the trenches of that one season did not align with the trenches of the previous or subsequent seasons.

In our own work we prefer to align the site grid according to our excavation strategy given the situation at the specific site. We measure magnetic or true north relative to the site grid and, if necessary, rotate the site grid at a later date to correspond with north (see Chapter 4). For example, if the site is at the base of a cliff, such as at Pech de l'Azé IV, we might align the east-west, or X-, axis to run parallel to it. In the case of Fontéchevade, which is a long, tunnel-like cave, we defined grid north to follow the long axis of the cave itself (see Figure 3.2). Aligning the grid to natural or architectural features can also help excavators to keep track of the proper orientation.

Similarly there are some advantages to retaining (0, 0, 0) for the origin of the site grid. The most basic of these is that it is certainly easy to remember. There is, however, at least one disadvantage to using (0, 0, 0), in that, unless the origin is carefully chosen to lie forever outside the extent of the site, you can end up with points having both positive and negative values. While both the total station and the data collection program are perfectly capable of dealing with negative numbers, our experience is that humans are less able to, particularly when negative numbers are mixed with positive ones. The main difficulty is that negative numbers appear to increase in the opposite direction of positive numbers. When negative and positive numbers are being used simultaneously,

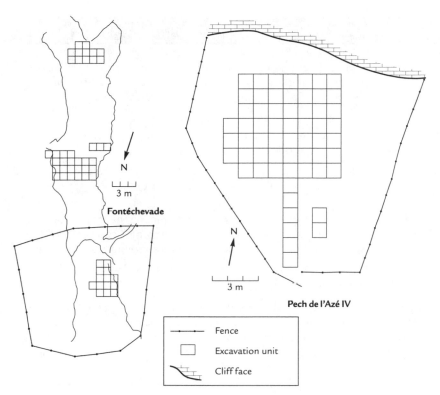

FIGURE 3.2   Grid orientations at Fontéchevade and Pech de L'Azé IV. Both maps are printed with grid north aligned toward the top of the page. At Pech de l'Azé IV, this roughly corresponds with magnetic north (shown by north on map), whereas Fontéchevade magnetic north is roughly opposite grid north.

the failure to note a sign can result in a mistake being made. We strongly suggest, therefore, using an arbitrary grid origin sufficiently large to ensure that no recorded points will have negative values. We often use (1000, 1000, 100) though in most cases (100, 100, 100) will suffice.

Just as it is useful to know where magnetic or true north is located relative to the orientation of the site grid, it is also useful to know where the site grid is located in a global system such as latitude/longitude or universal transverse Mercator (UTM). This can be easily accomplished by measuring the coordinates, using the local site grid, of a global benchmark or by taking a global positioning system (GPS) reading over a point in the local site grid. Every point in the site grid can then be adjusted by the difference between the global and local coordinates of the benchmark. It is important to emphasize, however, that it is possible, and indeed preferable, to establish completely arbitrary site grids that can be related to global systems of measurement at a later time. (See the accompanying box for tips on how to set up a new site with an arbitrary grid.)

SETTING UP A NEW SITE WITH AN ARBITRARY GRID

Your first station at a totally new site can be completely arbitrary and does not have to be permanent. If it is going to be a permanent datum, then you should verify the coordinates of that datum *after* the initial setup and from a different datum.

1. Set up the total station over your first point. Pound in two other datums that can be seen from this station and from each other.

2. Power on the total station. Point the total station in the direction you want to be the grid's north alignment, and set the horizontal angle of the instrument to 0.

3. Either with your software or by directly programming the total station, enter the coordinates of your location. When you enter the Z coordinate, be sure to first add the height of the instrument from the ground to its exact center.

4. Record the two datums you have created. These two datums can then be used for future setups.

If you want to use your initial setup datum as a permanent datum, set up on one of the other two newly created datums (using the other as the reference point), and then record your initial datum to verify its coordinates. If there is a small difference in the Z, it will represent the error in measuring the height of the instrument.

What we are really advising here is that you not be overly concerned with establishing a site grid that is, from the outset, tied into any global system or aligned with true north. Usually there are very practical considerations for aligning a grid and choosing the units with which you work. For instance, you probably want to align it according to natural or archaeological features, and you want to avoid having to deal with positive and negative numbers or with numbers that are too large to deal with effectively. After the fieldwork is done, you can always tie your site in with whatever global system is appropriate, so why let this consideration make things more difficult for you in the field?

WORKING WITH DATUMS

The way to manage and record a grid for future use is with datums. A *datum* is a survey point with a known X, Y, and Z, and it serves as a reference point for all of the mapping and point proveniencing. Every archaeology student learns right away about the importance of establishing a permanent datum, so there is no reason to belabor the point here.

However, most students are taught that every site should have at least *one* datum, what is known as the *primary site datum (PSD)*. In fact, every site should actually have *two* primary datums. This is because while one datum is sufficient to mark a known X, Y, and Z it does nothing to establish the orientation of the grid. Remember that a site grid requires two things: (1) a known point and (2) a reference angle. When the reference angle is based on a nonarbitrary alignment, such as magnetic or true north, the one point will suffice to record the grid, as long as the alignment can be reliably and accurately determined in subsequent seasons. In contrast, when an arbitrary grid is used, two points are needed, because two points determine a line, and that line defines the reference angle for the site. Thus, it is customary to publish a site map with at least two datums so that the proper orientation of the grid can be established (see Figure 3.3). In actuality, however, you will likely need many more datums to efficiently survey a site, to provide verification or checkpoints, and to serve as backups should something happen to the primary site datums.

To use two datums to set up your total station, you need to know the angle between them. This angle becomes the horizontal reference angle for your grid. When you think about it, however, while two points do define a line, and that line has a certain orientation in the site grid, there are really two angles that you could use. As Figure 3.4 shows, if you are standing on Point A and looking at Point B, then the angle is 33 41' 24"; but if you are standing on Point B and looking at point A, then the angle is 180 degrees different, or 213 41' 24". In trigonometry we say that one angle is the complement of the other. The complement of any angle can be computed by adding or subtracting 180 degrees. Whether you add or subtract 180 depends on whether the resulting value will be larger than 360 or smaller than 0 degrees or will fall somewhere between the two. While mathematically there is nothing wrong with angles larger than 360 or smaller than 0 degrees, some programs and most total stations accept only angles from 0 to 360 degrees.

In surveys, these two angles are given different names depending on where the total station is set up. The angle from the total station to any point is called the *foresight*. The angle from that point back to the total station is called the *backsight*. So, if we set up over Point A looking at Point B, then the foresight will be 33 41' 24". To set our horizontal reference angle, we need to turn the total station to Point B and set the horizontal angle to be 33 41' 24". If we turn the total station to the left until it reads 0 degrees, we will be looking directly at the Y-axis of the site. (See the box on page 74 for a discussion of practical considerations in setting up datums.)

THE BASICS OF STATION INITIALIZATION

We are now at the point at which we can go over the basic procedure for station initialization. It is actually quite easy if you have two datums and you can set your total station directly over one of them. Simply do the following:

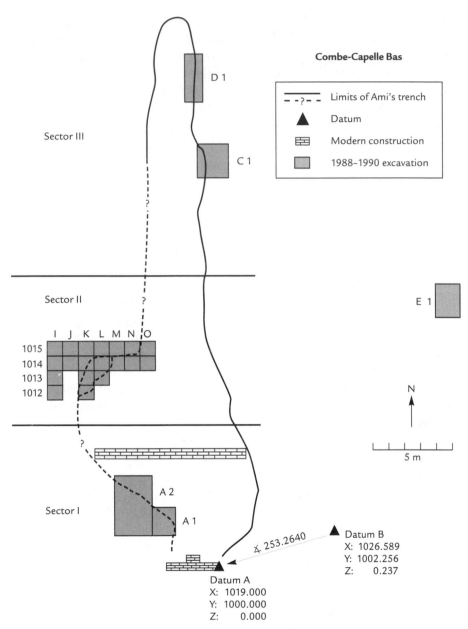

FIGURE 3.3   Map of Combe-Capelle Bas, France, showing the location and coordinates of the PSD (Datum A) and the reference datum (Datum B), as well as the angle between them

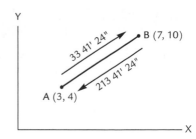

FIGURE 3.4   Foresight and backsight

1. After leveling the instrument over one of the datums, turn it to your second, or reference, datum.
2. Set the horizontal angle of the instrument to the foresight angle of that second datum.
3. Enter the X and Y coordinates of the datum over which you are set up.
4. Measure the height of the instrument from the datum, add that value to the Z of the datum, and enter that as the Z coordinate of the station.

After you initialize the station, you can set up other datums across the site. You do this by first pounding in the new datum and then measuring the X, Y, and Z coordinates. Unless you want to calculate the foresight trigonometrically, you should also make a note of the horizontal angle when you record the point. You can then set up over that new datum by using your first datum as a reference point and enter your horizontal angle as the complement of the foresight you noted.

There are three common errors that you can make when initializing a station. The first is to forget to take into account the height of the instrument, which will cause all of your measurements to be off in the Z coordinate value. A second error involves setting up your total station over an incorrect datum—that is, setting up the station with the wrong X and Y coordinates. This will have the effect of shifting the entire grid by the amount of the error (see Figure 3.5a). The third error involves catering a wrong horizontal angle. This will have the effect of rotating your grid relative to the defined site grid, with the point of origin (the point about which the points are rotated) being the datum that you set up on (see Figure 3.5b). Note that, if you set up over a wrong datum (you think you are setting up on a particular datum but are actually setting up on another), then all of your coordinates (X, Y, and Z) and your horizontal angle will be incorrect.

Although these problems can be fixed even after points are recorded (see Chapter 4), it is always a good idea to verify a station initialization immediately after you set up the instrument. You can verify the station simply by recording the coordinates of some other known point—the farther away, the better, since most errors associated with survey increase with distance. If the coordinates

SETTING UP DATUMS

There are some practical considerations in establishing permanent datums. First, and most obviously, permanent datums should be placed so that they are not likely to move or be buried for a long time to come. When you are working in caves, the cave walls make excellent locations for planting datums, though in some cases it may be objectionable to place objects in the cave wall. A small nail or a surveyor's pin with a clear X marked on its head placed in a large amount of cement makes a great datum. Obviously you should not put a datum in a tree or freestanding rock.

This, however, brings us to our second point. The more you protect a datum with large amounts of cement, the more likely it will become a target of vandalism. Certainly this is not the case everywhere, but acts of vandalism do happen, and it can be devastating to install a site grid and excavate for a season only to return the next year and find the primary datums removed from the ground. Thus, we suggest that, in addition to your standard datums, positioned to be useful to site survey, you place several other datums in less conspicuous locations and with somewhat less cement, so as to draw less attention to their location.

Third, it is important that you situate at least one datum in such a way that the total station can be set up over it. While it is theoretically possible to set up a grid by recording two datums from a third, unknown point, it is far easier to set up over one and record another. Thus, while a nail placed in a cement wall can serve as a good datum, it is better not to rely on two nails each placed in cement walls.

Fourth, the closer the datums are to the excavation or survey area, the better, since it will reduce errors that may result if several setups are required to bring the station into the working area. In some cases, of course, it is not possible to set datums on the site. Such is often the case when excavating in a farmer's field, where the excavation trenches are backfilled at the end of each season and the field plowed for a winter crop. In these instances you have to choose a location off-site.

Finally, try to arrange your datums so that the level of visibility among them is high. It is of little benefit to have multiple datums if you cannot see any of them from individual locations. It is best if at least three datums are all within one view field. In this way the total station can be set up on two of them, and the setup can be verified with the third.

If we seem overly concerned with this topic, it is because preserving your site grid for future archaeologists is an incredibly important but often overlooked aspect of documenting and archiving a field project. We have worked on sites excavated as recently as the 1970s where it was very difficult to find the original site datum and where the presence of only one datum meant that we had to estimate the orientation of the grid from the lines of the old trenches. Obviously this is less than ideal. But even if you are not concerned with future archaeologists, you still want to set up each day and each season as consistently and accurately as possible.

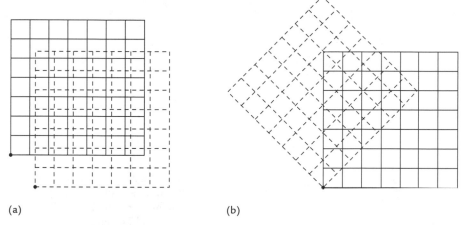

(a)   (b)

FIGURE 3.5   The desired grid (solid black lines) and the grid that results (dashed lines) from a station initialization (a) offset error in X and Y and (b) horizontal angle error

that you record for this point are not correct, then you can redo the setup and avoid the problem of having to fix points after the fact. Such verification on a third point should be done frequently throughout the day since instruments can easily go out of level. Also, if the tripod is accidentally kicked or moved, you must redo the initialization from the beginning, including centering and leveling the instrument over the datum.

EXAMPLES OF TOTAL STATION SETUPS

Mapping an Open-Air Site

Imagine that you are doing some survey work in the American Southwest and you come across a site on a desert mesa. The site consists of several clusters of houses with stone foundations visible on the surface. Let's also assume that this site is rarely if ever visited by people and is not in imminent danger of being destroyed by construction. Your immediate need is to produce a scale map of the site.

The first step in mapping the site with a total station is to establish the site grid. Start by finding a point on the site that can serve as the primary site datum (PSD) (see Figure 3.6). This point should be a little out of the way so that people will not accidentally step on it later, and it should be easy to see from other points around the site. Similarly it is preferable if you can see most of the site from this point so that you can accomplish as much of the mapping as possible while set up over the PSD.

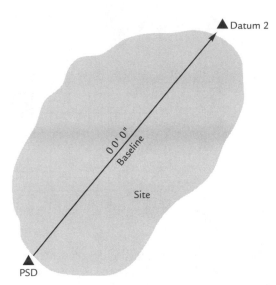

FIGURE 3.6   A map of a hypothetical site. The PSD is the primary site datum. The PSD and Datum 2 together form the baseline or reference angle for the site.

Next, set up the total station over the PSD. At this point you need to give coordinates to the point so that you can enter them into the instrument or the data collector's software. These coordinates can be completely arbitrary, so you have several options. In this example let's give the PSD coordinates of (1000, 1000, 100). In this way, unless the site turns out to stretch for a kilometer in the "wrong" direction, we can be sure that the whole site will fall into positive X and Y values. Likewise, assuming that there is less than 100 meters of vertical change in topography, all elevations will be greater than zero.

Next, you need to align the site grid in a particular direction. Here, too, you have a number of options, but in this example let's simply eyeball the site and determine how we would like it to look on a piece of paper in the printed report. In other words, let's find the long axis of the site and make that align with the long axis of our paper. So, from the PSD, point the total station in the direction that will correspond to the top of the paper. Now put a point in the ground, your second datum, along that axis. It helps to reduce angle errors if this second datum point is distant from the PSD. The best point will be one on the other side of the site but still close enough that the person holding the prism and the total station operator can easily communicate and that the tip of the prism can be easily seen resting on the datum point through the lens of the total station. Ideally the distance should be no less than 10 meters.

Once you have pounded the second point into the ground, aim the total station at this point and set the horizontal angle to zero. These two points together now define the site grid. The first point, or the PSD, sets the location of the grid, and the two points together form the reference angle that sets the orientation of the site grid. Together these two points form the site's baseline.

As a final step before you start mapping this site, you will need to compensate for the fact that the total station is not actually resting on the PSD, but is above it because of the height of the tripod. First, measure the height of the instrument, or station height, with a tape measure. For instance, if you gave the PSD an elevation of 100 meters and the station height is 1.35 meters, then the actual coordinates of the total station are (1000, 1000, 101.35), and all measurements will be relative to this point.

You are now ready to map this site, but probably the first point you should record is the second datum used to set the site grid reference angle. By recording the actual coordinates of this point (do not forget to subtract the height of the prism pole from all measurements), you will have created a point that can be used to install the total station in much the same way as it was installed over the primary datum (see the next section).

Moving to a New Location

Suppose that you were able to map most of the site with the total station set up over the PSD, but there is a far section of the site that is hidden behind some trees and could not be mapped. Thus, the station needs to be moved to a new location.

The first step in moving to a new location is to choose an actual location on the ground (see Figure 3.7). Pick a spot (1) that can be easily seen *from* the PSD, (2) from which you can easily see *back* to the PSD, (3) from which you can easily see the new area to be surveyed, and (4) from which you can see another datum that can be used to double-check the station initialization.

This may seem rather obvious, but you would be surprised how many times a point is selected that meets only two or three of these conditions. Also, when we say that you should be able to see the datum, we mean the actual datum. This is not absolutely necessary, since you can always use a long prism pole, but it is always better to set your reference angle by looking directly at the point on the ground. This is because, despite the best efforts of the person holding the prism pole, it might not be absolutely level, and so not directly over the datum.

Once you have selected a new point and pounded a datum into the ground, record its location with the total station and note the coordinates in your survey notebook. Also, note the horizontal angle between the total station and this new point. As we learned earlier, this angle, called the foresight, will be needed to set up on the new datum.

Now move the total station to the new datum and enter the coordinates of this point, compensating for the station height, just as you did in the first example

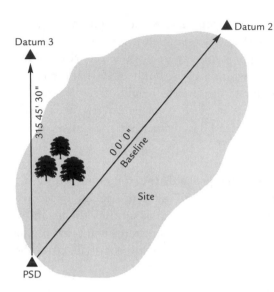

FIGURE 3.7   In this example, a cluster of trees is blocking the view of part of the site. Thus, a third datum is placed where (1) the area behind the trees can be easily surveyed, (2) the PSD can still be seen, and datum 2 can still be seen.

when you were installing the total station over the PSD. Once this is done, the total station will have the correct site grid coordinates, but you still have to align the site grid with the reference angle. You cannot aim the total station at the same point you used in the first example because the horizontal angle to this point is no longer zero and is not easily calculated without a bit of trigonometry. You need to set the angle back to the PSD where you just were. This angle is easily calculated as the complement of the foresight angle you recorded when you were at the PSD looking at this new datum. For instance, suppose that from the first datum to the new one you recorded a foresight angle of 315.4530. The complement represents the angle you should see when looking back to the PSD, or 135.4530. Now aim the total station at the PSD and set the horizontal angle to this value.

You are now ready to map the rest of the site. However, whenever you move to a new station, it is always best to double-check your new setup with a third point. In this case you can use the second or reference angle datum. We do not know the angle to this datum, but we do know its coordinates. It is an easy check of our setup, therefore, to record its location from the new datum and compare the calculated coordinates with the coordinates obtained earlier. While you are at it, you should note the horizontal angle to this point as well. This ensures that you will have a backup in case something happens to your PSD.

Determining Instrument Height Without a Hand Measurement

Though it is easy to do, we have never liked the idea of determining the station height by hand measurement. Even the least expensive total stations can maintain millimeter accuracy across large distances. There are some situations, too, in which millimeter control over elevations is very important. In our own work at Paleolithic sites, for instance, where each artifact is piece plotted with the total station, we have to keep very careful track of the elevations of artifacts and the levels they are in. Given the accuracy of total stations, it seems unnecessary and counterproductive to introduce relatively large errors at the start by using hand measurements to determine the instrument height.

When Using Two Datums   Although it may at first seem counterintuitive, there are simple ways to get around having to measure the height of the instrument above the setup datum, assuming that you have two datums with known coordinates on the site. The trick is to remember that the total station measures X, Y, and Z relative to the optical center of the instrument—not relative to the datum over which it is set up. Now, because the instrument should be set up directly over the datum, the X and Y of the total station will be equal to the X and Y of the datum itself. It is only the Z that will differ. And you can easily find that difference in Z by using the total station itself.

Figure 3.8 shows how it works. First, you set up over one of the datums, using its X, Y, and Z as the coordinates of the station and setting the horizontal angle as the angle to the second datum. Next, you record the position of that second datum. Because of the (unknown) difference between the height of the instrument above your setup datum, the Z coordinate of the second datum will also be in error. But the error will be equal to the height of the instrument. As the figure shows, if we set up the total station with the coordinates of (100, 100, 0), when we record the coordinates of the second datum we will actually get back coordinates of (90, 110, 3.5). The difference between the known Z of that datum (5) and the recorded Z (3.5) corresponds to the height of the instrument above our setup datum (1.5).

Note that this way of determining station height is accurate to the precision of the instrument and is much more accurate than determining it by hand.

When Initializing the Site   You can also use this trick when initially setting up your site. The difference is that we assign the first set of coordinate values, not to the PSD (as in our first example), but rather to the second datum used to establish the reference angle.

For example, imagine that the total station is set up over the PSD and the reference angle is set to zero with a second datum, just as before. This time, however, let's assign the coordinates of (1000, 1000, 100) to the second datum. Next, enter the coordinates of (0, 0, 0) into the total station or data collector program and record the coordinates of the second datum. For example, suppose that the total station tells us the reference angle datum has the coordinates of

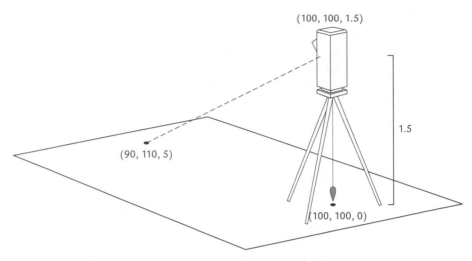

FIGURE 3.8   Determining station height with two known datums

(0.000, 10.900, –5.200). This means that the reference angle point is 10.9 meters along the Y-axis from your PSD, and it is 5.2 meters below the notch on the side of the instrument that indicates the vertical 0 point. The reference angle datum has an X value of 0.000 because we have set the horizontal angle to 0.0000 degrees between the two datums, thus ensuring that there is no difference along the X-axis.

We already know the second datum's coordinates, (1000, 1000, 100), because we assigned them to it, so we need to determine the coordinates of our instrument. We do this by subtracting the measured distance of (0.000, 10.900, –5.200) from the second datum's coordinates of (1000, 1000, 100), which gives the result of (1000, 989.100, 105.2). This is the position of the total station in the site grid. These coordinates are then entered into the total station to replace the (0, 0, 0) coordinates we originally used. If you have done this setup properly, when the reference angle datum is remeasured, it should return coordinates of (1000, 1000, 100), and you are ready to start mapping the site.

Note that this method directly calculates the coordinates of the total station, but it leaves the coordinates of the PSD on the ground immediately under the total station unknown. Well, this is not exactly true. We know the X and Y coordinates of the point of the datum itself (1000, 989.100) because the total station is directly over it. The Z, however, is unknown because the Z we have is at the center of the instrument and not on the ground. This does not present a problem for measuring points with this total station setup since the instrument has the correct site grid Z. But if we ever want to shoot to the PSD to install a new station somewhere else on the site, we will first need to find the actual elevation of this point. The best way to do this is to set up a third datum now that the station is initialized, move to that new datum (setting up with reference to what we are calling the second datum or reference angle datum), and record all three coordinates of the PSD directly.

Once you have completed this exercise, you will have three good datums on your site from which you will probably be able to survey most of the site. Furthermore, you can set up the total station on any of the three using any one of the other two and verify your setup on the remaining datum of the three. Once you understand and are able to apply this basic technique, you are ready to survey and map a site of any size.

Working Without Permanent Datums

Imagine another site in the middle of a plowed field somewhere in the Mississippi River valley. This site contains substantial deposits below the plow zone, and the excavation likely will continue for several summers. The problem is that after each season all the squares have to be backfilled so the owner of the land can plow and replant the whole field. This means that datums cannot be left in the field from season to season, and without the datums it will be extremely difficult to relocate the site and the previously excavated units.

Clearly the solution is to place a baseline, consisting of the PSD and a reference angle datum, just outside the field. In a best-case scenario, you would place it just inside some woods, where the trees would protect the datums from being run over by heavy farm equipment. Each summer the first step will be to set up the total station with these two baseline points as described in the first example. Once the total station is in the grid, you can start taking points in the field to locate the corners of the previous year's excavation units.

In theory it really does not matter whether the baseline you establish in the woods is at the start of the first field season or at the end, and it does not matter whether the horizontal angle along the baseline is 0.0000 degrees as it was earlier. Imagine that in the first season you set up the total station in the plowed field with a set of datums just as described earlier. Now, after a season of excavation, you need to place some datums in the woods in preparation for next year. The key is to select two points in the woods that (1) can both be seen from the middle of the field where you are currently set up and (2) have a clear line of sight between them. Record the coordinates and horizontal angles to both of these new datums. Now set up the total station on one or the other of these new datums by sighting back to the current datum in the middle of the field. Then look to the other datum in the woods and record the horizontal reference angle to this datum. While you are there, you can double-check by recording the coordinates of this other datum and comparing them with the previously recorded coordinates for this point.

If everything checks out, then you are all set for the next field season. When you arrive, relocate the two datums in the woods, install the total station on one or the other, and establish the grid using the methods described previously. The only difference is that, rather then entering an angle of 0.0000 degrees for the original horizontal reference angle as we did earlier, you need to enter the angle recorded previously. The point of this example is that the reference angle can be any angle. Once you set this angle and determine the coordinates of the total station, you can use the station to record new temporary datums in the middle of the field for that season.

There are two practical issues that you should consider, however. First, you should establish at least two baselines in the woods widely separated from each other in case something happens to one or the other of them during the off-season. Second, while it is theoretically possible to wait until the end of the season to establish a safe baseline, it is best to do it right away. It should be done immediately as a protection against anything happening to your temporary datums during the season. It is not unheard-of to have midnight visitors to the site kick over or remove the important datums.

DECIDING ON THE GRID ORIENTATION

Establishing North

If you are using an arbitrary reference angle for your grid rather than magnetic or true north, then at some point you will want to record the north angle so that you can include it on your map. Some total stations have a built-in compass, which makes this simple. Merely align the total station on magnetic north according to the compass and then note the horizontal angle on the total station's display. Suppose the angle is 315 30' 00". This means that your grid north (0 00' 00") is 44 30' 00" degrees off of magnetic north (360 00' 00" – 315 30' 00" = 44 30' 00"). To put a north arrow on your map, simply draw a line with an angle of 315 30' 00". To rotate all of your points so that the whole map is oriented on magnetic north, rotate every point by an angle of 44 30' 00" (see Chapter 4). Remember that when you rotate your points you also need to rotate your datums. The coordinates of each datum and the angles between datums will also change.

Recall, however, that magnetic north is not the same as true north, and true north is much more useful for integrating your map with other maps (see Chapter 9). To rotate to true north, you will need to consult a local map to determine the angle difference between magnetic and true north and then add or subtract this from your rotation factor (see Figure 3.1).

If the total station does not have a built-in compass, then the easiest way to record magnetic north is to place a good compass, such as a Brunton, on the tripod after you level it over a datum but before you place the total station on the tripod. Now turn the compass to magnetic north and have someone place a datum in the ground at a fair distance from the tripod on the north line. Install the total station on the tripod, place it in the site grid, resight this north line datum, and record the horizontal angle. This same technique can be used in combination with the techniques described in the first example to orient the original site grid on magnetic north.

Placing Your Grid into a Global System

As we have already discussed, it is usually more convenient to use a local coordinate system (i.e., an arbitrary one) for sites at the time of excavation. At some point, however, you will want to locate the site in a global coordinate system such as latitude/longitude or universal transverse Mercator (UTM) so that it can be placed on maps. In addition, you will want to determine the site's elevation relative to mean sea level (msl). Let's consider two methods for accomplishing this.

Today the easiest way to place your site on a map is with a Global Positioning System (GPS) (discussed in more detail in Chapter 2). Basically, placing the grid into a global system is as simple as placing the GPS unit on a datum (the PSD is best) and letting it record a series of locations that are then averaged into a best estimate or differentially corrected. For instance, suppose that you are using the UTM system. The GPS unit might return a coordinate of something like (634768.234, 2458320.879, 539.290) for your point of (1000, 1000, 100). This is enough information to place the site on a map with a single dot. However, this is not the same as having the site's grid being fully placed into a global UTM grid. If you want to place all of the mapped features onto the map, then the two grids (the local and the global) must be the same. This means not only shifting the XYZ coordinates but also aligning the reference angle of the two grids, much as was done in our third example with magnetic or true north.

First, you need to shift all of the site's points into the global grid. Subtract (1000, 1000, 100) from each point to reset everything back to zero (0, 0, 0), and then add the GPS measure to each point (634768.234, 2458320.879, 539.290). Alternatively you can calculate the difference between the local and the global grids and add this result to each point:

(634768.234, 2458320.879, 539.290) − (1000, 1000, 100) =
(633768.234, 2457320.879, 439.290)

Second, you need to calculate true north using the methods in the third example and then rotate all the points (see Chapter 4). When all of this is done, your site map can be drawn on a map published in UTM, and not only will the site be properly located on the map but the orientation of the site's features will match those of the UTM map. A wall, for instance, that runs along a ridge will match the topography shown by the underlying UTM map.

While all of this can be rather difficult, it is essential if the site is to be placed in a GIS and combined with other kinds of spatial data. It is important to keep two things in mind, however. On the one hand, you may not have to move the entire grid into a global system if the GIS requires only a single point for the analysis, as is often the case. Most regional, intersite GIS analysis is conducted with single-point representations of site locations. But if you want to have each feature of the site in the GIS, as would be the case when doing intrasite analysis, then the whole grid must be shifted.

If a GPS unit is not available or if the accuracy is not enough for your application, you can link your grid to a global grid by recording known global grid points, or benchmarks, in the local grid. This usually involves consulting a map for your site area and finding specific points that can be mapped. National-level datums are the best, because they are accurately measured by the federal mapping agency with techniques that are usually superior to the GPS measurements that you could take yourself. National-level datums are particularly useful for establishing your elevation since GPS units are somewhat less capable at measuring elevation than they are with X and Y coordinates. If datums are not available or if they are too remote from your site, then other landscape features such as roads, railroads, and power lines might allow you to shift your grid onto a global grid.

An Example from Northern France   In actual practice our experience is that relating your site grid to national grid points, like benchmarks, without a GPS unit can be one of the more challenging and rewarding aspects of archaeological survey. The reason we have not used a GPS unit to this point to tie our site grids to national grids relates primarily to our need for very accurate elevation information. This was especially true when we were working on Lower Paleolithic sites in the Somme Valley of northern France. Geologists working there have established a system to date archaeological sites by placing them on the correct river terraces. Terraces higher above the valley floor were cut by the river longer ago and are, therefore, older than terraces closer to the current level of the river. Thus, for purposes of establishing the age of a site, it is extremely important to know its elevation relative to the height of the river and other sites on other terraces in the valley.

After discussions with local archaeologists, we located a datum installed by the French equivalent of the USGS (United States Geological Survey) in the wall of a cemetery approximately 2 kilometers from one of our sites, Cagny-la-Garenne, and approximately 5 kilometers from another of our sites, Cagny-l'Epinette (each site is named after the village of Cagny, France). We started by initializing our total station in the local site grid for Cagny-la-Garenne. We then started working our way across the countryside, through a heavily wooded area, with temporary datums until we were finally able to see the datum on the cemetery wall.

We moved across the countryside using the same techniques described in our first example, about moving the station to a new location. First, we identified the next potential location. We selected points that were as far away from the current station as possible given the limits of our equipment and that were well positioned for the next place we knew we had to be. Once the new datum point was staked in the ground, we measured its location with the total station and noted the horizontal angle to this point (the foresight). Next, we moved to the new datum, installed the total station, and set the horizontal angle using the backsight (the complement of the foresight). Once the reference angle was set, we could establish the correct coordinates in the site grid by recording the location of the previous datum and calculating the new relative location.

Eventually, after several station initializations, we reached a place from which we could see the cemetery wall datum. We recorded the height of the datum by holding a prism against it at exactly the point indicated on the datum itself. This measurement gave us the difference between our local site grid and the national elevation relative to mean sea level.

Suppose, for example, that our measurement of the elevation of the datum (i.e., in our grid system) was 113 and the datum was marked in the French national system as 50 meters above sea level. This means that the difference in elevation between our grid and the French national system is 63 meters (the difference between the two systems, or 113 − 50). To place all of our excavated points in the global system, we then subtracted 63 meters from each point in our grid.

The story does not end there, however. In our description of how we moved across the landscape, notice that we did not verify each new setup by shooting to a third point. If we made any mistakes along the way, such as entering the wrong station coordinates or setting the wrong reference angle, the mistake would be perpetuated throughout the remainder of the survey. Since our goal was simply to record the elevation of the French datum, you could argue that errors in the horizontal angle or the X and Y coordinates did not matter—and you would be right. Nevertheless, in circumstances like this, it is common to check your work by tracing your path back to the original starting point where you can record a known point in your grid and check the difference. In survey parlance this is called *closing*.

Once we had verified the accuracy of our cross-country survey from Cagny-la-Garenne to the French datum, we worked our way through the woods and across fields to Cagny-l'Epinette. Cagny-l'Epinette already had its own site grid, but once we measured the difference between the l'Epinette and La-Garenne grids, then by extension we could determine the height of the l'Epinette archaeological layers relative to the French national system. In addition, it became a simple matter to directly compare the elevation of layers in the two sites.

When we finished we found significant discrepancies between the previously measured elevations and our measurements. Since the date of the site is determined by its elevation, the implications were important for Lower Paleolithic archaeology in northern France. Our goal in relating the results of this survey is not to criticize the work of others in this area. Rather, it is an example of how, in our experience, when a total station is used where standard survey and measurement instruments have been used before, the results can be surprising.

The previous discussion details how we were able to link the local elevation in our site grid to the nation elevation in the French global grid. The X and Y coordinates of the cemetery datum were not marked on the datum itself, but we likely could have determined them had we contacted the correct government agency. Similarly, in the United States, the USGS publishes the X, Y, and Z coordinates of all benchmarks.

SUMMARY

If you can complete the process of mapping an open-air site presented in the first example in this chapter, then you are ready to survey a site. The remaining examples are just variations on the basic theme. There are many more techniques we could discuss, but in our experience 99 percent of archaeological survey does not move beyond the techniques reviewed here. The following chapters discuss how to put these techniques to work mapping (Chapter 4) and excavating (Chapter 5) a site.

4 Making Site Maps

Now that you have learned how to use a total station to install a grid on your archaeological site, it is time to start making maps. In this chapter we discuss how to make topographic maps and explain a series of transformations that you may have to make to your data before you can complete your map. In the next chapter we examine how to use the total station to map features on a site, to lay out excavation units, and to piece provenience artifacts.

TOPOGRAPHIC MAPS

How Topographic Maps Are Made

Making a good topographic map used to be somewhat of an art. Surveyors would go into the field, record a few key points that described important changes in the topography, plot them by hand in the laboratory, write the elevations of each onto the map, and then begin a labor-intensive process of extrapolation to fit contour lines between these points. Today archaeologists can record hundreds and even thousands of points in days and process them on a desktop computer in literally minutes to produce high-quality topographic maps. Moreover, they can use software that costs hundreds of dollars rather than the software of professional cartographers that can cost thousands of dollars.

To understand how to make a good topographic map, it is probably best to start at the end of the process and work backward. In other words, we will first explain how a computer program processes topographic points to make a contour map and then discuss how best to record points in the field. The process is fairly complex in its actual operation, but relatively simple in terms of its logic.

The basic data for a topographic program are a grid of elevations. The grid is arranged, naturally enough, on the X- and Y-axes of the site. Intervals along the X-axis are called columns, and those along the Y-axis are called rows. Thus, a grid consists of a certain number of rows and columns. The spacing between the rows and columns (that is, the size of the interval) determines to a large extent the accuracy of the topographic map: the smaller the space, the more accurate the map.

When a topographic program is asked to make a contour map, it uses this regularly spaced grid of elevations to calculate where contour lines are drawn. The process is similar to the "connect the dots" game that children play by drawing lines between sets of numbered dots to make a picture. In this instance, however, the program draws lines connecting grid cells with the same elevation. Of course, not all contour elevations will be present in the grid; thus, the program also has to estimate where the contours will fall between grid cells. This estimation is relatively easy to do since the grid is regularly spaced.

The points you record in the field, however, will not be spaced on a regular grid. Thus, a topographic program must estimate the elevation of a grid point from your field points, a process known as interpolation. How a topographic program interpolates the field data—that is, what mathematical method it uses, how many points it uses, how far these points are from the grid point in question, and what effect distant points have on a grid point—are all factors that affect the final product. Some of the more common methods of interpolation are nearest neighbor, inverse distance, minimum curvature, and Kriging. Each of these methods will produce a different contour map with the same input data, and you will want to experiment to find the best results.

The nearest neighbor method works just as you might think. As the topographic program moves through the grid, it looks for the nearest recorded point to each grid point and assigns this value to the grid point. In its simplest form this method does not interpolate these values at all. In other words, the nearest recorded point is accepted without regard for trends in the data that might be apparent if multiple points were considered. Typically you can set a maximum distance so that if a recorded point cannot be located within this maximum distance to the grid point, then an elevation is not assigned. This prevents the program from making up data where none are available, but it can also create holes or islands of no data within the topographic map if the maximum distance is set too small. The topographic surface that results from the nearest neighbor method will be characterized by flat areas with abrupt changes from one flat area to the next (see Figure 4.1). This method tends to minimize variability or complexity in the underlying data.

The inverse distance method adds an awareness of trends in the data to the nearest neighbor method. This method considers several points in the neighborhood of a grid point and weights their effect on the grid point's assigned value based on their distance from the point. When a data point is nearly coincident with a grid point, then the grid point simply gets its value. Otherwise, all data points within a maximum distance are considered, and each is weighted as a function of its distance. This function can be linear, meaning that a point twice as far away has half the influence, or it can be exponential, meaning that a point twice as far away might have a quarter the influence. Thus, in addition to controlling

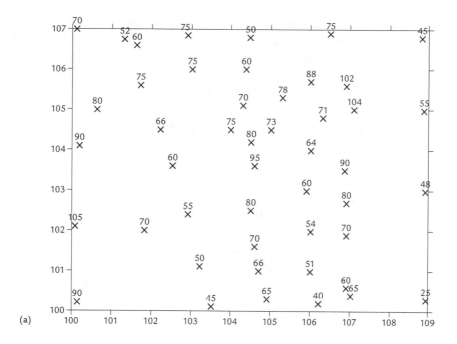

(a)

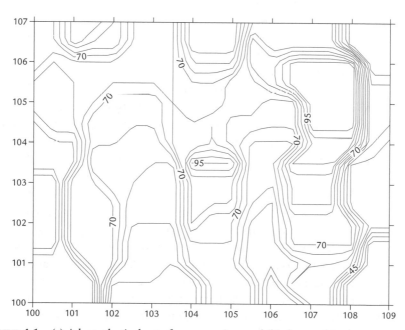

(b)

FIGURE 4.1   (a) A hypothetical set of survey points and (b) the resulting contour map when the points are converted to a regular grid using the minimum distance method

the search radius (the maximum distance for points that can be considered), this method also lets you adjust the distance function, which in turn can have a significant effect on the map that is produced. There is no way to objectively judge how the function and search radius should be set. Rather, you have to try various possibilities and compare the results with your expectations (see Figure 4.2).

The minimum-curvature method involves working with spline curves. Splines are a mathematical technique for drawing a curve that constantly changes to fit against control points along its path. Thus, spline curves are very good at showing trends in the surface, though they tend to emphasize local detail as opposed to larger trends. How closely the curve fits to the data points is another variable that can be controlled with this method, and this in turn affects how closely the map sticks to the original data points. The maps produced with this method tend to be aesthetically pleasing due to the smoothness of the calculated curves (see Figure 4.3). However, they also tend to include curves even when the underlying data do not lend themselves to curves.

Kriging is a fairly complex set of procedures that attempts to overcome some of the limitations of the other methods. One of its principal advantages is that it includes methods for evaluating the results of weighing near and far data points and the distribution of these points dynamically as it moves through the data set and selects the set of factors that most closely match the underlying data (i.e., reduce the error factor). In general, Kriging produces very good maps (see Figure 4.4). Its main downside, and the main recommendation for the other methods, is the time it takes to process large data sets. Depending on the type of Kriging performed, the number of data points, and the number of grid cells to be calculated, Kriging can take from minutes to days.

Today, however, this is less an issue as even the most basic personal computers have the processing power to quickly interpolate thousands of points. In the late 1980s, the best field computer had an 8-bit processor that operated at 10 MHz. Our daily routine was to upload the new topographic points before dinner and start the interpolation process to run overnight so that we could see the results the following morning before going back into the field. We hesitate to say how fast today's laptops operate because by the time you read this they will be twice as fast as when we wrote these words. The bottom line is that today you can easily upload topographic points and create a map during your lunch hour. It is even possible, and sometimes advisable, to use a laptop in the field to view the topographic map while the total station is still set up. This sometimes saves hours of work because you can immediately see any errors or gaps and fix them right away.

Note that the regular grid used by topographic software is the same thing as a digital elevation model (DEM) as used in GIS, a topic that will be covered in more detail in Chapter 9. This is a very important concept because it means both that contour grids can be easily moved into a GIS and viewed and manipu-

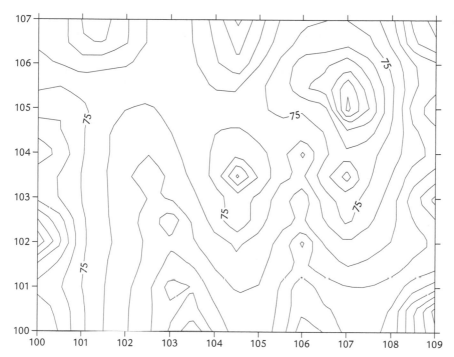

FIGURE 4.2   The same set of survey points introduced in Figure 4.1 converted to a regular grid using the inverse distance method

lated there and that GIS layers can be moved into topographic programs and turned into contours.

Strategies for Recording Topographic Data in the Field

To a large extent, how a topographic map looks depends on the method employed in the topographic software, but if you do not record the correct data points in the field, then no amount of software manipulation is going to make a good map. For instance, if there is a depression on the site, obviously you need points from inside for it to register on the map. Less obvious, perhaps, is the fact that you also need points around the outer edge of the depression. Otherwise, the topographic software will blend the depression with the surrounding terrain and make it look much smoother than it actually is (see Figure 4.5 on pages 94–95).

Since topographic software requires regular grid points, it might seem as though the best approach would be to record points in the field, as much as humanly possible, on a regular grid. But there are a couple problems with this approach. First, in some cases it might be a huge waste of time. In general, points are not required when the slope of the topography does not change. Imagine

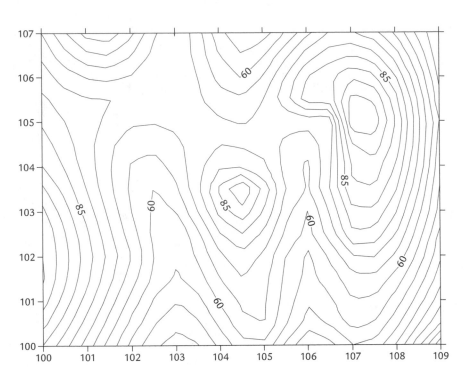

FIGURE 4.3   The same set of survey points introduced in Figure 4.1 converted to a regular grid using the minimum curvature method

making a topographic map of a flat surface like a ball court. Obviously points in each of the four corners would be enough for a topographic program to extrapolate the contours. This is true even if the plane of the ball court is steeply sloping. The important consideration is only that the surface is flat, which means the slope does not change. The contrary rule, therefore, is that more points are required when the slope changes or when there is more relief in the topography. A second argument against taking regular grid points is that dramatic changes in the topography often occur between grid points. In these instances the abrupt change must be clearly defined with points. Usually this means taking points along the top and at the base of the topographic feature.

Even if the topography is fairly constant, you will still need to take some survey points because of the search radius issue we mentioned when comparing the various topographic methods. You need to have at least one data point within the search radius of each grid cell. If you plan on using a very small grid cell spacing because you need to show very small, local changes in the topography, then you will need to either keep your search radius high or increase the density of points recorded in the field despite consistent topography. Otherwise, your map will have blank areas.

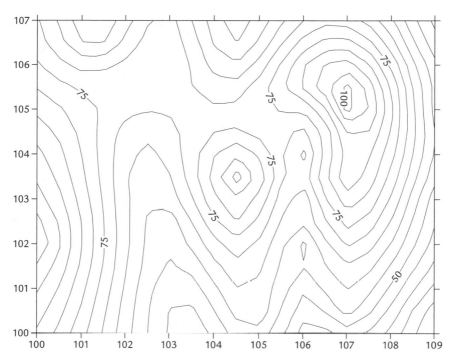

FIGURE 4.4 The same set of survey points introduced in Figure 4.1 converted to a regular grid using the Kriging method

In addition to grid cell spacing and search areas, you need to keep in mind the contour interval you expect to use in your finished map. If a mound or depression in the survey area is only a meter deep, then contours of less than a meter will be required for it to appear on the map. This means that across your survey area you need to take a point when the topography changes by a meter or more.

Generally it is best to employ a combination of methods for taking survey points. First, take lots of points in and around features that need to appear on the map. Take far more than you think you will need since taking points once in the field is far less time consuming than getting to the field in the first place. Second, take points regularly spaced regardless of a lack of change in the topography—this will help to ensure that you have a survey point within your search radius. Third, take additional points as you note changes to the topography.

Remember also that, despite the best plans for how to take points across an area, vegetation and undergrowth will have a large impact on what you do. If vegetation is heavy in your area, the winter months are usually the best time to survey. Otherwise, you may be limited to surveying in lines cut with a machete radiating from the total station. Of course, the farther these lines extend from the total station, the most distant they become from one another. Thus, you

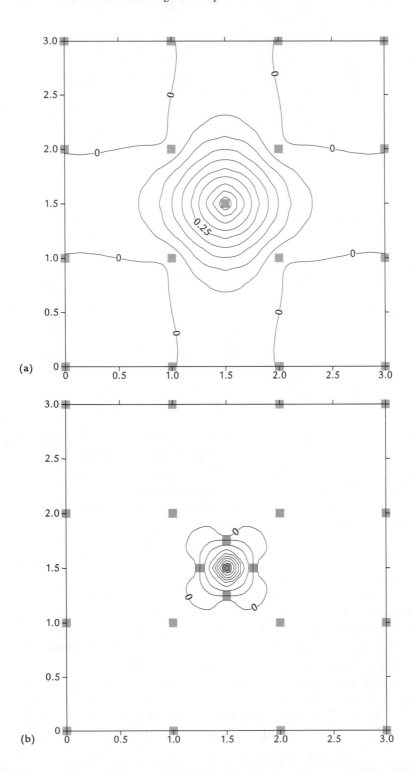

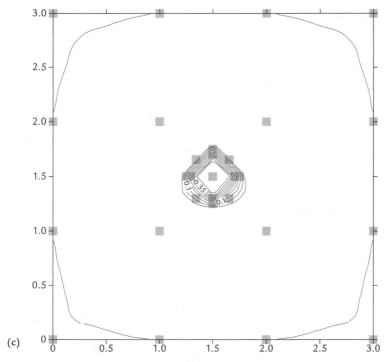

(c)

FIGURE 4.5   In this figure a hypothetical pit 0.5 meter deep and 0.5 meter across is being mapped. In (a) points are recorded every meter and a single point is recorded at the bottom of the pit. In (b) four points are added around the edge of the pit. Though this improves the appearance, more points are needed. Thus, in (c) four more points are recorded around the edge and four points are recorded around the edge inside the pit to show that it has a flat floor.

will need to move the total station frequently across the area to create a system of intersecting lines that together provide good coverage.

Reviewing Your Map

Even with a good point-taking strategy in the field and a good computer program to analyze the data, producing a topographic map can be a tricky undertaking. Often the map will not agree with your impression of how the terrain looks. Sometimes your impressions will be wrong and, for instance, a certain hill is not nearly as steep as you thought it was as you climbed it each morning with all your equipment. It can also be a question of perception. Three-dimensional surface maps are particularly adept at flattening changes in elevation. This is why most programs allow for something called vertical exaggeration, wherein all of the elevations are temporarily scaled (multiplied) by some factor to make them more apparent (see Figure 4.6). As a result, the map will have two scales: one for the

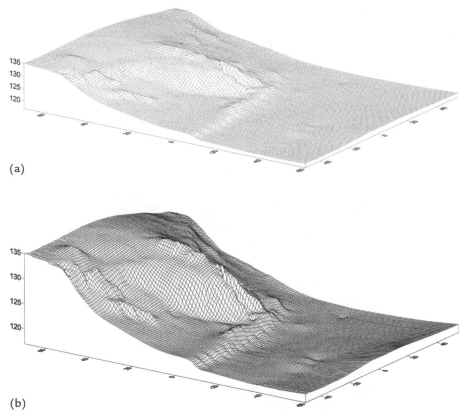

(a)

(b)

FIGURE 4.6   (a) A three-dimensional reconstruction of the area around the cave site of Fontéchevade, France. You can see the cave entrance in the center of the map. Three-dimensional grids like this are constructed from the regularly spaced grid calculated by the topographic software. It is the same grid that can be used to make topographic maps. While this representation of the cave is accurate, it does not visually reflect the dominance the cave entrance seems to have on the topography when you visit the site. (b) The same data set but with a vertical exaggeration factor of two. Having mapped the site ourselves, we can tell you that despite the exaggeration factor this map looks much closer to our own impressions of the topography.

X and Y coordinates and another for the Z. There is nothing wrong with doing this, and it can be quite effective in some instances, but the map must be clearly marked to indicate as much.

Maps also can be wrong. In our own work we have found that we are rarely satisfied with the results of our first effort. Inevitably certain topographic features are lost or minimized when the topographic software mathematically crunches the data, and the solution is almost always to record more points in and around the features in question so that we can reduce the grid spacing and bring out the feature. Thus, the mapping process should be looked at as a series of steps. Just how many steps you go through will depend on the complexity of the topography and the level of detail you are trying to extract. For this reason it is very important that you take the hardware and software needed to process the data points into the field with you. In the best-case scenario you will make a draft topographic map each night so that you can quickly identify and remap problem areas before it becomes difficult to get back to them.

Another important reason to process the data at the end of each day is to spot errors. All kinds of errors can occur but the three most common involve the setup itself, lost horizontal reference angles, and prism pole heights. Topographic mapping, as opposed to feature mapping or the point proveniencing of artifacts, typically requires that you frequently move and initialize the station, and each time you do so there is a chance for serious mistakes. The potential mistakes are too numerous to list, but the bottom line is that a series of topographic points recorded from a bad setup will all be wrong. Sometimes the errors can be corrected. For instance, if you enter the wrong datum into the total station, you can use the difference between the wrong one and the correct one to offset the points. Other times it is more difficult or even impossible to correct the mistake, and you have to delete the points and rerecord them in the field. Note that the key to recognizing and recovering from mistakes is good note taking.

A lost horizontal reference angle means that at some point the horizontal angle was set incorrectly. This has the effect of arbitrarily turning the orientation of the grid and can have disastrous consequences if not immediately recognized and corrected. Thus, it is common practice to periodically check that the angle is still correct by sighting back to a datum. It is especially useful to do this before taking down the total station to move to another station or before recording a new datum. If you can calculate the error in your angle, then you might be able to correct the mistake. Later in this chapter we will discuss how to rotate points by a given angle.

Prism pole height errors are easy to make and, depending on the magnitude of the error, the variability in the topography, and the number of affected points, sometimes difficult to detect. In a typical scenario a pole is raised to a new height to see over an obstacle and then lowered a few points later to its original height. The total station operator can forget to switch to the new height or forget to switch back to the original height afterward. Note that pole height errors affect only the elevation of the point and not its X or Y coordinates. It is always best to delete or edit the incorrect points immediately upon recognizing the problem.

GENERATING PROFILES FROM CONTOUR MAPS

Sometimes it is useful to show the topography of the site with a series of profiles in addition to a contour map. A profile shows the topography from the side in a vertical cross-section, and this is usually done along a straight line across the landscape though sometimes profiles are constructed along a series of connected line segments that trace a nonlinear feature of the landscape (e.g., a cliff that first crosses the site in one direction and then turns in another direction). One way to make a profile is to use the total station to record a series of points across the landscape. To make sure the points are in a straight line, you can stretch a heavy cord or rope along the profile line to guide the person holding the prism. It's a good idea to take points at fairly regular intervals, especially as the topography changes.

We have used this technique to good effect to create profiles of caves, and particularly of cave roofs. First, we stretched a rope from the front of the cave to the back along the line we wanted for our profile. Next, we walked the line with the prism pole taking points on the ground. Then we removed the leveling bubble from our prism pole and turned it upside down. In this way we could extend the prism pole until its tip touched the roof of the cave and then level the pole. Next, we retraced our steps taking points from the roof using the upside-down pole. To get the correct elevation from our total station data collector, we entered the pole heights as negative numbers. This way, when the program subtracted the pole height, it actually added the pole height to the measured elevation of the prism, which gave us the elevation of the roof of the cave. When we put these two profiles together—of the floor and the roof—we had a profile of the cave (see Figure 4.7).

Alternatively, if you have created a topographic map, then most topographic software will let you automatically calculate a profile from the map. This means that you can decide exactly where the profile lines will run despite the roughness of the actual topography and any obstacles that might have existed. Once you decide on the end points of the profile line, the software takes care of the rest by analyzing the grid of topographic points and interpolating new points along the profile line (see Figure 4.8).

Note that when you actually plot the profile, you need to be aware of what you place on each axis (see Figure 4.9). Obviously what is normally the Y-axis becomes the Z-axis in this case. What you place on the X-axis is less clear. If your profile is exactly parallel to the X-axis, then you can use the X coordinate of each profile point. Likewise, if the profile is exactly parallel to the Y-axis, then you can use the Y coordinate of each profile point. In all likelihood, however, a profile of the topography will run across your site on a diagonal such that it crosses both the X and Y grid lines. In this case, if you use either the X or the Y coordinate of the profile point, you will in effect be projecting the profile against the X- or the Y-axis, and this projection will distort the profile by shortening its actual length.

In these instances the only solution is to use, not the X or Y coordinates, but instead the distance from the first profile point to each successive profile point. Some programs do this automatically. When you calculate a profile, the program

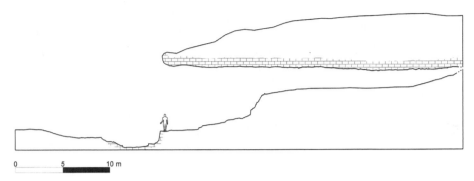

FIGURE 4.7   Profile produced for Fontéchevade

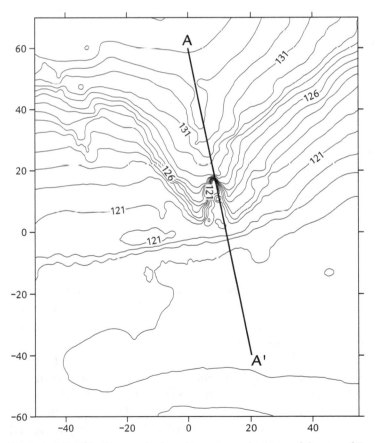

FIGURE 4.8   The line marked on this topographic map of the site of Fontéchevade marks the path the topographic program follows to compute the profile shown in Figure 4.9.

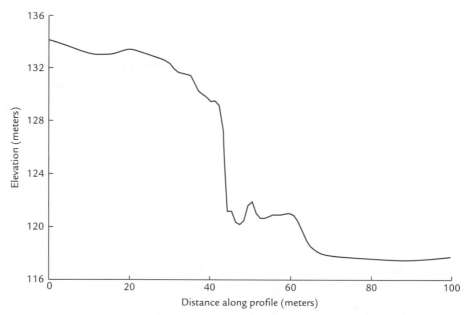

FIGURE 4.9   The profile shown here is based on the grid data used to draw the contour map in Figure 4.8. The X-axis represents the distance along the profile line. The Y-axis is the calculated elevation along the profile line.

returns the X, Y, and Z coordinates of each profile point and also the distance along the profile. If the program does not do this, then you can calculate it yourself using the Pythagorean theorem, because this distance along the profile line is essentially the hypotenuse of a right triangle. The spreadsheet in Table 4.1 shows how this can be done. In this example, to draw the profile, you need to do an XY plot where the X-axis is represented by column E and the Y-axis by column D.

Remember, too, that if the profile does not show the changes in the topography that you expected, you might need to use a vertical exaggeration factor. In the preceding example we can accomplish this by first subtracting the minimum of all elevations from each elevation and then multiplying this difference by some factor. In Table 4.1 the formulas given in rows 10–12 are for row 5, but they can be copied into rows 6–8 to make the complete spreadsheet. The formula in column F subtracts the minimum of all elevations from each elevation. The formula in column G then multiplies this difference by the Z scale factor in the cell G2. In this way you can easily change the scale factor and judge its effect on the resulting profile. Note that when you make the profile, column G becomes the Y-axis and now the elevations are not at all related to your actual site grid. As we discussed before, this is not a problem, but you will need to note this along with the vertical exaggeration factor when you publish the profile.

TABLE 4.1   Calculation of a profile

	A	B	C	D	E	F	G
1	Starting X	100					
2	Starting Y	100				Z scale factor	3
3							
4	Point No.	Profile X	Profile Y	Profile Z	Distance	Z Diff.	Z Scaled
5	1	100.00	100.00	102.34	0.00	2.30	6.90
6	2	101.23	103.76	101.39	3.96	1.35	4.05
7	3	102.94	105.03	103.42	5.83	3.38	10.14
8	4	103.85	106.12	100.04	7.23	0.00	0.00
9							
10	Where distance = sqrt((b5-b1)^2+(c5-b2)^2)						
11	Where Z diff. = d5-min(d$5..d$8)						
12	Where Z scaled = f5*g2						

SHIFTING AND ROTATING

When making a map you may need to alter or adjust the points after you have established a site grid and recorded points. Perhaps you made an error during part of your mapping and recorded some points with the wrong station coordinates. Or maybe you have since recorded a known benchmark and want to shift your elevations into the national grid so that the finished topographic map will have correctly labeled contours. Or perhaps you need to merge your points with points taken by someone else using a different grid system. To solve these problems, you need to know how to shift and how to rotate your survey points.

Shifting the X, Y, and Z

Shifting data points or the entire site grid in any of the three axes (X, Y, Z) is a simple matter of adding or subtracting the necessary change to the relevant field. Let's imagine that you set up your site as shown in Figure 4.10, with the original site datum set at an arbitrary (10, 10, 10), and that you have recorded a series of points relative to it. Later, on the basis of a survey to a known benchmark, you determine that the actual coordinates of your datum should be set to (20, –25, 100). For each of the coordinates, determine the adjustment to make in the old coordinate value by subtracting the true (or new) value from what currently exists. In this instance, the differences are as follows:

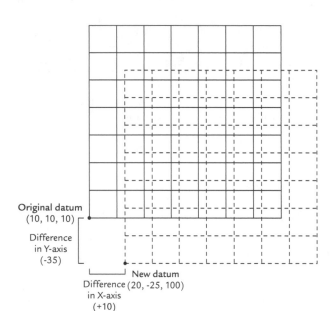

Original datum
(10, 10, 10)

Difference
in Y-axis
(-35)

Difference
in X-axis
(+10)

New datum
(20, -25, 100)

FIGURE 4.10   Shifting X and Y

Difference in X = 20 (true value) – 10 (existing value) = +10 (adjustment for X values)

Difference in Y = –25 – 10 = –35

Difference in Z = 100 – 10 = +90

In other words, for example, to place the X coordinate of the current site grid into the new site grid, you need to add 10 to each point. If you are doing this work in a spreadsheet, you can create three new columns for the updated values of X, Y, and Z. You would then write three formulas to add these differences to the existing X, Y, and Z values.

Rotating the Grid

Rotating a grid is a little more difficult since it involves some trigonometry and not just addition and subtraction. There are three steps to rotating a grid: (1) Determine the amount of change, or the rotation angle, that you wish to make, (2) choose a point around which you want to rotate the grid, and (3) perform the calculations.

In the previous chapter we discussed how you might install a site grid with an arbitrary orientation that meets with your research goals or with the layout of the site but is not aligned with north. We then discussed how you can record the angle to magnetic north (using a compass) or absolute north (using Polaris, the North Star). So, for instance, you might find that, given your site grid, north is at an angle of 30 degrees. If you want to rotate the grid such that grid north is equal to this north, then you will have to rotate the grid 30 degrees. This is because grid north is equivalent to the positive Y-axis, which is equivalent to 0 degrees. Thus, the difference between the orientation of the site grid and north is simply the angle to north (30 – 0 = 30).

Sometimes it is more difficult to determine the rotation angle. Suppose that you want to overlay your topographic map onto an existing map that includes a larger region and lots of features that you did not record but would like to include in your map. Unfortunately the two maps are at an angle to each other, so one has to be rotated to fit the other. Usually the other map will be oriented on north, so one solution would be simply to follow the steps outlined in the previous paragraph and rotate your site grid onto north as well. But for this example let's assume that the other map is also on some arbitrary and unknown orientation.

What you need in this case is a straight-line feature that is common to both maps—for example, roads, fences, walls, or power lines. The trick is to determine the angle one of these straight-line features makes in its respective grid. As we demonstrated in Chapter 2 in the discussion of how points and angles are related in a grid, you can do this if you know two points on the line. (See the accompanying box, which explains how to calculate an angle based on two points.)

You will need to compute this angle in both grid systems. Suppose, for instance, that a road is exactly 25 degrees in your site grid and 135 degrees in the other map's grid. The difference between the two is 110 degrees. You need to either rotate your grid clockwise 110 degrees or rotate the other grid counterclockwise 110 degrees. Note that rotating a grid counterclockwise 110 degrees is the same as rotating it clockwise 250 degrees because 360 degrees makes a full circle (360 – 110 = 250).

Defining the Point of Rotation or Origin   When a set of points is rotated, the rotation occurs around a specific point, what is called the *origin*. Depending on the location of the origin relative to the points to be rotated, the results will differ. Compare, for example, the two rotations shown in Figure 4.11, on page 106. In both cases we are going to rotate a mapped site (the shaded portion). In the left-hand figure the rotation is done about an origin point (primary site datum, PSD) that lies outside of the mapped site, and the PSD itself remains unchanged. In the right-hand figure the rotation is done about the center of the group of points (the origin being the midpoint of the Xs and the midpoint of the Ys), and in this case the location of the PSD changes. In effect, these two rotations show the effects of rotating around the original datum (keeping the location of the datum constant) and of rotating all of the points including the datum itself.

Which kind of rotation you do depends entirely on your situation. The first kind, however, is especially useful when the total station has been initialized with an incorrect horizontal angle. If this happens, then you should rotate the points around the coordinates of the datum that was used as the station's datum.

CALCULATING AN ANGLE BASED ON TWO POINTS

The angle between any two points can be easily calculated with trigonometry. To do this, refer to the accompanying figure, where X1 is the X value for Point A, Y2 is the Y value for Point B, and so forth. First, determine the lengths of all of the sides:

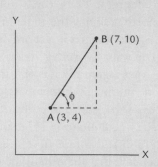

> Side_Adjacent = X1 – X2
>
> Side_Opposite = Y1 – Y2
>
> Hypotenuse = SquareRoot(Side_Adjacent ^ 2 + Side_Opposite ^ 2)

Next, calculate the cosine and sine:

> Cosine = Side_Adjacent / Hypotenuse
>
> Sine = SquareRoot(1 – Cosine ^ 2)

Now, get the angle and convert it to degrees:

> Angle_in_Radians = ArcTangent(Sine / Cosine)
>
> Angle_in_Degrees = Angle_in_Radians * 57.2958

We know that the angle from Point A to Point B in the figure must be between 0 and 90 degrees because Point B is in the positive X and positive Y direction relative to Point A. However, if we are standing on Point B looking at Point A, the angle is the complement; in other words, the angle from Point B to Point A must fall between 180 and 270 degrees. It is important to understand the relativity of this relationship. While the angle from the origin of the grid to Point A must be between 0 and 90 degrees, the angle from Point B to Point A must be between 180 and 270 degrees. In other words, an angle between two points is relative to those two points only.

The angle returned by the above formula always falls between –90 and 90 degrees. It therefore needs to be offset to between 0 and 360 degrees depending on the direction of the line:

> If Side_Adjacent < 0 and Side_Opposite <= 0, then
>   Angle_in_Degrees = Angle_in_Degrees + 90

The second kind of rotation may be more appropriate if, for example, you want to rotate the entire site grid to correspond to true north. Obviously in this case you want to note the new coordinates of all of the datums so that future setups will reflect the new grid orientation.

Performing the Calculations   Once you establish the angle of rotation and point of origin, you can do the actual rotation through a simple transformation

If Side_Adjacent < 0 and Side_Opposite > 0 then

    Angle_in_Degrees = 90 – Angle_in_Degrees

If Side_Adjacent > 0 and Side_Opposite <= 0 then

    Angle_in_Degrees = Angle_in_Degrees + 270

If Side_Adjacent > 0 and Side_Opposite > 0 then

    Angle_in_Degrees = 270 – Angle_in_Degrees

Finally, convert the decimal degrees to degrees, minutes, and seconds:

Degrees = Integer(Angle_in_Degrees)

Seconds = Integer((Angle_in_Degrees – Integer(Angle_in_degrees) * 3600)

Minutes = Integer(Seconds / 60)

Seconds = Integer(Seconds – Minutes * 60)

Using the example presented in the figure, we would compute the angle (ϕ) as follows (using an Excel spreadsheet):

	A	B	C
		X	Y
1		X	Y
2	Point 1	3	4
3	Point 2	7	10
4			
5	**To Compute:**	**Formula**	**Result**
6	Side Adjacent	B2-B3	−4
7	Side Opposite	C2-C3	−6
8	Hypotenuse	SQRT(C5^2+C6^2)	7.211
9			
10	Cosine	C5/C7	−0.555
11	Sine	SQRT(1-C9^2)	0.832
12			
13	Angle in Radians	ATAN(C10/C9)	−0.983
14	Angle in Degrees	C12*57.2958	−56.310
15			
16	Corrected for Quadrant	C13+90	33.690
17			
18	Degrees	INT(C15)	33
19	Remaining Seconds	INT((C15-C17)*3600)	2484
20	Minutes	INT(C18/60)	41
21	Seconds	INT(C18-C19*60)	24
22			
23	Corrected Angle (ϕ)		33 41' 24''

of the X and Y coordinates. First, calculate the sine and cosine of the angle of rotation (being sure to convert it to radians and making sure the angle is in decimal degrees):

SINANGLE = SIN(Angle in Degrees * 1.74532925199433E-02)

COSANGLE = COS(Angle in Degrees * 1.74532925199433E-02)

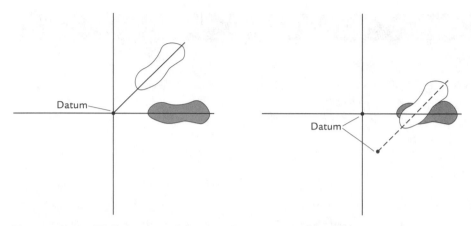

FIGURE 4.11   Two rotations of the same data. On the left, the site (shown in gray) is rotated around a datum located outside the site (the black dot). On the right, the site is rotated around a point within the site. As a result, the datum is rotated as well.

For each record, subtract the X and Y from the X and Y of the origin:

TEMPX = X – Xorigin

TEMPY = Y – Yorigin

Then recalculate the new X and Y based on the rotation angle:

NEWX = (TEMPX * COSANGLE + TEMPY * SINANGLE)

NEWY = (TEMPY * COSANGLE – TEMPX * SINANGLE)

Finally add the coordinates of the origin back to the rotated points:

NEWX = NEWX + Xorigin

NEWY = NEWY + Yorigin

CHANGING MEASUREMENT UNITS

Most maps are in meters, or feet, or degrees. Converting between meters and feet is relatively easy, whereas converting between either meters or feet and degrees is very complex. We will consider only the former.

Converting from meters to feet or vice versa is similar to applying a vertical exaggeration factor as discussed previously in this chapter. First, we need to know the conversion factor:

1 meter = 3.2808 feet

1 foot = 0.3048 meter

This means that to convert meters into feet you need to multiply each coordinate by 3.2808.

Thus, if your PSD has the meter coordinates (100, 100, 100), it becomes (328.08, 328.08, 328.08) in feet. Conversely a PSD in feet of (100, 100, 100) becomes (30.48, 30.48, 30.48) in meters once each coordinate is multiplied by 0.3048. Likewise, you can adjust all of the points in your database simply by multiplying each by either of these factors, depending on which way you are converting.

SUMMARY

Advances in computer technology have made it relatively easy to make a topographic map of your site. In most of the sites we have surveyed over the years, it has taken us about a week or two to create a good topographic map. Processing the points and putting the final touches on the map for publication takes about a day.

The math and the thought processes involved in shifting and rotating grids can be a little complex at times. For instance, one map might give angles but not individual coordinates, and another might give the coordinates but not the orientation angle. And one map might be in feet and another in meters. If you are lucky, several features on your map will overlap with features on the other map. These features might be part of the solution to the problem, or they might merely provide a handy check to make sure you have done things right. Perhaps the single biggest issue in combining maps is not scale or orientation but the accuracy of each. You may rotate and shift your map onto a large-scale map only to find that sites fall on the wrong side of streams or, worse yet, in the middle of lakes rather than on their margins.

Now that we have installed a site grid and made a topographic map of the site, it is time to start excavating. In the next chapter we will discuss how to use the total station to excavate a site and how to create the databases you need to store the resulting data.

5 Excavation and Point Proveniencing

A total station can do more than merely map surface architecture or the topography of a site. It can also replace tape measures and line levels in day-to-day setup and excavation of archaeological units; it can locate test units and then map the individual finds from within those units; and it can even be used to draw the profiles of the excavated units. In this chapter we discuss these topics and more. The discussion builds on the material presented in previous chapters and thus assumes that you are familiar with that material.

DEFINING EXCAVATION UNITS

Many different kinds of excavation units can be used on an excavation, and it is a relatively straightforward task to set them up with a total station. The more difficult task is deciding what kind of units to use, how to name them, and where to place them. We will ignore this last point since it is more related to the research design and layout of the site than it is to computer applications. It is important, however, to bear in mind that there are several reasons for defining excavation units—some more historical than functional, reflecting the traditions of fieldwork in a particular region.

In terms of their function in an archaeological excavation, there are three basic reasons to define excavation units: (1) to control where excavation takes place (i.e., to define clear and explicit parameters of the excavated area), (2) to provide one level of context for the finds (i.e., to identify artifacts as coming from one unit or another), and (3) to provide a means of point proveniencing by using the unit boundaries as secondary datums (e.g., to fix the location of finds within a unit by measuring from the western and southern edge of the unit). This last reason becomes completely irrelevant with the use of a total station, and so we will focus here on the role that units play in a largely computerized excavation.

Setting Up Units

In setting up excavation units on the ground, it is always a good idea to use the total station to fix the corners of each one independently rather than relying on hand methods. By using the total station you can avoid cumulative errors in laying out your units (caused by measuring the limits of each successive unit from the previous one), and it is much easier to maintain an exact orientation of the units in relation to the overall site grid.

Whenever possible, you should define units that are oriented with the site grid. Then you can decide on the four corners of the unit and find those points on the ground with the total station. Let's say that we want to define a series of 1-meter units, as shown in Figure 5.1. For unit A3 the four corners will have coordinates of 0 and 2 (for the "southwest" corner), 1 and 2 (southeast), 0 and 3 (northwest), and 1 and 3 (northeast). Beginning with the northwest corner, place the prism close to where the boundary should be and record the point. Depending on what X and Y values you get back, adjust the location of the prism accordingly. This usually takes a few tries, but eventually you will determine the location of the corner relatively precisely, and you can then pound in a nail or stake to mark the corner. Find the remaining corners in the same way. To define the next unit, B1, simply find the northeast and southeast corners, and so forth. Keep in mind that the placement of the nail or stake does not have to be exact to the nearest millimeter, since future points will be measured with the total station, and not in relation to the unit boundary.

Sometimes you will want to excavate in units defined in terms of surface features, such as rooms or pit-houses. In this case you first stake out the unit and then record its boundaries. Depending on the regularity of the unit, you should record as many points as required to adequately define it.

In either case, keep in mind that you should be aware that a unit, once defined, can change. For example, imagine that we originally define a unit as a trench measuring 2 meters by 3 meters. If we want to increase the length of this trench by 1 meter, we can either define a new unit (measuring 2 meters by 1 meter) or redefine the original unit to be 2 meters by 4 meters. Likewise, it is possible to define units within units. We may, for example, define a room as a unit but then define different features found in the room as units in themselves.

You probably will want to save the coordinates of the unit boundaries because, depending on the data collector software you are using, the total station may also be able to determine automatically the unit from which a particular find comes based on its X, Y, and Z coordinates. This can be a real time-saver in that you don't have to type in the unit for each point, and it can also reduce the number of errors when you forget that you switched from one unit to another.

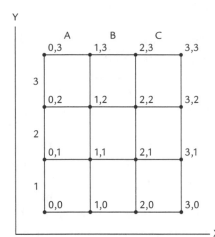

FIGURE 5.1   Unit corner coordinates

Naming Units

In theory any arbitrary name is as good as any other, because the unit is defined in terms of its physical location (the coordinates marking its boundaries) rather than its name. Nevertheless, you should give some thought to naming your units appropriately. "Appropriate" in this case means convenient in terms of how you view the units and how cumbersome the unit names are. The three most important functions of unit names are (1) to give some indication of the location of the unit, (2) to give some indication of when the unit was excavated, and (3) to maximize the efficacy of recording the unit name on artifacts, labels, and so on.

In French Paleolithic archaeology, most sites are set up as in Figure 5.1 or as in a standard spreadsheet, with letters going across and numbers going down. Just as in a spreadsheet, any given 1-meter square is assigned the name of the intersecting column letter and row number (A1, B3, etc.). At one of our sites, Combe-Capelle Bas, we actually used this system in conjunction with a series of rectangular trenches and test pits (see Figure 5.2).

POINT AND AGGREGATE PROVENIENCING

For many years archaeologists have been concerned with the accurate recording of where objects are found during excavation, and over time the level of precision in proveniencing objects has increased. The degree of precision that you strive for, however, represents a trade-off between the time it takes to record the provenience and the amount of information you hope to retrieve. In school you are taught that each archaeological site is unique and that it is destroyed in the process of excavation, which means that you have a responsibility to document it

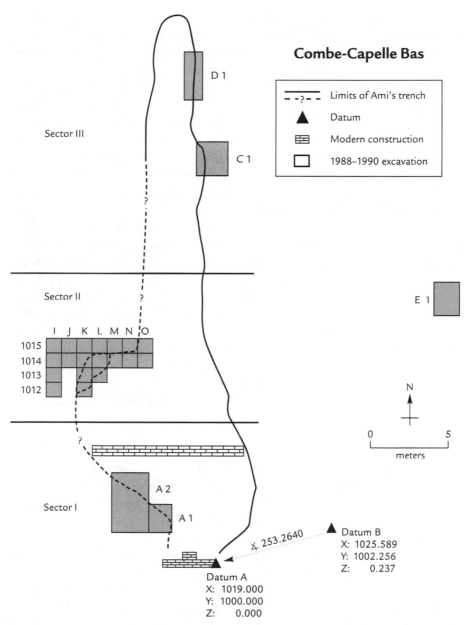

Combe-Capelle Bas

– –?– –	Limits of Ami's trench
▲	Datum
⊞	Modern construction
☐	1988–1990 excavation

Sector III

D 1

C 1

Sector II

E 1

I J K L M N O

1015
1014
1013
1012

N

0   5

meters

Sector I

A 2

A 1

✗ 253.2640

▲ Datum B
X: 1025.589
Y: 1002.256
Z: 0.237

Datum A
X: 1019.000
Y: 1000.000
Z: 0.000

FIGURE 5.2   Units defined at Combe-Capelle Bas

as completely as possible. But it is practically, as well as theoretically, impossible to collect "all the data," and so you have to reach a compromise in choosing which observations to take and which to neglect. This dilemma carries through to the three main aspects of archaeological excavation and reporting: (1) which objects are to be recovered, (2) what observations of their archaeological context are to be noted, and (3) what analytical observations of the recovered objects are to be made. It is that second aspect which concerns us here.

There are two basic ways of recording provenience: (1) *point proveniencing*, whereby each individual artifact is recorded in place in its own location, and (2) *aggregate proveniencing*, in which several artifacts are collected and together given a single provenience location. Aggregate proveniencing typically is used when excavation and recording is carried out with lots or spits, or when small finds are bagged together according to quarter-square/level. There are several pros and cons to both of these recording systems, and, in fact, most excavations employ both, depending on the class of artifacts.

Obviously point proveniencing comes closest to the ideal of reconstructing a site with all of the artifacts in their original positions. It also has a number of advantages in terms of databasing. Not the least of these is that each artifact can easily be considered as a separate record with its own unique identifying number, which in turn allows for archaeologists to build relations among different database tables. At the same time, however, field recovery is much more efficiently accomplished with aggregate proveniencing, and in many situations knowing the exact location of each artifact fragment is simply not worth the effort that would be expended in point proveniencing. We will not concern ourselves with issues of why or when one method should be used over the other, but rather will focus on how best to handle each for purposes of databasing.

Point Proveniencing

There are not many database issues surrounding point provenience data. In a simple database design each object (i.e., artifact) is represented by one set of coordinate data (X, Y, and Z), and each represents one record in the database table containing the provenience data, as in Table 5.1.

These basic data in themselves allow us to map the precise locations of the artifacts, and in many instances this is sufficient. However, with only one record or one set of coordinates per object, the view of the artifact distribution is somewhat distorted. For example, we lack information on artifact orientation—both vertical orientation, or inclination, and horizontal orientation, or declination—and, if certain artifacts are large, their overall size and shape will not be apparent. The solution is to record more than one point per object (perhaps two points, one at each end of the object) or several points that outline the overall shape. The effect of this can be quite good (see Figure 5.3).

Note, however, that with such an approach we will be creating more than one record in the database table for each recorded object—what in Chapter 1 we called a many-to-one relationship. Since each of the multiple points still refers to

TABLE 5.1   Point-provenienced objects

ID	X	Y	Z
1	12.544	14.232	-5.42
2	12.553	14.235	-5.47
3	12.751	13.875	-5.34
4	12.760	14.853	-5.39
5	12.761	14.845	-5.38

TABLE 5.2   Multiple provenience points per object

Unit	ID	Suffix	X	Y	Z
A1	1	0	3.926	27.935	-2.009
A1	1	1	3.873	28.1	-2.036
A1	1	2	3.874	28.096	2.037
A1	4	0	3.995	27.786	-2.284
A1	5	0	3.378	27.966	-2.073
A1	6	0	3.26	27.873	-2.099
A1	7	0	3.132	27.906	-2.08
A1	10	0	5.218	28.032	-2.469
A1	10	1	5.224	28.101	-2.463

one object, the ID number will have to be the same, which in effect results in duplicate ID numbers. The way to get around this is to number each of the multiple shots sequentially and to store that sequential "shot number" (what we call the suffix) in its own field, as shown in Table 5.2. Here, we see that artifact A1-1 has been recorded with three points, and artifact A1-10 with two; the rest are one-shot artifacts. Unique IDs in this table are then formed by combining UNIT + ID + SUFFIX. In an analysis table for these same artifacts, the suffix is unnecessary since Unit and ID alone will identify the record observations for each object. This is why the suffix is kept in a separate field.

Recording a separate shot number has several benefits. First, by following the values of SUFFIX, it is possible to preserve the order in which the shots were taken, or if necessary, to change that order. Some mapping software will connect the points that define an object, but as is apparent in Figure 5.4 on page 116, the order of the points can have a considerable effect on how the object maps. In this case, having a separate suffix for each shot allows us to identify which shots are out of order and to edit them appropriately.

A second benefit of having a separate shot number field is that it allows us to choose "representative" shots for different needs. For example, if we are

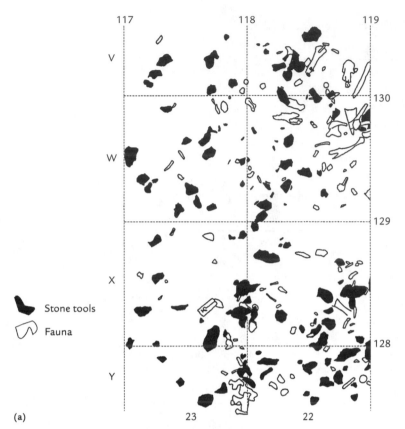

FIGURE 5.3   Comparison of (a) a hand-drawn map and (b) a computer-generated map of several excavation units at Cagny-l'Epinette

interested in mapping the artifacts to look for patterns of differing artifact densities, using all of the points recorded can give misleading results: an area with lots of multiple-shot points would appear to be denser than an area where most artifacts were recorded with one point only. In this kind of mapping, we could therefore choose to plot only points where SUFFIX=0, which would give us one point per artifact.

Aggregate Proveniencing

There are many different ways of databasing aggregate lots, and many important issues surround the use of aggregated data. For simplicity we will refer to aggregated data as lots, even though that term has a much broader usage. Assuming that spatial distribution (horizontally or vertically) is important, then it is necessary to define lots in terms of their location on the ground. Usually

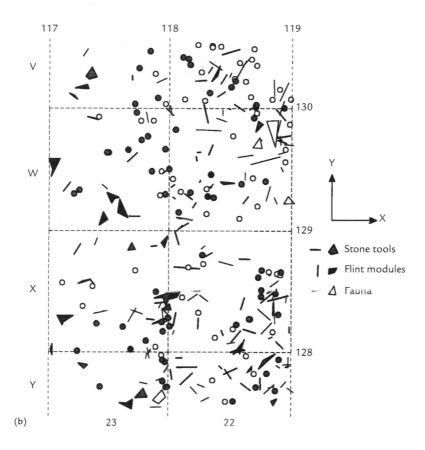

- ▲ Stone tools
- ▰ Flint modules
- △ Fauna

(b)

this is done with reference to the excavation unit (or a portion of that unit), depth, and stratigraphic context.

Let's say, for example, that a site is set up with a series of units 1 meter square, as shown in Figure 5.5. Retouched stone tools and diagnostic sherds are point provenienced, but flakes and other debris from stone tool manufacture and nondiagnostic sherds are put in bags (a separate bag for lithics and ceramics). Bags are changed every 10 centimeters of depth or every time the stratigraphic layer changes, and there are four sets of bags, one for each quarter-square. Each quarter-square is given a letter designation of A, B, C, or D, as shown in the figure. A simple table design for these quarter-square bags, or lots, of stone tools and ceramics might look like the one shown in Table 5.3, with analytical fields for COUNT and WEIGHT added.

There is no problem in the design of this table in that it gives us everything we need. That is, we know where each bag came from, and we can, for example, easily count all of the stone tool debris for a given level. We will, however,

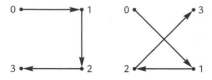

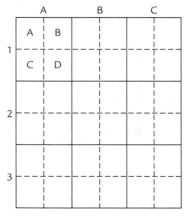

FIGURE 5.4   Connecting multiple provenience points. The order in which the points are taken will affect how the object is drawn.

QuarterSquares CV5

FIGURE 5.5   Defining aggregated lots based on quarter-squares

encounter problems when we try to integrate these data with other, point-provenienced data (because the coordinates of each bag are not defined in terms of the global X, Y, and Z coordinate system, as they are for the point-provenienced data) or if we attempt to define relations between this table and other ones (because of the lack of unique UNIT-ID identifiers). We also have a certain amount of duplicate data.

There are several ways of handling these problems. The first is to convert these raw data into a format that is more compatible with the point-provenienced data. The second, and preferable, way, is to alter the strategy of data collection so that from the beginning the aggregated data share a format with the point-provenienced data.

Transforming these data into a format that is more compatible with the point-provenienced data involves two tasks. One is to decide what to use as the X, Y, and Z coordinates. By definition, of course, aggregated data come from an *area*, and so cannot easily be accommodated by a single set of coordinates. Accepting this fact, we can, however, choose a point that can be used to represent the area. The best choice for the X and Y coordinates is to use the midpoint of the quarter-square since, in this case, the most we can be off in either the X or Y direction is a quarter-meter. In contrast, if we choose one of the corners of the quarter-square to represent it, then objects that fall near the oppo-

TABLE 5.3   Aggregated data by quarter-square, depth, and level

Unit	Lot	Level	Ending Depth	Class	Count	Weight
A1	A	Layer 1	–1.6	Lithics	77	56
A1	A	Layer 1	–1.6	Ceramics	83	45
A1	A	Layer 1	–1.7	Lithics	74	18
A1	A	Layer 1	–1.7	Ceramics	50	63
A1	A	Layer 1	–1.8	Lithics	85	31
A1	A	Layer 1	–1.8	Ceramics	18	92
A1	B	Layer 1	–1.6	Lithics	21	51
A1	B	Layer 1	–1.6	Ceramics	32	85
A1	C	Layer 1	–1.6	Lithics	23	54
A1	C	Layer 1	–1.6	Ceramics	2	13
A1	D	Layer 1	–1.6	Lithics	73	74
A1	D	Layer 1	–1.6	Ceramics	1	6
A1	D	Layer 2	–1.7	Lithics	16	99
A1	D	Layer 2	–1.7	Ceramics	17	55

site corner will be off by a half-meter in both the X and the Y. Using the midpoint of the area is best, therefore, because it involves the least amount of average error. In this case we are more or less forced to use the ending depth as the Z value. Note that if we record both STARTING DEPTH and ENDING DEPTH for each lot, however, we can use the midpoint of these two depth measurements to calculate a more accurate Z value of the lot.

Calculating the midpoint of each lot is relatively easy. To get the X and Y values of Lot A, we take the value of the Y coordinate of the southwest corner of Unit A1 (2.000) and add 0.75 to get the Y of the lot midpoint, and we add 0.25 to the X coordinate of the southwest corner (0.000) to get the X of the lot midpoint. Likewise, we add 0.75 to both the X and the Y of the southwest corner of Unit A1 to get the X and Y values of Lot B, and so forth for each lot from each unit. Our transformed table looks like the one shown in Table 5.4.

Now we have coordinate values for our lots in terms of X, Y, and Z in the site grid, but we have not yet integrated these data into the table containing the other points. Before we can do this step, however, we have to make some other decisions.

Let's begin by taking a look at a table containing the data for the point-provenienced artifacts (see Table 5.5). In this table each artifact is given a separate ID number, with the suffix serving as the shot counter when there are multiple points taken for a single artifact. Thus, each artifact is uniquely identified

TABLE 5.4   Calculating midpoint X and Y coordinates of quarter-square lots

Unit	Lot	Level	Ending Depth	Class	Count	Weight	X	Y	Z
A1	A	Layer 1	−1.6	Lithics	77	56	0.25	2.75	−1.6
A1	A	Layer 1	−1.6	Ceramics	83	45	0.25	2.75	−1.6
A1	A	Layer 1	−1.7	Lithics	74	18	0.25	2.75	−1.7
A1	A	Layer 1	−1.7	Ceramics	50	63	0.25	2.75	−1.7
A1	A	Layer 1	−1.8	Lithics	85	31	0.25	2.75	−1.8
A1	A	Layer 1	−1.8	Ceramics	18	92	0.25	2.75	−1.8
À1	B	Layer 1	−1.6	Lithics	21	51	0.75	2.75	−1.6
À1	B	Layer 1	−1.6	Ceramics	32	85	0.75	2.75	−1.6
A1	C	Layer 1	−1.6	Lithics	23	54	0.25	2.25	−1.6
A1	C	Layer 1	−1.6	Ceramics	2	13	0.25	2.25	−1.6
A1	D	Layer 1	−1.6	Lithics	73	74	0.75	2.25	−1.6
A1	D	Layer 1	−1.6	Ceramics	1	6	0.75	2.25	−1.6
A1	D	Layer 2	−1.7	Lithics	16	99	0.75	2.25	−1.7
A1	D	Layer 2	−1.7	Ceramics	17	55	0.75	2.25	−1.7

by a combination of UNIT + ID, and each point by a combination of UNIT + ID + SUFFIX. Each point has, of course, its own set of X, Y, and Z coordinates.

To combine the lot data with the data in this table, we first have to consider how to provide an ID name for each lot. The name of the lot (A, B, C, or D) will not work because it is repeated; that is, several lots may have the same combination of UNIT+LOT. We will be better off, therefore, if we can come up with some arbitrary values for ID for the lots, making sure that each lot will be unique in terms of the UNIT+ID combination.

One trick we often use to assign arbitrary ID values is to produce a string of random letters. If we define the field ID to be a character field five characters wide, then the random-letter ID value can consist of five characters. If each letter in the ID name is chosen randomly, the odds of getting two records with the same five-letter permutation are very low—1 in 11,881,376 to be exact. To get a random letter, use the RAND function combined with the CHR function as described in Chapter 1, remembering that the ASCII code values for the letters A–Z are between 65 and 90:

```
RandomLetter=CHR(INT((90 - 65 + 1) * RAND () + 65))
```

If we do this for each separate lot, we can uniquely identify them with the same UNIT-ID combination that we use for the other points. Note, however, that the two bags (lithics and ceramics) from the same quarter-square and depth

TABLE 5.5   Point-provenienced objects (multiple points per object)

Unit	ID	Suffix	Level	X	Y	Z
A1	1	0	Layer 1	0.73	2.06	–1.79
A1	1	1	Layer 1	0.75	2.09	–1.42
A1	2	0	Layer 1	0.86	2.64	–1.75
A1	2	1	Layer 1	0.76	2.68	–1.27
B1	1	0	Layer 1	1.6	2.6	–1.98
B1	2	0	Layer 1	1.53	2.49	–1.90
B1	3	0	Layer 1	1.78	2.73	–1.15
C3	1	0	Layer 1	2.89	0.2	–1.79
C3	2	0	Layer 1	2.27	0.84	–1.97
C3	2	1	Layer 1	2.32	0.92	–1.04
C3	2	3	Layer 1	2.24	0.86	–1.57

TABLE 5.6   Assigning random-letter ID values to the lots

Unit	Level	Class	Count	Weight	X	Y	Z	ID
A1	Layer 1	Lithics	77	56	0.25	2.75	–1.6	OWAQH
A1	Layer 1	Ceramics	83	45	0.25	2.75	–1.6	OWAQH
A1	Layer 1	Lithics	74	18	0.25	2.75	–1.7	ZXBPA
A1	Layer 1	Ceramics	50	63	0.25	2.75	–1.7	ZXBPA
A1	Layer 1	Lithics	85	31	0.25	2.75	–1.8	BXLYO
A1	Layer 1	Ceramics	18	92	0.25	2.75	–1.8	BXLYO
À1	Layer 1	Lithics	21	51	0.75	2.75	–1.6	KYFRD
À1	Layer 1	Ceramics	32	85	0.75	2.75	–1.6	KYFRD
A1	Layer 1	Lithics	23	54	0.25	2.25	–1.6	KFMUV
A1	Layer 1	Ceramics	2	13	0.25	2.25	–1.6	KFMUV
A1	Layer 1	Lithics	73	74	0.75	2.25	–1.6	MJKDB
A1	Layer 1	Ceramics	1	6	0.75	2.25	–1.6	MJKDB
A1	Layer 2	Lithics	16	99	0.75	2.25	–1.7	VEHBP
A1	Layer 2	Ceramics	17	55	0.75	2.25	–1.7	VEHBP

have the same ID value (we will explain why in a moment). Since we now have actual X, Y, and Z values, we can also eliminate the fields for LOT and ENDING DEPTH. The results are shown in Table 5.6.

The best way to combine these two data sets is to go an extra step and put the analytical data of the lots (the CLASS, COUNT, and WEIGHT fields) into their own separate table. We can then relate these two tables (Table 5.7 and

TABLE 5.7   A table of point-provenienced artifacts and lots

Unit	ID	Suffix	Level	X	Y	Z
A1	1	0	Layer 1	0.73	2.06	−1.16
A1	1	1	Layer 1	0.75	2.09	−1.40
A1	2	0	Layer 1	0.86	2.64	−1.38
A1	2	1	Layer 1	0.76	2.68	−1.75
B1	1	0	Layer 1	1.6	2.6	−1.63
B1	2	0	Layer 1	1.53	2.49	−1.16
B1	3	0	Layer 1	1.78	2.73	−1.87
C3	1	0	Layer 1	2.89	0.2	−1.64
C3	2	0	Layer 1	2.27	0.84	−1.54
C3	2	1	Layer 1	2.32	0.92	−1.43
C3	2	3	Layer 1	2.24	0.86	−1.18
A1	OWAQH	0	Layer 1	0.25	2.75	−1.6
A1	ZXBPA	0	Layer 1	0.25	2.75	−1.7
A1	BXLYO	0	Layer 1	0.25	2.75	−1.8
A1	KYFRD	0	Layer 1	0.75	2.75	−1.6
A1	KFMUV	0	Layer 1	0.25	2.25	−1.6
A1	MJKDB	0	Layer 1	0.75	2.25	−1.6
A1	VEHBP	0	Layer 1	0.75	2.25	−1.7

Table 5.8) by the combination of UNIT+ID, where ID is the newly created random-letter ID value. Notice that, by using the same random-letter ID for both the ceramics and the lithics samples, we can combine them as one record in the LOT table, and that same ID will point back to the point provenience table.

Note that you can avoid having to convert the lot data by recording lots in the field at the time of excavation. To do this, simply record the location from which the lot was taken (with multiple shots if necessary) and assign a unique ID number to the lot as if it were a point-provenienced artifact. From then on, the data can be treated as shown here. (See the accompanying box for a discussion of the use of "bucket shots" in excavations.)

CONVERTING HAND-RECORDED PROVENIENCE DATA

Throughout this discussion we have assumed that you are setting up a site for the first time and can make decisions about how it will be done. Clearly this is not always the case. There exists today vast amounts of information from previously excavated sites that is waiting to be computerized and analyzed using modern

WORKING WITH BUCKET SHOTS

In our own excavations we treat lots as any other point-provenienced artifact and record the provenience of the lots with the total station. Our most common lot represents screening samples from which we collect small lithic fragments and small faunal material. During excavation we place all of the sediment and small finds from a restricted area of the unit (normally about a tenth of a meter square) and within the same level into a 7-liter bucket. When the bucket is filled, the center of the area from which its contents were excavated is also provenienced with the total station; the bucket itself is assigned a two-part identifying number; and the level and other information noted is recorded, as with the numbered artifacts. The identifying number of the buckets is composed of the excavation unit followed by a random combination of letters as described above. In the case of these "bucket shots," the field data collection computer prints up to four tags, labeled "Coarse Lithics", "Fine Lithics", "Coarse Fauna", and "Fine Fauna", which accompany the bucket to the screening station.

After screening, all of the worked flint and animal bone are then recovered from each mesh size and bagged along with the corresponding computer-generated tag indicating the identifying number of the bucket. Thus, the site coordinates from where that portion of sediment was excavated became associated with each aggregate of small finds.

The proveniencing and assigning of identifying numbers to each bucket of sediment offers many advantages. Each bucket of sediment represents a relatively uniform volume, and each is fixed in space in the three-dimensional coordinate system. In this way we can obtain the exact volume of sediment removed from each level. This, in turn, is useful for computing relative densities of numbered artifacts and small finds. We also assign coordinates to the small finds (or to any other object that was overlooked during the excavation), which enables us to do precise spatial analysis of their distribution. In addition, if any artifacts larger than our normal cutoff size are found with the small finds, they are given new artifact numbers and they retained the coordinates of the bucket itself, the level from which it came, and the other accompanying information.

TABLE 5.8   A lot data table

Unit	ID	Lithic Count	Lithic Weight	Sherd Count	Sherd Weight
A1	OWAQH	77	56	83	45
A1	ZXBPA	74	18	50	63
A1	BXLYO	85	31	18	92
A1	KYFRD	21	51	32	85
A1	KFMUV	23	54	2	13
A1	MJKDB	73	74	1	6
A1	VEHBP	16	99	17	55

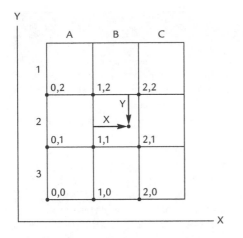

FIGURE 5.6 How the measurements of objects were taken, measuring X from the western edge of the unit and Y from the northern edge

techniques. We have done a fair amount of this ourselves, and the results can be quite rewarding. Certain issues must be dealt with, however.

One of the things you might have to do is convert hand-recorded point proveniences to a computer mapping system. The final structure of the database will look just like those we have already discussed. The important issue here, however, is that hand-recorded points have their own coordinate system. Thus, they need to be converted from the unit's coordinate system to the site grid.

Let's say that we have the records from an older excavation that consisted of nine contiguous 1-meter excavation units, as shown in Figure 5.6. During the excavation of this site, measurements of the finds from each unit were taken from the northern (Y) and western (X) boundaries and recorded as whole-number centimeters from each edge boundary. The records for these artifacts thus consist of UNIT name, ID number, X (in centimeters), and Y (in centimeters) (see Table 5.9). What we want to do is convert these measurements into our site grid based on a PSD located in the lower left-hand (southwest) corner of Unit A3 with coordinates of (0, 0).

This data set really poses three different problems: (1) The measurements are from individual unit boundaries, and not a single PSD; (2) as they are recorded, the measurements are in whole numbers, rather than as the proper fractions of a meter; and (3) the Y measurements are, in effect, taken from a direction opposite our desired grid orientation. Thus, we are going to have to do a number of things to convert these data properly.

First, we have to determine the meter intervals that represent the local datum for each unit relative to the overall site grid. In Figure 5.6 these are the points at the southwest corner of each unit, with the coordinates given in terms of the overall site grid. In other words, based on these local datums, we know

TABLE 5.9	Hand-recorded objects*		
UNIT	ID	X	Y
A1	1	8	94
B1	2	75	91
C1	3	86	36
A2	4	36	12
B2	5	60	40
C2	6	50	51
A3	7	78	27
B3	8	89	80
C3	9	27	16

*X and Y represent measurements from the western
and northern square boundaries, respectively.

that the finds from Unit B1 should have X coordinates between 1 and 2 meters, and Y coordinates between 2 and 3 meters.

The conversion of the X coordinates is straightforward. Taking each unit one at a time, we add the X of the local datum for that unit to the ratio of the original value divided by 100 (this converts the original value into fractions of a meter). To convert the Y coordinates, we do the same thing, but first we subtract the original Y values from 100 (to convert it to a measurement from the southern rather than the northern boundary). The results are shown in Table 5.10.

Obviously, for a large set of records from many squares, you will not want to do this conversion by hand. Each of the steps we just outlined, however, is easily converted into formulas given in Chapter 1. Since each unit has a different set of coordinates, this part of the conversion is a bit more difficult to write as a general formula. Thus, you might have to select and alter the records of one square at a time using a query (e.g., Unit = "B1").

SPECIALIZED RECORDING

Many other kinds of things are recorded spatially during an excavation, and most of the concepts that we have already covered apply to them as well. During our own excavations, we do virtually all recording by adjusting the values of UNIT, ID, SUFFIX, LEVEL, and CODE (a short description indicating the type of object or measurement). We will present some examples of these to illustrate our overall approach. Keep in mind that our ways of handling these various specialized needs are not necessarily the best way in different kinds of situations, but they do work well for us.

TABLE 5.10   Transforming X and Y values to meters based on position relative to the PSD

Unit	ID	X	Y	New X	New Y
A1	1	8	94	0.08	2.06
B1	2	75	91	1.75	2.09
C1	3	86	36	2.86	2.64
A2	4	36	12	0.36	1.88
B2	5	60	40	1.60	1.60
C2	6	50	51	2.50	1.49
A3	7	78	27	0.78	0.73
B3	8	89	80	1.89	0.20
C3	9	27	16	2.27	0.84

Topographic Points

In our excavations we typically record three different kinds of topographic points. The first kind are surface topographic points, which we use to prepare a contour map of the site and its surroundings. The second kind are level topographic points, which we record on the top of each stratigraphic level. These points, when combined after the excavation, can be used to prepare a contour map of the surface of each buried level. The third kind of topographic points we record are feature points, which we use to outline major natural or anthropogenic features within the site. All of them incorporate the use of random-letter strings for the ID values.

For surface topographic points we typically assign the word "TOPO" as both the UNIT and CODE value and "SURFACE" as the value for LEVEL. Since there is no need to join individual points when plotting, we typically do not use multiple shots for the same UNIT-ID, so SUFFIX remains at 0 for all of the points. It is thus an easy task to query the database for the points that will be used to produce a contour map (e.g., CODE = "TOPO" AND LEVEL = "SURFACE").

For level topographic points it is possible to follow the exact same strategy. In this case, however, the LEVEL field should contain the name of the stratigraphic level whose surface is being recorded. Also, to avoid confusion with the surface topographic points, we tend to assign to UNIT the name of the excavation unit where these points are being recorded.

We use feature points to locate and draw outlines of major features of the site or perhaps the boundaries of the site or other relevant landmarks (stream or road boundaries, the base of a cliff, etc.). Because we want the computer to join the series of points, we increment SUFFIX as we follow the edge of the feature in question. UNIT and CODE are assigned values that will subsequently help us identify the kinds of features represented by these points.

Stratigraphic Profiles

It is often useful to record the boundaries between stratigraphic layers as seen in section, as a series of points taken along the upper surface of each layer. The name of the layer should be assigned to the LEVEL field. The ID value can be a random-letter value, but each subsequent point measured along the level boundary should be given an incremental SUFFIX value. The CODE field can be assigned a value of "PROFILE", for example, to help isolate these points from other level topographic points.

Unit Boundaries

Because the measurements that define an excavation unit boundary should be clearly associated with that unit, the name of the unit should go into the UNIT field. For purely historical reasons we assign the ID field a value of "LIMIT" for these measurements, and we increment the value of SUFFIX for as many points as it takes to spatially define the unit. CODE is assigned a value of "UNIT".

Datums

In the field we assign names to all of our datums (Datum1, Datum2, Main, Side, etc.). When a datum is defined, the UNIT field contains this name, and both the ID and CODE fields contain the value of "DATUM". Because a datum is always a single point, the SUFFIX field is given the value of 0.

Samples

We provenience all samples collected in the field with the total station. These include geological, pollen, geophysical, dating, and other samples. Our strategy for defining the fields for these measures may differ according to the needs of the specialist taking the samples. For example, if a column of samples is being taken, the UNIT field may contain the name of that column as determined by the specialist, and each individual sample from the column is given an incremental ID number. A specimen to be used for dating may be given a normal UNIT-ID, just like any other artifact. Typically we note in the CODE field what kind of sample was taken.

SUMMARY

Of course these are not the only issues you will encounter in computerizing the collection of data in the field. We hope, however, that in the preceding chapters we have provided a foundation on which you can build a customized system for your excavation. While there are definite traditions in archaeology, no one excavates in exactly the same way, and each site has its own particular requirements. The key is to design a system that is flexible enough to accommodate the peculiarities of each site and to deal with the unexpected.

Next we will discuss how to analyze the excavated materials in the laboratory. When these data are combined with the spatial data, it makes for a powerful database that can easily be analyzed and published.

6 Entering Laboratory Data

In the laboratory the primary goals are to gather as much data as needed, as quickly as possible, with as few errors as possible. In this chapter we discuss a number of techniques to accomplish these goals. Some of them involve specialized hardware like electronic calipers connected directly to the computer so that measurements can be recorded automatically. Other techniques, such as pull-down menus and authority files containing lists of correct or valid responses to data entry questions, involve software that can be applied to most database management programs.

WHERE YOU ENTER YOUR DATA

One of the more basic issues that we need to consider is where you actually put the observations that you record from your artifacts. In the old days (which do not quite date back to the Paleolithic), you would have had no choice but to design a paper form on which to record your observations. Later, when you wanted to summarize a particular observation, you would have to sift through those forms and tabulate the results. When computers came on the scene, most researchers continued with paper forms, or coding sheets, but developed various code sets for their observations that could easily be computerized using the technology available at the time.

Using coding sheets typically means assigning numeric or letter codes to observations. For instance, rather than enter the species of a particular bone as "Bos primigenius", this species is given a code number of "063", and this number is entered in the computer. There were a number of reasons for handling data this way, but at the time the two most important were storage space and punch cards. From the discussion in Chapter 1, you know that it takes a lot more storage space to save the species name in a text field than it does to save the code number in an integer field. Punch cards, however, were just as important a factor since they structured how data was entered into a computer. Punch cards could hold 80 columns of ASCII data. If you wanted to get all the observations for, say, a particular bone, on one punch card, then codes like "063" for "Bos primigenius" were the only way to make it happen.

With the invention of the personal computer, and particularly the portable or laptop computer, archaeologists started entering their data directly into computers, abandoning punch cards. But some archaeologists continue to use paper forms for various reasons. For example, some do not want to, or simply cannot, take a computer into the field or wherever the artifacts to be studied are. Some still do not fully trust computers and prefer to have a hard copy of their data that can be easily stored for the ages.

In this chapter, however, we will assume that you want to enter your data directly into a computer, because otherwise you simply cannot take full advantage of the techniques we present for making data entry more efficient and more error free. But this still does not fully answer the question of *where* you put your data. A word processor? In a spreadsheet? A specialized data entry program? A database?

Though we have seen many people do it, entering your data into a word processor is not the best way to go. The reason is that most word processors add all sorts of internal formatting information to the file, unless you specifically indicate that you want to save the file in "Text" or ASCII format. If you do not save the file in ASCII, then there is little you can do with the data outside of that program, and it can be very difficult to translate a word processor table into a spreadsheet or a database table.

Spreadsheets offer a lot more advantages for entering data, and many people do it this way. Spreadsheets are certainly simple to set up, use, and modify as you go along. As we discussed in Chapter 1, the columns of a spreadsheet are the equivalent of database fields and the rows are the equivalent of database records. When you want to add a new field, you need only insert a new column. And, with some planning and preparation, particularly in how you name your columns, you can convert your spreadsheet into a database after you complete your analysis. While you can do some analysis of your data in a spreadsheet, ultimately you will want to transfer your data to a database program where it can be merged with other archaeological data from the project.

We use a specialized data entry program that we wrote years ago, and we know of others that are commercially available. What these programs do, and what spreadsheets do not, is provide you with a lot of shortcuts that make data entry faster and with error reduction techniques that make them more accurate. Also, these programs are often better able to interface with measurement devices like electronic calipers and scales, though this is less of an issue than it once was. And they are usually easier to configure to your data entry needs than a more generalized database program. The downside is that for these same reasons such programs tend to have more limited applications and to require some customization to very specific data entry needs. Specialized data entry programs usually assume that, once you enter your data, you will be transferring them to a database.

Database programs also provide you with the tools to design data entry screens. Depending on the program, this can be a time-consuming process, and it will likely require learning more about the program than you had anticipated. It means, however, that you will be able to tap into the full power of the database to enter your data efficiently and accurately. Even if you do not design your own data entry screens, most database programs have default data entry screens that either resemble a spreadsheet in which multiple rows are displayed simultaneously or that present one record at a time to enter.

DATABASE DESIGN

Database design is the first step to recording laboratory data. In setting up your database, you will, of course, need to decide which observations on your artifacts you are going to make. Unfortunately we cannot help you with that since there are an infinite variety of research questions; we will simply assume that you know what observations you want to make. What we can help you with is the next step, which is figuring out how to translate those observations into a set of database fields that (1) store the information efficiently, (2) make the retrieval and analysis straightforward, and (3) integrate easily with what others are doing with the material from this site. This is what we mean by database design. A little later we will discuss the design of a data entry form that will make entering data into this database easy.

Artifact analysis involves some of the same kinds of database design issues as for the field system discussed in Chapter 1 and again in Chapter 5. Foremost of these is the determination of the unit of analysis (the "case" or database record). Typically each individual object is defined as the unit of analysis, and the fields represent the various observations that are made on each object individually. Consider Table 6.1, for example, in which the same observations (DATACLASS, LENGTH, WIDTH, and THICKNESS) are made for each stone tool. Such a simple table, with a one-to-one relationship between objects and records, poses no real concerns for data entry, computer storage, or analysis.

It is easy to imagine a more complicated table, however. Consider, for instance, a study of stone tools in which we are interested in characterizing the type of retouch and the length of retouch on each retouched edge of a tool. Some tools, of course, can have more than one edge retouched, and so we have to be prepared to deal with multiple edges (and corresponding multiple observations) on a single piece.

TABLE 6.1   A simple stone tool table design

Record #	Unit	ID	Dataclass	Length	Width	Thickness
1	C13	50	FLAKE	33.685	23.41	9.335
2	C13	54	CORE	25.29	17.34	6.15
3	C13	66	SCRAPER	31.25	16.33	7.335
4	C13	118	FLAKE	27.27	16.595	5.69
5	C13	120	SCRAPER	47.53	19.46	8.745
6	C13	123	FLAKE	31.89	35.475	9.305
7	C13	132	CORE	39.16	26.48	8.445
8	C13	140	NOTCH	30.125	19.8	7.645
9	C13	145	FLAKE	27.165	19.165	5.515
10	C13	149	FLAKE	28	18.305	6.595
11	C13	152	CORE	31.015	20.13	6.375
12	C13	163	SCRAPER	28.335	17.705	6.875
13	C13	165	FLAKE	26.1	23.36	7.63
14	C13	174	NOTCH	33.59	26.825	9.675

TABLE 6.2   Analysis of multiple-edged tools, but stored in a one-to-one table

Record #	Unit	ID	Type	Retouch 1	Length 1	Retouch 2	Length 2	Retouch 3	Length 3
1	A1	1	Scraper	Light	22.54	Medium	41.84		
2	A1	2	Scraper	Heavy	40.23	Heavy	38.52	Medium	26.87
3	A1	3	Notch	Notch	12.83				

One approach to this problem is to keep the stone tool as the unit of analysis and to create a new record for each object. The different retouched edges on the tools can be handled with individual fields reserved for each of the possible edges. This is probably the most straightforward approach, and the resulting table might look something like Table 6.2.

Again, this structure is easy to conceptualize and relatively easy to deal with during data entry. However, there are two issues to consider. One has to do with the amount of space that will be wasted if we assume that most tools have only one retouched edge. With today's computers, however, this efficiency consideration is not as important as it once was. The second, and more important, issue has to do with analysis. Imagine, for example, how difficult it would be to find the average length of all retouched edges using this structure. Or imagine the

TABLE 6.3   Redesigned table with each retouched edge as a record

Record #	Unit	ID	Type	Edge Number	Retouch	Length
1	A1	1	Scraper	1	Light	22.54
2	A1	1	Scraper	2	Medium	41.84
3	A1	2	Scraper	1	Heavy	40.23
4	A1	2	Scraper	2	Heavy	38.52
5	A1	2	Scraper	3	Medium	26.87
6	A1	3	Notch	1	Notch	12.83

difficulty of determining the percentage of retouch types (heavy, light, medium, notch) on all edges; we would have to combine the totals resulting from three separate queries on fields Retouch1, Retouch2, and Retouch3, respectively. No statistics program handles operations across multiple fields very well, especially when there are a number of missing values.

In an alternative approach, shown in Table 6.3, we can make the unit of analysis the individual retouched edges. In this case we can easily include several database records for each stone tool, although we can have only one record for each retouched edge. This design makes it very simple to do analysis on retouched edges. Here each record is an edge, and multiple edges on a tool are distinguished with a simple counter (EDGE NUMBER). To determine the percentage of each retouch type, we need only query the Retouch field, and calculating the average length of a retouched edge is a straightforward matter. This design is also more efficient as there are no empty fields.

At the same time, certain other kinds of queries are more difficult using the format in Table 6.3. For instance, with this table, while it is easy to learn how many scraper edges there are (5), it is more difficult to know how many artifacts are scrapers (2). Likewise, it is a fairly complex process to find out how many tools with "Heavy" retouch on the first edge also have two or three retouched edges.

Which approach is best, then? Unfortunately there is no one "best" format since it depends on what you want to do with your data. If you are doing a specialized study focusing on retouch, you should probably use the format in Table 6.3. But if you are inventorying a large collection of stone tools and making many observations besides those relevant to retouched edges, you should probably stick with the design in Table 6.2. Fortunately these two designs are not mutually exclusive. In a relational database design you can use both tables and link them on the unique identifier UNIT-ID.

A similar situation arises with individual teeth in jaws and cut-marks on bones. In a database for analyzing animal bones, each record typically represents

TABLE 6.4   Table with each jaw as a record, with separate fields for each tooth

Unit	ID	Taxon	Left Upper Incisor 1 Length	Left Upper Incisor 1 Width	...	Left Upper Molar 3 Length	Left Upper Molar 3 Width
A1	6	Bos sp.	12.43	11.03		14.7	11.37
A1	7	Bos sp.					
A1	8	Bos sp.				14.2	10.98

TABLE 6.5   Table with each tooth as a record

Unit	ID	Tooth	Length	Width
A1	6	LeftUpperIncisor1	12.43	11.03
A1	6	LeftUpperMolar3	14.7	11.37
A1	8	LeftUpperMolar3	14.2	10.98

a single bone. Teeth that are still attached to a jaw, however, each require their own set of observations and measurements. One approach is to place a set of fields for each tooth in the database (see Table 6.4), but for every bone that does not have associated teeth (which is most bones), these fields will be blank. Even on jaws, most teeth will be missing. Thus, an alternative approach is to create a separate table just for measuring teeth (see Table 6.5) and to organize it the same way as in Table 6.3. The two tables—one for the bones and one for the teeth—can then be related on the basis of UNIT-ID. This also works better for dealing with isolated teeth.

Cut-marks on bones are even trickier because at least with teeth you can predict how many there will be. With cut-marks you have no idea, and the number could be fairly high. You can take a guess and set aside a certain number of fields in each bone record to record potential cut-marks, but as soon as you do that you might come across a bone that exceeds your set number. This means modifying the database design partway through the data entry, something that you really want to avoid. Thus, cut-marks, like retouched edges and teeth, are probably best placed in a separate table and then related back to the main table that contains the rest of the information about that particular bone.

Consider a study of an Old Kingdom Egyptian cemetery consisting of individual tombs. These tombs will contain all sorts of objects: stone tools, ceramics, metals, and so on. One approach is to create table wherein each record represents a tomb. In this table the fields may indicate the presence/absence or the types of various kinds of artifacts. This design might make it very easy to compare tombs. Alternatively, separate tables can be created for each artifact class, and these tables can then be linked back together to rebuild the contents of a tomb. While the latter is a bit more complicated to design and implement, in the long run it will allow much-needed flexibility in terms of analysis.

There are, of course, an infinite variety of research questions, as well as the kinds of data that are relevant to them. We can give only a few examples here, but the key point is that deciding on your basic unit of analysis is important and will have consequences for your subsequent analysis of the data. Also, keep in mind that, while one kind of organization may make sense for purposes of data entry, an entirely new kind of organization may be required for the analysis. Usually this will involve simply rewriting a table into a new format. And, finally, remember that there is nothing wrong with having multiple formats simultaneously.

MORE ON UNIQUE ARTIFACT IDENTIFIERS

Individual Objects vs. Aggregates

One of the fundamental concepts that allows you to structure your data in different ways is that of unique artifact identifiers. Without unique identifiers it is impossible to associate database records with particular objects or sets of objects and to separate one record from the next. It is also, of course, extremely important that the objects themselves be stored with their identifier in a permanent way. For most objects this means writing the identifier directly on the object. In this way, when you analyze the object, you can relate new observations to the data already stored in the computer for that object. Obviously, if you lose the identifier for an object, then you cannot add any data collected in subsequent analyses of that object to previously collected data.

When working with a collection, and especially an older one, or with any material that does not include individual artifact identifiers, it is often tempting to collect analytical data without worrying about entering individual identifiers. Suppose that you are interested in the weights of the stone tools from a lithics collection. The easiest way to do this is to weigh each object, enter the weights into a spreadsheet, and then run your statistics program.

In itself this is fine—unless you subsequently decide that you want to know whether the scrapers are heavier than the notches. If you did not record the identifier of each piece when you were recording weights, then you cannot go back now and check each object, note whether it is a scraper or a notch, and add that information to your spreadsheet. If the objects themselves do not have identifiers written on them, or if you did not enter the identifiers along with the weights, you have no way of knowing which weight you entered earlier corresponds to which tool. You will, in effect, have to reweigh each piece and this time note the tool type as well.

Everyone falls into this trap one time or another in the course of doing research, and it can result in an enormous waste of time. The lesson to be learned is that it is always better to enter an identifier for each object when you go through a collection, even if you do not have any plans at the time for adding new information later on. Even when you are dealing with a collection of pieces that are not individually identified, it is a good idea to make every effort to assign identifiers to them.

This brings us back to the issue of aggregated data, which we touched on in Chapter 1 and again in Chapter 5. In most excavations, archaeologists recover some combination of (1) individual artifacts, each of which has its own unique identifier, and (2) groups of artifacts bagged together (as aggregates or lots), with all of the members of the group assigned the same identifier. As we discussed in the preceding chapter, there are many good reasons for aggregating certain field data this way, the most important one being for excavation efficiency. There are, however, a couple of issues that you should address when first designing such a system.

In most cases a single series of numbers or identifiers are used for both artifacts and lots. Thus, ASP-3412, for instance, might refer to a single flint knife or to a group of 12 flint blades. If you use the same set of identifiers for both individual and aggregated finds, it is best to include a separate count field indicating the number of objects being grouped together. Among other things, you can use a count field to track objects.

Another approach is to use a separate series of numbers for lots and artifacts. Some excavations have a lot number series and a separate artifact number series, so, for example, Artifact 3412 is not the same as Lot 3412. This system is perfectly workable, but it still has important drawbacks. First, it requires that you maintain two separate series of numbers, which means, in effect, that the probability of making a mistake with the unique number series is doubled. Second, it makes it more difficult to move objects from one group to the other. Suppose that you later discovered that a particular lot is actually two artifacts, each of which deserves its own artifact number. This means that you have to drop the lot number (leaving a hole in the lot number series) and add two new artifact numbers to the artifact series.

A more serious problem in using aggregated data arises during analysis, when you might want to enter information about individual items within a lot. Since each object within the lot shares the same provenience information, there is no problem relating your new observations to provenience. However, a problem discussed earlier in this section—adding new data for objects previously analyzed—is still an issue. One simple way to handle this is to add a new field (e.g., ITEM

NUMBER) to your database that corresponds to specific items in the lot. Each item in the lot should, of course, then be labeled with this item number.

Issues in Maintaining Unique Identifiers During Analysis

As you assign unique identifiers in the field, whether to individual artifacts or to lots representing groups of artifacts, you have to make an entry in a provenience table that records the find location of each. This table becomes, in effect, the "master provenience table" for the excavation. In our own work we refer to this as the context table. Then, as analyses are done in the laboratory, you enter the results into a separate table. Each record in these analysis tables must contain the unique identifier so that the records can be linked back to the master provenience table. An issue, however, arises when, during the course of analysis, it is discovered that new artifacts or lots need to be added to the master table.

First, the person doing the analysis may not have the right to add new records to the master table. Typically this table, or an analogous one, is maintained by a single individual, often called the excavation's registrar, who takes the requests for new records from all of the people doing the analysis. This is important because, if one person is not ultimately responsible for maintaining the integrity of the master provenience table, then chaos can quickly result, with different individuals working independently on their own materials, adding records and deleting them.

Second, the master provenience table may not be physically accessible to the person doing the analysis. For example, the analysis might be conducted in one country and the master provenience table may be in another country. The analyst might be working solely from a paper listing of the master provenience table indicating the artifacts that need to be studied and their proveniences. If this is the case, then the analyst may hit a roadblock each time a new artifact number is needed.

One solution is to give the analyst a block of numbers to use as needed, but this leads to several new problems. One is that it creates holes in the number sequences when a block of numbers is not completely used. While this is not a serious matter, it has several downsides. It becomes difficult, for instance, to know whether a record is missing from the database because of an error or because it was intentionally skipped. Sometimes people deal with this problem by inserting a kind of "this record left intentionally blank" record in the database simply to note the holes. Holes also have the disadvantage of disassociating the final identifier number with the number of artifacts in the database. In other words, when you assign, say, number 100,000 to an excavated artifact, it does not mean that there are 100,000 artifacts in the database. While this is simply an aesthetic consideration, do not underestimate aesthetic considerations when working with archaeologists!

Another problem with assigning blocks of available numbers is that careful record keeping is required so that the same block of numbers is not given to two different researchers. Unless blank records are immediately inserted denoting that the records and their associated unique identifiers have been allocated to someone, then there will be no way simply to look at the master table and know what record to give someone. And disaster results if the same block is given to two different analysts. Hours of work will be lost while bags of artifacts are relocated and relabeled to correct the problem.

A third problem with adding new records to the master table is that information has to be duplicated. Suppose that a particular feature at the site has been excavated and that it produced a bag of animal bones, ceramics, and stone artifacts, each of which was given a lot number and sent off to the respective analyst for analysis. These three lots are entered into the master table as separate records, each of which will be identical because of their shared provenience. They will differ only in the field that indicates the contents of each lot. Subsequently, imagine that the ceramicist discovers two beautiful pots that can be reconstructed from the sherds. Both of these pots, had they been discovered intact during excavation, would have been given their own artifact numbers in the master table. Thus, at this time the ceramicist requests two artifact numbers from the registrar, who in turn finds the next available numbers and adds two records to the master table. These records too will repeat all the provenience information of the original three ceramic, animal bone, and stone artifact records. This is clearly an inefficient method of handling things, and is one prone to all sorts of errors as provenience information is copied or reentered each time.

One alternative that addresses this problem and many others discussed in this section is to allow analysts to add their own unique item number series to the artifacts. In the case just outlined, for instance, imagine that the ceramicist is working with Lot 3412. Thus, Lot 3412.001 would include all of the sherds, Lot 3412.002 the first reconstructed pot, and Lot 3412.003 the second pot. In this way the ceramicist has a unique identifier for each record in the ceramics database table, and each of these records can be easily linked back to the master table to obtain the proveniences using the root part of the identification number (Lot 3412). No extra effort is needed on the part of the registrar, and the ceramicist can work completely independently of the registrar. Furthermore, all the analysts can maintain their own sequence of suffix numbers based on their own research criteria. For instance, the ceramicists may want to divide a bag of ceramics based on the type of ware, the decoration, or the possibility of reconstruction into a single vessel, the faunal analyst may want to divide a bag of bones based only on species, and the stone tool analyst may want to give each stone artifact above a certain size threshold its own identifier while leaving the rest as Lot 3412.001. In this system the item numbers restart with each lot or artifact number. Thus, they do not stand on their own and need only the respective lot or artifact number to be a unique identifier.

WORKING WITH REFITS AND CONJOINS

One of the more challenging things to track in an artifact database is refits and conjoinable pieces. We just discussed how to deal with sherds from a single provenience that refit into a single vessel, but what if the sherds come from multiple proveniences? Clearly you cannot simply lump all the sherds into one provenience or the other since the fact that they come from two different proveniences might be very important in interpreting the formation of the archaeological layers. The same is true for stone tools. The fact that, say, three flakes from one layer can be refit back onto a core from another layer is important information that cannot be lost and must be somehow recorded into a database so that it will be available for later analysis.

All of the flakes or sherds from each provenience need to be grouped together and given their own identification number. Thus, we could have Lot 3412.002, which contains 5 sherds that refit with 12 sherds from Lot 3498.005. The ceramicist may then create a new table and a new series of numbers to denote vessels, giving the refit vessel a vessel number and placing a series of records for this vessel in the vessel table linking it to each of the lot numbers (see Table 6.6). In this way the ceramicist can keep track of the number of vessels discovered at the site and, by linking back to the master table, can view the proveniences represented by each. The same can be done with the stone tools. In this case the lithic analyst might create a refit table to track the elements of a particular refit.

Refits and conjoins introduce another challenge to the database system. Usually the analyst will want to physically refit the pieces together or at least bag them together. Since the artifacts will be separated from their bags, each piece obviously must be labeled with its unique identifier. The difficulty comes in tracking the physical location of these artifacts. Typically the master table is used to track the storage location or disposition of the artifacts from a particular provenience. Thus, the storage location of all ceramics from Lot 3498 is noted in the master table. But if some of the sherds from Lot 3498 are taken from the rest and stored separately, then it becomes necessary to create a new record in the master table to track these artifacts separately.

VARIABLES, OBSERVATIONS, AND FIELDS

Now that you have decided what kinds of observations will go into each table for your analysis, it is time to start creating those tables. In Chapter 1 we discussed some basic rules in naming fields. Specifically you should choose names that are long enough to convey some information about what is contained in that field, and you should avoid using spaces and special characters (like # and %). Be especially careful to avoid using the characters ? and *, because these typically mean something else to computer software and can be quite confusing.

TABLE 6.6 Table of refitted vessels	
Vessel #	Sherd Lot
1	3412.002
1	3498.005
2	2762.010
3	1234.023
3	1234.024
3	4323.003

In Chapter 1 we also reviewed the kinds of fields that exist in most databases. It should be clear from that discussion what kind of field you will want to use in most cases. For instance, if you are taking a length measurement that has decimal places, then you need to use at least a single precision number. If you are working only with integer values, then an integer field will suffice. There are, however, some traps and pitfalls in creating fields and assigning field types that you need to be aware of.

Numeric vs. Text Fields

When the data are numeric, most people's first thought is to create a numeric field, but this might not be the best choice. To illustrate, consider zip codes and phone numbers, both of which consist of numbers but are not really numbers in the same way that, say, artifact length is a number.

First, zip codes are always five digits. For instance, the zip code for Chesterfield, MA, is 01012. The first zero in this zip code, what we call a leading zero, is obviously important, since a four-digit zip code of 1012 is not valid, and the first zero distinguishes Chesterfield, MA, from Chester, GA, which has nearly the same zip code—31012. We need to store all five digits in order to know the proper zip code. In most database programs, when you enter 01012 into a numeric field, the leading zero will be removed and the number will be displayed as 1012. Thus, even though zip codes consist entirely of numbers, using a numeric field will not work because the leading zeros will be removed.

Telephone numbers can have the same problem with leading zeros, and they also have an embedded hyphen, which can be interpreted by the computer as a minus sign. We have seen this mistake made many times. Someone enters the telephone number 367-0081, and the computer dutifully performs the subtraction and stores the number 286 (literally 367 minus 81). Again, you can easily overcome this problem by storing telephone numbers in text fields rather than in numeric fields.

As an archaeological example, consider coding sheets. We have seen examples of coding sheets that run from 001 to 999 rather than from 1 to 999. Using a three-character text field will allow you to enter 012. Another example is radiocarbon dates. A typical radiocarbon date might read 890 ± 50, in which 890 is the actual date and 50 is an error factor associated with that date. If you want to enter the dates in that form, with the ±, then you have to use a character field. But this will restrict your ability to work numerically with the dates (e.g., to find the average date). A better solution here is to create two fields, one for the date (RE_DATE) and one for the error factor (RE_ERROR). When you print the dates you can put the ± back using an expression like this:

    STR(rc_date) & "±" & STR(rc_error)

Another, even more subtle, way in which text and numeric fields differ in relation to the use of numbers becomes evident when you do not enter a number. In a numeric field some databases will show a blank numeric field as a zero and others will show it as empty or null. In a text field a blank field either is null or contains only spaces. For instance, when you enter the artifact type for a stone tool, despite the fact that it is always a number between 1 and 63 based on your coding sheets, you should place it in a text field so that stone tools without an artifact type will be displayed as blank and not zero. Again, this is primarily a matter of aesthetics, but since there is no such thing as a stone tool type 0, you don't really want that in your database.

Zero raises another dilemma when designing your database and entering your data. In a numeric field like WEIGHT, zero might well have a meaning very different from a blank numeric field. In other words, an object may weigh so little that its weight is zero according to your scale. If it is important to distinguish objects that weigh zero from objects not yet weighed, then it is important that the database program keep the numeric field blank until a value is entered. Otherwise, if it automatically fills each numeric field with a zero when the field is created, it will be impossible to distinguish objects that weigh next to zero from objects not yet weighed and yet both zeros will look the same in the database. Temperature is another good example. Entering a value of 0 degrees means something other than that you did not take a temperature measurement. We will return to the question of how to code missing data a little later in this chapter.

Another thing to keep in mind is that you cannot enter text into a numeric field. This may seem obvious, but sometimes it is not. It may turn out that 99.99 percent of the time the value that is entered into the field is numeric, but occasionally a text value is required. If this is the case, then you have to either use a text field or add another field to the database to take care of those rare special cases.

Finally, remember that you have to take into consideration how the field will sort. If you put numbers in a text field, they will not sort in numeric order unless you format them correctly. As we discussed in Chapter 1, basically you need to pad the numbers with leading blank spaces or zeros to get a proper numeric sort. While this is not difficult, particularly with the use of a few functions, it is something to consider.

In short, the basic rule of thumb is that, if you want to do math or make plots with the values in the field, then the field has to be numeric. Otherwise, you can use a text field.

Free Text Fields

For the purposes of our discussion, we need to further subdivide text fields based on how the data are to be entered into the field. With free text fields you can type in whatever you want up to the size of that field, whereas with menu fields you must select from a list of predetermined choices. Some databases are now sophisticated enough that they allow the menu choices to be included as part of the definition of that field. But other programs view all text fields as identical, and it is up to the data entry portion of the program to determine whether the text is entered from a menu or as free text. We will discuss menu fields in more detail when we examine ways to reduce data entry errors.

Some might consider this to be an extreme judgment, but we view free text fields as a bad thing. The principal reason is because free text fields, in which you can enter whatever you like, are almost impossible to analyze. Consider this example of a description in a free text field of a piece from a stone tool database: "a scraper with two retouched edges—one of which is heavily retouched and the other lightly retouched—on an exotic piece of raw material; note also it appears to have been burned." Clearly our understanding of this description will be much better than a computer's. From the computer's point of view, this information will be much more useful if it is divided into a series of fields: TOOL TYPE (scraper), NUMBER OF RETOUCHED EDGES (2), RETOUCH INTENSITY 1 (heavy), RETOUCH INTENSITY 2 (light), RAW MATERIAL TYPE (exotic), BURNED (yes).

Here is another example taken from a ceramics database: "white stoneware with blue stamp-pressed decoration and cracked glaze." A better way to database this information is with a field for COLOR (white), FABRIC (stoneware), DECORATION (yes), DECORATION TYPE (stamp-pressed), DECORATION COLOR (blue), GLAZE (yes), and GLAZE CONDITION (cracked). Note that DECORATION and GLAZE are Boolean fields and the rest are menu fields. The more you can assign your data to separate fields, the more useful the information will be during analysis.

That said, we realize that you might want to add a COMMENTS field to your database. Just be aware as you write things in this field, that they will be very difficult to systematically retrieve afterward and next to impossible to analyze. Finally most database programs put a limit on the amount of text that can be entered into a text field, such as 255 characters. If your text exceeds this limit, some programs offer another kind of field called a memo field. Memo fields typically do not have a length limit, but there is a catch: They can be difficult to include in reports, and some database programs limit their use in queries. The latter is especially important. For example, if you want to locate all records in which you made a comment about the need to draw or photograph the artifact, you can write this query:

INSTR(Comments,"draw") > 0 OR INSTR(Comments,"photo") > 0

This expression will be true when the COMMENTS field contains the word "draw" or the word "photo". Note that the INSTR function will likely be your most useful function for searching through the contents of a free text field like COMMENTS. Think of it as the equivalent of the FIND function in a word processor. In contrast, if the person doing the data entry instead mentioned the need to "illustrate" the object, you might not find it.

Menu Fields

Many observations about artifacts can be converted from free text input to menus, which are basically predefined lists of "acceptable" choices. In entering an observation in a menu field, you simply select one of the choices offered. This not only speeds data entry (the entry of a long term can be as simple as one mouse click) but also standardizes the data and reduces errors.

Menu fields are often used in archaeological recording because a large part of archaeological analysis involves placing artifacts into various predefined groups or attributes. Lower and Middle Paleolithic stone tools, for instance, are categorized into 63 types. Thus, in the data entry screen, you can select the stone tool type from a menu of 63 choices.

Sometimes, however, menu lists become so large that they are cumbersome and actually slow the speed of data entry. In other words, with a large menu it may take more time to sift through the menu selections than to enter the information directly. Take, for instance, taxon identification in animal bone analysis. At first glance the best way to set up this field is with a single text field. Thus, you might have a field called TAXON that contains the genus and species combination "Bos primigenius" for a cow bone. On the one hand, entering taxa by hand is time consuming, and the likelihood of spelling errors increases. On the other hand, depending on the variety of taxa represented at the site, a menu list of valid taxa can be prohibitively long.

The solution is to divide TAXON into two fields: one for genus and one for species. The menu lists associated with each of these two fields will be smaller than the combined list, because neither genera nor species are unique. That is, there are many different species of Bos, but with the fields split into two, the GENUS field will have only one Bos selection, thereby reducing the number of menu options that you need to sort through to find the correct one.

We can take this a step further and make it even more efficient by linking the SPECIES menu field to the selection made in the GENUS field. If all possible species are displayed in the SPECIES menu, then even when you enter Bos for the genus you will have to sift through species that are only appropriate for other genera. What you really want are only the species relevant to Bos. To accomplish this, you need to create another table in your database—a look-up table (discussed later in the chapter) that contains a list of valid taxa. Table 6.7 shows what this table might look like.

Given this table, you need to instruct the database program to build the menu list for genus from the unique values in the GENUS field. In this case, rather than a list of seven possible menu choices, you will have only three: Bos, Equus, and Rangifer. Next, you need to instruct the database program to build the menu list for SPECIES from the unique values in the species field, but only for those records in which genus is equal to what has been entered into the GENUS field of your data entry table. As a result, you will have a menu of only two (for Bos), three (for Equus), or two (for Rangifer) choices depending on whether the bone is Bos, Equus, or Rangifer.

Unfortunately we cannot tell you exactly how to do this in your database program because every program will handle it differently. We can tell you, however, that it probably involves queries. Typically you create a query that selects the records you need from the look-up table and then associate this query with the menu list in your data entry screen. It can be a little tricky at first, but the benefits from designing it this way are tremendous. In addition, this concept can be easily extended to include more than two fields. In the case of TAXON, you could add FAMILY and ORDER to further narrow a potentially large list of genera. And TAXON is not the only field in which this concept applies; it is generally applicable to any hierarchically organized observation. Artifact types, for instance, are sometimes organized this way.

Boolean Fields

Boolean fields, which store only a true or a false, are often overlooked in database design, yet they can be quite useful and are very efficient. Remember that true and false are merely "computerese" for 1 and 0, respectively, which is what is actually stored in a Boolean field. But 1 and 0 can stand for other binary pairs such as yes/no and present/absent.

One of the best uses of Boolean fields is when you have a series of check-off observations in which more than one can be true. Consider the analysis of

TABLE 6.7 Taxon look-up table	
Genus	Species
Bos	sp.
Bos	primigenius
Equus	caballus
Equus	hydruntinus
Equus	sp.
Rangifer	sp.
Rangifer	tarandus

alterations to bones. You might want to note whether each bone has been burned, chewed, or sawed. One option is to create a text field called ALTER-ATION with a menu of options including "Burned", "Chewed", and "Sawed". But what if a bone is burned *and* chewed. You could include all possible combinations in your menu list, or you could make a series of individual Boolean fields called "Burned", "Chewed", and "Sawed". Then you simply check off the ones that apply.

Boolean fields arranged like this are easy to analyze. If, for instance, you want to look at only the burned bones in the collection, you write a query that looks like this:

Burned=True

To look at all burned and sawed bones, the query looks like this:

Burned=True AND Sawed=True

To look at bones that are either burned or sawed, the query looks like this:

Burned=True OR Sawed=True

Missing Data

The proper handling of missing data, such as when a particular observation cannot be made on an object, is an important element of good database design. Quite simply, you have to be able to tell the difference between an observation that could not be made and a legitimate value.

In some cases the fact that most database programs recognize null or empty fields as a valid entry in a field may make the difference for you. In other words, you might be able to rely on null or empty values to distinguish between measurements not made versus measurements made with a result of zero. We prefer not to do this, however, because it is too risky. While your particular database system might be able to handle the difference, the difference might be lost when you transfer your data to another program for analysis. Thus, we try to set aside special values or codes to make these distinctions.

Let's consider numeric fields first, which pose the greatest problem simply because not entering a value might inadvertently result in a value of 0 being stored in the database. Imagine a numeric field that contains the number of retouched edges on stone artifacts. In this case a value of 0 would mean that no edges were retouched, a value of 1 would mean that one edge was retouched, and so on. Clearly you do not want to have a missing observation (perhaps due to the fact that a piece is so fragmentary that you cannot tell if it has any retouched edges) default to 0; you would rather not count that piece at all. The best option here is to enter a value of –1 or some other obviously invalid value that cannot be confused with a valid entry. Likewise, with a variable like temperature, an entry of 0 or even –1 has a very definite meaning, so you might want to use something like –9999 to indicate that a measurement is missing.

Sometimes a value of 0 is perfectly appropriate as a missing value, as in the case of length or weight. When you weigh very small objects, however, they may actually show a weight of zero (depending on the precision of the scale). In this case you enter not 0 (which would mean "missing"), but the smallest value that the scale allows. Thus, if the scale measures to the nearest gram, you enter 1 gram for objects that weigh less than 1 gram. In this way you reserve 0 for cases in which you are not able to take the weight—for example, when a stone tool has a clump of breccia still attached to it.

Text fields are a little easier to handle. The simplest approach is usually to leave the field blank, but doing this still does not allow you to tell the difference between "I looked at that object and couldn't make that observation" and "I haven't yet looked at that object" and "I looked but forgot to make that observation." The easiest solution is simply to enter something like "NA" for "not appropriate" or "no answer" or "not available."

One of the most important rules in any empirical field is that no data are better than bad data. If you are unsure of an observation or measurement, it is always better to assign a missing value than to take even an educated guess at the value.

DATA ENTRY

Now that you have settled on the observations you want to make and set up a table with appropriate fields, it is time to start filling the table with data. As noted previously, the best way to enter your data is to use either a specialized data entry program or the tools provided with your database program.

If you use a specialized data entry program, it should either write the data you enter directly to the fields you have created in your database table or write a file that can be easily imported into your database. In the latter case, the most common exchange format is an ASCII comma-quote delimited file. Sometimes ASCII files are called text files, which means that the data are written in a standard format without any special codes recognizable only to certain programs. You can tell whether a file is in ASCII format if you can easily read it when you look at it in the most basic word processor (e.g., Notepad in Windows). A line of data in the comma-quote delimited format will look something like this:

"A1","23","SCRAPER",32.739,19.452,12.432

This is a list of six fields, each one separated from the other by a comma. The first three fields are text fields. We know this because they are enclosed in quote marks. Remember from Chapter 1 that for computers, text values are typically placed in quote marks. Note that the second field looks like a number, but from the quote marks we know that it was entered into a text field. The last three fields are numeric fields and do not require commas.

This comma-quote delimited format can be read by nearly any program on nearly any computer system (Mac, PC, Unix). It is as close to a universal standard as we have in the computer world, and it has been that way for decades. There are, of course, some wrinkles. In Europe commas are used to separate the decimal portion of a number from the whole portion (e.g., 1000.234 is written as 1000,234). Obviously this means that one number will be read as two numbers in two fields. Thus, another common format for exchanging data between programs is space delimited, in which spaces are substituted for commas. Thus, the line above will read this way:

"A1" "23" "SCRAPER" 32.739 19.452 12.432

Note, too, the importance of quote marks for preventing errors. Consider this line:

"A1" "23" "COMPLETE TOOL" 32.739 19.452 12.432

Without the quote marks the space between COMPLETE and TOOL would be mistaken by the computer for two fields. Similarly, quote marks allow you to include commas without causing problems (e.g., "KATRANIDES, DAPHNE").

Electronic Instruments

One of the best ways to speed data entry and reduce the number of errors is to avoid keyboard data entry altogether. For instance, a number of brands of

SERIAL, PARALLEL, AND USB COMMUNICATIONS

One of the oldest, and still commonly used, communication standards is *serial* (or RS-232) communication. In serial communications high/low signals are transmitted along a wire, with each high or low (determined by the voltage level) indicating a 0 or 1, or a bit. Bits are sent one at a time along the wire, which is why it is called serial communication. At least three wires are needed—one to send information, another to receive information, and a ground wire. The basic concept of serial communication is simple, but a number of complications can arise when you try to connect two devices in this way.

The first problem is the physical connection, as there are many kinds of serial connectors. The most common are DB-9 (nine pins) and DB-25 (twenty-five pins) connectors, which must be connected in pairs—the male connector (the one with pins) fits into its female counterpart. Adapters allow you to convert a DB-9 to a DB-25, and vice versa, and gender changers allow you to connect two connectors with the same gender.

The second problem is that two devices being connected have to expect the stream of data to be transmitted in the same way. There are a number of parameters affecting transmission, and all of them must be set the same for both devices:

- Word length: usually 7 or 8 bits are defined as the length of a word (or byte).

- Stop bit: the data are surrounded with a start bit and a stop bit, which let the receiving device know when data are about to be sent and have been sent, respectively. The duration of the stop bit can vary from 1 to 1.5 to 2 bit periods, though 1 is a common standard.

- Parity: this is a way of checking to make sure that the data were received correctly. It works by counting the number of 1s in the word and adding an extra bit, the parity bit, to make the number of 1s either even or odd. In this way, if a bit is changed during transmission, the count will likely not match the parity (unless by chance two bits are switched in opposite directions). In addition to even and odd parity, "none" can be used to ignore parity checks.

- Baud rate: this is the transmission speed, as measured in bits per second. Typical baud rates are 1200, 2400, 4800, and 9600, and the maximum is about 115 kilobits per second. The integrity of the data is often enhanced by lowering the transmission speed.

Finally, there can be a problem related to which pin a device uses to send data and which pin will receive data. Most instruments that connect serially with a computer are designed so that the pin or wire that the computer uses to send data is connected to the receive pin on the instrument. A problem arises, however, when the two machines have identical pin configurations, since the send pin on one device will connect with the send pin on the other. Imagine, for example, that you have two phones and receive calls on each of them at the same time. The two callers actually want to speak to each other, so you put the two receivers together. If you line them up normally, the speaker on one will be facing the speaker on the other, which will not work. But if you turn one of the receivers upside-down, then the microphone of one will be facing the speaker of the other, and it will work.

You can overcome the problem in connecting two devices (usually two computers) in the same way, by reversing the send and receive wires. This is done with a *null modem*, a simple device that can be connected to the cables linking the two machines, as shown in the accompanying figure.

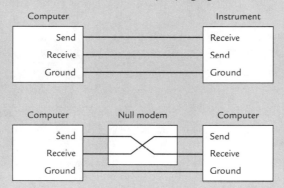

Serial communication is not a very speedy way of sending data, however, since one bit has to follow the other. In 1981, IBM developed another form of communication, which bundled eight wires together, with each wire sending one of the bits making up the word, or byte. So, instead of sending 8 bits one at a time, as in serial communication, this new way sent all 8 bits at the same time. This kind of communication, which is used most often with printers and scanners, is called parallel communication. Most computers have at least one serial and one parallel port or connector. Even if they are not labeled, you can still distinguish them because on the back of computers parallel ports are always female and serial ports are always male.

University serial bus (USB) is a much faster standard for communications than serial or parallel and is quickly replacing both of them. Currently USB can operate in two speed modes: 12 megabits-per-second (mps), which is commonly used for printers, scanners, and cameras, and 1.5 mps, which is used for mice or keyboards.

Besides providing increased speed, USB eliminates many of the headaches that are common in serial communication. There are no parameters to set and no worries about null modems or gender changes. There are only two kinds of USB connectors: a flattish one (type A), which is typically used on computers, and a squarer connector (type B), which is often used to connect to an instrument. Also, up to 127 different USB devices can be connected to a computer at the same time through the use of multiple-port USB hubs. The primary disadvantage to USB is that there are significant restrictions on the length of cables that can be used—5 meters for full-speed USB devices and 3 meters for low-speed devices.

A related standard is IEEE-1394, commonly known as firewire, which is both faster and more expensive.

FIGURE 6.1 Electronic calipers connected directly to the computer's communication or keyboard port provide a fast, efficient way to record measurements. Electronic scales also can be easily connected to a computer.

electronic calipers or scales can attach directly to the computer (see Figure 6.1). To take a measurement, you simply press the Send button and the data are passed to the computer so that they can be inserted into a waiting database field. Electronic instruments such as these not only greatly speed data entry but virtually eliminate keyboard entry errors. (See the box on pages 146–147 for a discussion of how electronic devices "communicate.")

Most electronic instruments are relatively easy to use, but there are several things you should be aware of. One thing common to both calipers and scales is that you have to make sure that your units (English vs. metric) remain appropriately set. Another issue has to do with the zero setting. On calipers they typically read 0 when the jaws are closed, but with scales you may wish to weigh objects within a container. You can set the scale to ignore the weight of the container by setting the tare of the scale while the container is on it. Usually you set the tare with a button, but you can also set it by having the container on the scale when it is powered on.

One issue with calipers in particular has to do with their power requirements. Usually they are powered by small, specialized batteries, and, depending on where you are working, they can be difficult to find. Thus, you should pack several spares. Also, electronic calipers have a tendency to get dirty, so you should clean them regularly.

Bar Codes

Another useful and perhaps underutilized tool is bar codes. Bar codes, like those found on practically all products sold in stores, are particularly useful for encoding identification numbers for artifacts or bags of artifacts.

A bar code is a series of vertical lines (called bars) and spaces of different widths. The bars and spaces collectively are referred to as "elements," which are grouped together in different combinations to represent different characters. There are, however, a number of ways in which this can be done, resulting in a number of different bar code types (see Table 6.8). One of the more common is called Code 39 (or Code 3 of 9), which has nine bars and spaces; three are wide, and the other six are narrow. Standard Code 39 can represent a full range of capital letters, numbers, and special characters. Enhanced Code 39 can represent both upper- and lowercase letters. In addition to the information contained in the bar code, many types also include special start/stop code characters—for example, the * (asterisk) in Code 39. You should leave at least ¼ inch of white space to the left and right of the code; this helps the reader pick out where a bar code begins and ends.

For most types, the size of the printed bar code will vary proportionately to the number of characters represented (see Figure 6.2). The size of the bar code is also affected by its density, which refers to the width ranges of the elements. Lower-density bar codes have wider elements and take up more space when printed. The thinner the elements, the less space required and the higher the bar code density. But, there is a trade-off between the size of the bar code (as reflected by its density) and its readability. Lower-density bar codes are more reliably printed and more consistently read than higher-density bar codes because minor variations (due to printing errors or damage) are much more serious with high-density bar codes.

One of the main drawbacks of bar codes is that you need a computer to decode their information, and over time the bar code can become damaged and unreadable. It is very important, therefore, that you not rely totally on them. When printing a bar code of an artifact identification number, for instance, you should include a plain-text version of the identification number with the bar code, as shown in Figure 6.2. In this way the label will still be readable despite changes in computer and bar code technology. The software used to print bar codes takes care of this automatically.

Several different kinds of instruments can read bar codes. The least expensive is a wand, which looks like a thick pen or laser pointer (see Figure 6.3). You

TABLE 6.8   Common bar code formats

Bar Code Type	Variable Length	Allowable Characters
Code 11	Yes	0–9
Codabar	Yes	0–9 $+.:/
Plessey	Yes	0–9 A–F
MSI	Yes	0–9
2 of 5	Yes	0–9
UPC and EAN	No	0–9
Code 39	Yes	0–9 A–Z./+-%$Spc (2-character pairings for full ASCII)
Code 128	Yes	Full ASCII
Code 93	Yes	0–9 A–Z./+-%$Spc (2-character pairings for full ASCII)

FIGURE 6.2   Bar codes. The size can vary by the number of digits contained and by their density.

pass the wand over the bar code, and the results are sent directly to a computer via a keyboard wedge, USB, or serial cable. (See the box on page 152 for a brief discussion of keyboard wedges.) Wands are inexpensive, but they can be a little tricky to use, and you will have to practice a bit to get good results.

Easier to use but more expensive are bar code guns. You aim the gun at the bar code, and it automatically "reads" the information and passes it to a computer via a communications port (serial or USB) or a keyboard wedge. Bar code guns come in two types: CCD and laser. CCD guns have a digital camera inside that takes a photo of the bar code and decodes it. To function they typically have to be within about 6 inches of the bar code. Laser guns are like those seen in supermar-

FIGURE 6.3   Scanning a bar code with a wand

kets. A beam of laser light scans the object, locates the bar code, and then decodes it. Laser guns are very fast and do not need to be within 6 inches of the object, but they are a bit more fragile than the CCD devices and they cost more.

There have been some efforts to print bar codes directly onto artifacts using an ink-jet technology developed to print information on, for instance, eggs, but many types of artifacts are not suitable for this technique. Typically, therefore, bar codes are printed on labels that are then applied to the bag containing the artifact(s) or placed on a tag to be included in the bag.

Data Entry Errors

Errors can certainly affect the quality of your results, and there are many different kinds of errors. Some of these stem directly from how you operationalize your variables, or how you define how observations are recorded. The more subjective an observation is, for example, the more likely random errors will be introduced during data entry. And, of course, no matter how careful we all try to be, sometimes a convergent scraper will be incorrectly typed as a Mousterian point. While we cannot deal here with those kinds of issues, we can address the more common errors that result from mistakes in typing.

It's important to recognize that this is a much more serious problem than you might think. Keyboard errors during data entry range from simple typos in text fields (e.g., entering "LITICS" instead of "LITHICS"), which are usually

KEYBOARD WEDGES

Some instruments send data to a computer via the computer's keyboard port and a hardware interface called a *keyboard wedge*. The interface is connected between the instrument and the keyboard, and translates the signals sent from the instrument into keystrokes. This means that the measurements are inserted into any program without the need for special software. You simply go to the field where you want the data to be placed, and press the Send button on your instrument; the data appear exactly as if you typed them on the keyboard yourself. Note that these systems work on both laptops and desktop computers, and they work with your standard keyboard. Bar code readers, calipers, and electronic scales are all capable of working this way.

not difficult to find and fix; to typos in numeric fields (e.g., entering "152.23" instead of "125.23"), which are more difficult to find and which can affect your results; to mistyping the identifier of an object (e.g., entering it as "C12-1234" when the object is actually "C12-1235"). This latter error is the most serious because it will affect all of the observations being entered (associating them to the wrong artifact) and, in fact, renders both artifacts useless (i.e., "C12-1235" has the wrong data entered, and "C12-1234" has no data entered).

If a text field is free-form, then there is little you can do to prevent keyboard errors. By using menus, however, you automatically ensure that the user can input only one of a list of possible alternatives and that each entry will be spelled and otherwise formatted correctly. While it does not avoid the problem of someone accidentally picking the wrong option, it does completely eliminate other kinds of problems.

For numeric fields it is possible to define acceptable ranges on individual entries. For instance, you usually exclude all negative numbers for measures like length, width, thickness, and weight. There is also likely an upper range for these kinds of measures that you can spot and reject at the moment of data entry. If you are measuring Archaic stone tools, for example, it is highly unlikely that you will find one larger than a meter, and so you can immediately catch an entry missing a decimal point (e.g., a length entered as "2429" instead of "24.29"). Of course, if you use an instrument connected directly to the computer, then the instrument itself will eliminate virtually all such errors.

In working with artifact identifiers, you also want to be sure that you do *not* (1) use the same ID for two different objects, (2) enter the wrong ID for an object under study, or (3) analyze the same object twice. We will begin our discussion with the problem of creating duplicate IDs.

You can actually create two kinds of duplicates. The first results when you label two artifacts with the same ID number. This is what we call true duplicates, because there really are two objects with the same ID. Note that under most circumstances this represents a mistake in artifact labeling. The best way to avoid labeling problems is to verify the labeling process. (See the box on page 154 for a discussion of how to check identifiers.) You create another kind of duplicate when you enter the same artifact ID into the database more than once because either you misread or mistyped the ID or you analyzed the same artifact twice by mistake.

Using the same artifact ID twice is both annoying—because it is a waste of effort—and erroneous—because it will incorrectly alter your analysis of the data afterward. There are various methods for avoiding this problem, but they all essentially involve indexes and/or look-up tables.

Remember from Chapter 1 that indexes are ordered lists made from a field or a combination of fields in your table. Because they are ordered, it is easy to quickly find a record in your table by first looking for it in the index. Each record in the index contains something called a pointer that links it back to the appropriate record in the table. As we discussed in Chapter 1, one of the most basic indexes that all tables will have is based on the unique ID that identifies each record. This is typically called the *primary key* or *master index*.

In most database systems the primary key has an additional property, namely, that duplicate cases are not allowed. If this property is not an inherent part of the master index, then the database system probably will allow you to specify that the entries in the index must be unique. So, every time you enter a new artifact into the computer, an entry with that artifact's unique ID is made in the master index. If you try to enter that same artifact ID again, the database system will automatically reject it and give you an error message. Database systems have this feature built in because the maintenance of valid, nonduplicate IDs is essential in a relational database. If you structure your data with a primary index based on the artifact identifier, then the problem of assigning the same ID to two different objects is automatically taken care of—the database simply will not let you do it.

Another way to handle this, which is a little more cumbersome but with additional benefits, is through the use of a *look-up table*. In its basic form a look-up table is a list of all of the valid IDs in a collection. In some respects this is analogous to a menu field, but the sheer number of valid IDs makes it impractical to handle in this way. Instead, every time you enter a new artifact ID into the system, the look-up table is queried to see if that ID already exists. If it does not, the new ID is added to the look-up table. If it does already exist, then you know you are dealing with a duplicate entry.

Rather than make a separate table of valid IDs, you could merely read the list of valid IDs from the master Context table for the excavation. As artifacts

CHECKING IDENTIFIERS

Given that unique identifiers are essential for maintaining the integrity of the database system, special attention must be given not only to the process of assigning numbers from the database and to entering these numbers correctly when doing analysis but also to the process of labeling artifacts. In our own work in the French Paleolithic, for instance, we give each stone artifact larger than 2.5 centimeters a unique identification number. When we first started databasing our excavations and analysis, the analysts in the laboratory soon noticed and then complained about duplicate identification numbers. The reason they noticed these duplicates was that their data entry program checked each time they entered a unique identifier to make sure they had not already analyzed that particular piece. This check was put in place to prevent them from inadvertently looking at the same bag of artifacts twice, but when they further investigated each duplicate problem they discovered two completely different artifacts with exactly the same identification number. Eventually they determined that these duplicates were being created when the artifacts were washed and then labeled. For example, rather than writing "A1-1265" on an artifact, someone had written "A1-1256", making it a duplicate of the real A1-1256. It is hard to know how extensive this problem was. But we estimate that the duplicate error rates were surprisingly high, perhaps more than 10 percent, and our work with other collections since that time, collections processed and labeled by others but never databased, confirm this high figure. Frankly we suspect that duplicate artifacts are a huge problem with these kinds of collections. And unless some other information can be found to indicate which of the identically labeled artifacts is the properly labeled one, we are obliged to remove both of them from our analysis. In other words, 10 percent or more of a collection can be lost to duplicates.

As a result, we implemented a system wherein, after a set of artifacts has been labeled and before the artifacts are separated from the paper tag with their ID number, a person other than the artifact labeler reads aloud the ID number of each artifact while the labeler confirms this against the paper tag. If any problems are noted, be they reversed digits or illegible digits, the artifacts are relabeled. This simple procedure has drastically reduced the number of mislabeled artifacts and therefore the number of problems we have later in our analysis databases.

are excavated, you assign ID numbers and enter proveniences into the Context table, making this table a master list of all of the artifacts that have been recovered. Later, during analysis, when an ID is entered, it can then be validated by checking the input ID number against the Context table. This is an extremely important step that will drastically reduce the number of mistyped IDs.

Usually you can take this concept a step further by applying the same hierarchical techniques we just discussed in dealing with menu fields. For instance, the analysis of the bone typically will be done separately from the analysis of the stones. If there is a field in the Context table that indicates whether the artifact recovered from the field is a bone or a stone (we call this the Code field), then the list of valid IDs can be reduced from all artifacts to all bone artifacts. In this way, when the faunal analyst enters a valid ID but one that has already been assigned to a stone tool, it will be caught.

In addition to making data entry go faster and eliminating errors, look-up tables are important from a data management and documentation perspective. It becomes a simple matter to add new choices to the menus because you only have to add new records to the look-up table; the data entry screen will automatically take care of the rest. Often this has the added advantage of allowing someone more knowledgeable in databases to create the original data entry screen design. The maintenance of the actual menu lists can be done by the person doing the actual artifact analysis even if that person only knows how to add records to a table. Furthermore, when the look-up table is printed or otherwise included with the publication of the results of the analysis, it is a handy method for documenting the analysis. In this way other researchers can see the full range of possibilities from which the data were entered (see metadata in Chapter 10).

To summarize, controlling for problems with IDs involves different techniques. When you enter a new object for the first time, the ID number should be compared with the current list of IDs to make sure that it does not already exist in the database. And when you analyze objects, you first want to check that the ID does occur in the master table (which verifies that it is a valid ID) but that it does not already exist in the analytical table that you are currently using (which prevents the same object from being analyzed twice).

As we have already discussed, if artifacts are collected in lots, then the analyst will have to add some kind of suffix or additional ID to create a unique ID. Thus, for example, the link back to the Context table to check for valid IDs might be on A1-234 (UNIT-ID), whereas the check for duplicates in the analysis table might be on A1-234-02 (UNIT-ID-SUFFIX). (See the box on page 156 for a general discussion of how to debug communication problems.)

Finding and Fixing Data Entry Errors

Once errors enter the database, they can be very difficult to find, but a number of techniques can help. One of the best ways is to scan through lists of unique values built from your various text fields. You can make these lists using something called a unique query. As you learned in Chapter 1, queries retrieve a set of fields and records from your table. A unique query retrieves only the unique values of your fields—in other words, a list of the distinct values in the database. Sometimes this feature is called "totals" since it can also be used to count how many instances there are of each unique value. Generating such a list is one of the best ways to locate problems in a database table. For each erroneous value you find in the

DEBUGGING COMMUNICATION PROBLEMS

A potential nightmare in working with computer equipment in the field and in the laboratory involves cabling and communications. To illustrate, let's consider the process of connecting a total station to a data collector—in this case a laptop. The first step in debugging communications problems is to establish that you are using the correct cable with the correct communications settings. The easiest way to do this is with a communications program. However, if you are uncertain whether you have the correct cable, we strongly suggest that you first test the communications between the total station and the computer with a communications program.

Most computers have a communications program of some type built into the operating system. In Windows 98, for instance, it is called HyperTerminal. Usually these programs are designed to dial a modem and connect over the phone lines to another computer. However, you can also use them to connect directly, via serial cable, to a device plugged into the serial communications port.

To do this, cable the total station to the computer. Then run the communications program and change the communication settings to match those listed in the total station's documentation. In many cases, finding the proper settings in the documentation can be quite difficult. For the Topcon total stations that we use, the settings are 1200 baud, 7 data bits, 1 stop bit, and even parity. Now, record a point with the total station. After the point has been recorded, the data should appear on the communications program's screen.

If data appear on the computer screen but are unreadable, then there are two possibilities. First, most total stations send data in ASCII or plain text form, so it should be readable, but some may send the data in a coded, binary form that will be unreadable. If this is the case, then it might be difficult to determine whether the communications settings are correct. At the very least, however, you can be sure that the cables are correct.

Second, the communication settings may be incorrect. If the baud rate is not correct, for instance, in most instances data will be transferred but will be unreadable. Double-check the communications program and the total station to ensure that the settings are identical. If you do not have a manual with recommended settings, then you will have to simply try some settings. We recommend starting with something fairly slow, such as 1200 baud with 7 data bits, 1 stop bit, and even parity. If you do not know and cannot set the communication settings on the total station, then you will have to try every combination of baud rates, data bits, stop bits, and parity. This can be very time consuming and frustrating, but eventually you should be able to find the right combination. Of course, you might be better off trying to find someone who knows the correct settings.

unique list, you can then create a new query to select only those records with the erroneous value so that they can be corrected.

While this technique works well with text fields, it works less well with numeric fields such as LENGTH, WIDTH, and THICKNESS. One thing you

If data do not appear on the computer screen, then the problem probably lies with the cables. One of the most common cable problems is solved with something called a null modem. Imagine, for instance, that you have a situation in which you have one cable from the total station that ends with a 9-pin female connection—perfect for connecting to the serial port of a standard PC. However, imagine as well that you have a PC or data collector with a nonstandard serial port that also requires a special cable that ends with a 9-pin female connection. Obviously the two 9-pin females cannot be connected to each other without a gender changer. A gender changer, in this case, is a small item with two 9-pin male connectors at either end. In this way the cables from the total station and the data collector can be connected to each other. But this is not the end of the story. If you simply connect the cables in this way, then the talk wires of one cable will be connected to the talk wires of the other, as will the listen wires. Recall that a null modem is a small connector that reverses the wires inside so that the talk wires are connected to the listen wires of the other cable, and vice versa. So, if the communications are not working, try using a null modem.

Another obvious thing to check is the port number. A lot of computers have more than one communications port, so you will need to specify which one you are using in the communications program (along with the baud rate, parity, data bits, and stop bits). If you are unsure which port you are using, or if you suspect that the port might not be functional because of some hardware problem or some software conflict, you can try plugging something else, such as a serial mouse, into the port to test it. Note that if you unplug a mouse to connect a total station the port might not work until you reboot the computer. This is because the mouse software will have a lock on the port.

Be sure that the communication settings are correct and that the communications program is in some sort of "direct connect" mode. Also be sure that you actually recorded the point with the total station and that the total station is set to pass the data rather than store them internally. Most total stations distinguish between measuring a point and recording a point. In the former case the coordinates are displayed on the total station's display but are not stored internally or passed to a computer.

There are enough variables in this discussion to make it sound as if debugging is hardly worth the effort. We can only say that the first time you connect to devices you need to be prepared to spend some time making it work. Thereafter, however, once you have identified the correct cables and communication parameters, serial communications can work very reliably.

can do is sort your database on the numeric fields using indexes. This enables you to look at the beginning and end of the sorted lists to spot values that are either too small or too large. You can spot many typos this way, but it works only with the most extreme outliers.

Sometimes a little analysis can help you find errors. If you compare the values of the fields RETOUCH LENGTH (which records the length of a retouched edge on a stone tool) with LENGTH (the overall length of the tool), you should not find any cases in which the RETOUCH LENGTH is greater than the LENGTH. Or, by multiplying LENGTH, WIDTH and THICKNESS of your artifacts you can calculate their volumes. Volume and weight are strongly correlated, so by plotting your records with volume on one axis and weight on the other, you may spot outliers. Note, however, that this can be a tricky process. Sometimes there will be cases that are clearly wrong and can easily be eliminated. In many other instances, however, the potentially bad cases will merge gradually with the rest of the data points. If you assume these cases are incorrect, you run the risk of eliminating good data and potentially important variability in your data set. Thus, this "outlier" technique must be used with care.

If you were unable to check for bad artifact IDs as they were entered, there are some techniques you can use to identify them afterward. For instance, since the IDs should be unique, you can check for duplicate cases in your analysis table by building a unique list of IDs. Obviously the number of entries in this list should equal the number of records in your table. If the two do not match, it means that one or several IDs have been duplicated. To find out which ones have been duplicated, you will likely have to add a count to each unique ID. In other words, you need to total the number of instances of each ID. The total should be only one for each ID, but if you have duplicates some will have a total of two or more.

As for invalid IDs or IDs that belong to another class of artifact, you need to establish a relational link between your analysis table and the master Context table and then look for (1) records that do not link and (2) records that link but show a different kind of artifact class. You can accomplish both with one query. First, suppose that the Context master table and the Ceramics analysis table are related on UNIT and ID, and suppose that the field in the Context table that records what kind of artifact was excavated (e.g., ceramics, stone tools, and animal bones) is called Dataclass. After linking the two tables on ID, you write a query to display the following fields:

Ceramics.Unit, Ceramics.ID, Context.Dataclass

This tells the computer to display the UNIT and ID fields from the Ceramics table and the Dataclass field from the Context table. When a UNIT-ID exists in the Ceramics table but the query cannot find the corresponding UNIT-ID in the Context table, the returned value for Dataclass will be empty or null. Otherwise, if it can be found, this query will list the Dataclass, and you can look for instances when something other than "Ceramics" is listed. To make this task even easier, you can add the following condition to your query:

Dataclass<> "Ceramics" OR Dataclass=""

This tells the computer to list only those records that either cannot be found or are not ceramics. Note that empty quotes ("") are a common way of indicating empty or null. In some systems you might also write this as Dataclass=Null or with the function Isempty(Dataclass) or Isnull(Dataclass).

SUMMARY

This chapter has given you some ideas on how to make your data entry go faster and produce better results. And you should now be ready to stop filling spreadsheets with your data and to turn instead to a database. Unfortunately, as they say, "the devil is in the details." In the past, for instance, connecting calipers to computers was a virtually insurmountable obstacle for many, but with the growing popularity of keyboard wedges this is changing. Nevertheless, it will take you a while to learn how to implement the general concepts presented in this chapter. But the effort will likely save you a lot more time down the road. One type of data we have not talked about in this chapter is images. Not only are images useful for recording the process of archaeological excavation and the resulting objects, but increasingly they are becoming a source of data analysis as well. In the next chapter, we discuss images—how they are acquired and what issues they raise for databases.

7 Digital Images

Because archaeology is an "object-oriented" discipline, the use of images is important in a presentation of results. Although illustrations and photographs traditionally have been a mainstay of archaeological reporting, the development of digital images has had a major impact in the field. Again, this is a rapidly changing area. Our emphasis here will be on what underlies digital images and how they can be acquired. We will not consider how to analyze images, a process that may eventually be standard in archaeological analysis.

For the purposes of this chapter, an image is a digital representation of a thing, place, or person or a digital equivalent of a photograph. These kinds of images, known as *raster* images or *bitmaps*, are composed of dots, or *pixels* (short for *pic*ture *el*ements). By coloring the various pixels differently, an image is produced. In contrast, *vector* images are based on an entirely different concept in that, instead of saving a pixel-by-pixel image, they save instructions on how to draw the image. In other words, each dot, line, or polygon that makes up the image is saved as a set of relative coordinates or an equation so that, in effect, the image is redrawn every time it is displayed. Plots produced from the kinds of spatial data generated during an archaeological excavation are examples of vector images. The primary advantages of vector graphics over bit-mapped images are in their scalability (the resolution of the image remains the same at whatever scale) and their ability to display three-dimensional views. The biggest disadvantage is simply that vector images are not suitable for producing lifelike photographic images. We will discuss vector images more in Chapter 9.

RASTER IMAGES

Resolution

A raster image has a certain *resolution*, defined as the number of pixels across (the width) and the number of pixels down (the height). It also has a certain *color depth*, which represents the number of possible colors that each pixel can display

FIGURE 7.1 A bit-mapped image, with each pixel set to a particular shade of gray

(see the next section). The picture is composed by setting the color value of each individual pixel (or a shade of gray, as in Figure 7.1), in which each small square represents one pixel.

The resolution and color depth of an image determine its quality. As the resolution increases and/or the number of colors increases, the quality of the image improves. The same is true of film. Slower films have more, and smaller, grains of color, which is another way of saying a higher number of pixels or higher resolution. Large-format films are of a higher quality than standard films because their larger size means that they, too, have more pixels and so a higher resolution.

There is a difference, however, between the intrinsic quality of a computer image as defined by its resolution and color depth and the quality that we see when it is displayed or printed. A high-quality photograph of an artifact printed on bad paper or enlarged to the size of a poster may look quite bad. The same is true of raster images. When a high-resolution image with lots of colors is printed on a black-and-white printer, it may look bad. The problem is a conflict between the intrinsic and the display resolutions of the image.

This means that when considering image quality, you must also consider the quality of the display. To get a high-quality representation of an image, you should ensure that the image and the display resolution are compatible. As a general rule, the image quality should meet or, preferably, exceed by a factor of

50 percent the quality of the display. Let's see how that works, starting with displaying images on a computer screen.

Computer Displays   The quality of a computer display is defined exactly like a raster image. In fact, you can think of the computer screen as a raster image. First, the screen has a certain resolution defined by the number of pixels across and down. At the risk of dating this book, common screen resolutions for PCs are 640 × 480, 800 × 600, 1024 × 768, or even higher. Do not confuse this with the physical size of the screen. A bigger screen in terms of the number of inches does not mean higher resolution. This is because the size of the screen is determined by the physical dimensions of the monitor, whereas the resolution of the screen is determined by the video graphics card in the computer. The video graphics card is what determines how many pixels can be represented on the screen.

Thus, a larger monitor will not increase the resolution or the quality of your displayed images. In fact, contrary to what you might think, a larger monitor will probably make the displayed images look worse. This is because, without increasing the number of pixels in the image, you have increased the size of each pixel, resulting in an image that looks chunky or pixilated. For a sharp image, it is actually better to have a small monitor with lots of resolution. This is why the picture on tiny portable televisions often looks better (i.e., sharper) than that on full-size ones—the same number of pixels are shown, but they are packed into a smaller physical space, meaning that each pixel is smaller and thus the overall image is clearer. Taking our original drawing of the tools in Figure 7.1 and shrinking the size of the individual pixels makes the picture smaller, but it also makes it look sharper (see Figure 7.2).

Besides determining the resolution of the screen, the video graphics card sets the number of colors that are displayed. As we will see when we discuss image file sizes, the memory required to display the image on your computer screen is the product of the resolution and the number of colors. Thus, graphics cards usually allow some flexibility. High resolutions can be obtained if the number of colors are decreased, and vice versa.

Now, let's say that we have an image with an intrinsic resolution of 640 × 480. On a low-resolution 640 × 480 screen, this image will fill the entire screen, with each pixel of the image represented by one pixel on the screen (see Figure 7.3). On a higher-resolution 1024 × 768 screen, this same image will take about a third of the screen (see Figure 7.4). If the monitor size in both cases is the same, then the image will appear sharper on the 1024 × 768 screen because each pixel itself is smaller. Thus, increasing the resolution of the display is one way to make your images look better, but they will occupy less of the screen.

What will happen if you simply resize the original image to fill the screen of the 1024 × 768 monitor? The answer is that the image will not appear any better.

FIGURE 7.2   A resized image with smaller pixels

FIGURE 7.3   A 640 × 480 image displayed on a 640 × 480 screen

FIGURE 7.4   A 640 × 480 image displayed on a 1024 × 768 screen

To fill the larger screen, pixels need to be added to the image, but there is no new information to put in those extra pixels. In effect, you can expand the image only by duplicating what you already have. The only way to have the same quality when filling a 1024 × 768 screen is to start with an image of that resolution.

What will happen when you decrease the resolution of an image? The general rule is this: as long as the image resolution is *smaller* than the screen resolution, decreasing the size will result in a sharper image. However, if the resolution of the image is *larger* than the screen, then decreasing the size will result in a loss of information contained in the image. In other words, pixels will be lost. Imagine trying to display a 1024 × 768 image on a 640 × 480 screen. If you maintain the original resolution of the image, you will be able to see only a third of the image. In order to decrease the size of the image so that it fits on the screen, you have to eliminate about two-thirds of your original pixels and the information they contain (see Figure 7.5).

What this means is that displaying a high-resolution image on a low-resolution screen does not produce a better image than displaying an image that originally matches the screen resolution. In fact, reducing the resolution of an image may actually degrade its quality simply because the computer is deciding which pixels to keep and which to eliminate.

FIGURE 7.5   A 1024 × 768 image reduced to 640 × 480

There is, however, one important reason you might want to digitize an image at a much higher resolution than you will normally display that image: A higher-resolution image will allow you to zoom in and still retain a high-quality image. What we mean by "zoom in" is to show a smaller portion of the image on the same area of the screen. The effect is to show a close-up of the image or a portion of it.

Normally, if you zoom in on an image that has an intrinsic resolution that matches the screen's resolution, the effect will be the same as showing a low-resolution image on a high-resolution screen. Suppose, for example, that you halve the scale of a 640 × 480 image on a 640 × 480 monitor, which means that you will display 320 × 240 pixels of the image on the 640 × 480 pixels of the monitor. In this case your image will be grainy or pixely.

The effect will be different if you start with an image with a 1280 × 960 resolution. Displaying the entire image on this monitor means that you will have to drop half of the pixels, but by halving the scale of the image (to 640 × 480) you will see only a quarter of the image but will see all of the pixels. Thus, the image quality will still be good. The maximum zoom that still retains the best quality is when the image resolution equals the screen resolution.

Printed Images   Printers make the process of comparing image resolution and display resolution a little more straightforward by standardizing resolution to the physical size of the output. Printers measure resolution in terms of the number of dots per inch (dpi). This is the measure of resolution that is commonly used when printing an image because we end up with a physical image that has an actual size (unlike a monitor, which can be any number of sizes). The concept of dots per inch is exactly the same as pixels per inch.

In printing an image of a certain resolution, you have to decide what print resolution is needed to have the result a certain size. Suppose you begin with an image that is 500 × 300 pixels. If you print it on a 100-dpi printer, you will have made an exact copy and come out with an image measuring 5 inches by 3 inches. Alternatively, if you want an image only 2.5 inches across on this same printer, then half the pixels will have to be dropped. Fortunately most printer software is sophisticated in terms of how pixels are dropped (using a process of averaging adjacent pixels), which can make the reduced image look even better. In fact, it is often recommended that you begin with an image that has 50 percent more resolution than you want to use when printing it. Thus, to print at 100 dpi, you might scan the original image at 150 dpi.

What if the printer can print a 200-dpi image but the image is scanned at 100 dpi? In this case the image will look as good as it can since the printer resolution exceeds the image resolution, and it may even look a little better than it would on the 100-dpi printer because some printers fill in the extra pixels by interpolating from the original image. Interpolation can sometimes make the image look better by, among other things, making jagged lines smoother.

To summarize, deciding on what resolution to use for your images should be based entirely on what you want to do with them. If you are only going to be looking at them on a computer monitor, then you should try to match the resolution of the monitor (unless you want to be able to zoom in). If you eventually want to print your images, then you have to be concerned with both the printed image size and the printer's resolution. For instance, this book is published at 300 dpi. This means that, for an image that measures 6 inches across, the original image is 300 (the printer dpi) × 1.5 (add 50 percent) × 6 (the width of the printed image in inches), or 2700 pixels in width. As we will see, this much resolution comes at the price of file size. Remember that increasing the size of an image will not reveal more detail unless the original display resolution is lower than the image resolution. So, if you are going to want to zoom in for additional detail, then your initial resolution must be higher.

Note that scanning an image is conceptually just the opposite of printing it. In other words, scanners operate within a certain range of resolution measured in dpi. When you scan an image at a resolution of 100 dpi, you are recording 10,000 pixels (100 × 100) per square inch of the original image. If you begin with an image that is 5 inches across and 3 inches high, the scanned digital image

TABLE 7.1   The relationship between the number of bits used to store color and the maximum number of colors that can be displayed

Number of Bits	Number of Colors
1	2
4	16
8	256
15	32,768
16	65,536
24	16,777,216
32	4,294,967,296
48	281,474,976,710,656

will be 500 pixels across and 300 high. So, what you want to do when scanning an image is to set the resolution of the scan to at least the resolution that you want to have when you view or print the image.

Color Depth

The other major factor affecting image quality is color depth, or the number of colors that can be displayed by a single pixel. Color depth is commonly measured in terms of how many bits are used by each pixel to store the color information. Remember that a single bit has a value of either 0 or 1. To represent larger numbers, you have to string together several bits to arrive at a binary representation of that number. The number of colors that can be displayed by a pixel is thus determined by how many bits are used to store the numbers that represent the various colors used, as shown in Table 7.1.

For color images the higher the number of colors the more lifelike and realistic the image. This is simply because, with more colors available, the transition from one color to the next can be more gradual. Today 24-bit color, often referred to as true color, is commonly used. Pure black-and-white images, such as line art, can use a single bit. Another use of 1-bit black and white is for scanning text. However, in most instances what we commonly think of as black and white is really a series of different shades of gray, or what is called gray scale. Gray-scale images are typically adequately handled with 256 different shades or a mere 8 bits.

There are a number of ways of expressing color, or what are called color models. A popular color model is *RGB*, in which individual colors are defined in terms of the relative contributions of red, green, and blue. In 24-bit color each of these components can have 8 bits (3 × 8 = 24) or 256 shades (0–255). Thus, for instance, the brightest pure red is formed by mixing shade 255 of red with the darkest shades of (or lack of) green and blue (255, 0, 0). White is formed by mixing the brightest shades of red, green, and blue (255, 255, 255), and black is formed by mixing the darkest shade of each (0, 0, 0). Equal amounts of red, green, and blue form shades of gray between black and white.

Some systems now support 48-bit color, which means that each shade can be represented by 16 bits or 32,768 shades. However, the graphics display cards in most computers can handle only 24-bit color (or sometimes 32-bit color). When an image has higher color depth than can be displayed on a given monitor, the computer maps the actual color onto a smaller palette of colors, usually by substituting the color that comes closest. In this case data are, in effect, lost when the image is displayed.

Another common color model is *CMYK*, which consists of combinations of cyan, magenta, yellow, and black. This is the model used for most color printers. A color ink jet printer, for instance, has four inkwells for each of the colors in the CMYK model. By coating the paper with varying amounts of cyan, magenta, and yellow, all colors can be formed. Although placing the maximum amount of each of these colors on the paper would yield black, a separate supply of black ink is also included to save on color inks and to produce a more effective black. When an RGB image is printed, the printing software converts or maps each pixel from red, green, and blue into a corresponding CMYK representation.

FILE SIZES

One of the biggest issues surrounding raster images is the size of the files they require, which can easily become several megabytes and in some instances can exceed 100 megabytes. Of course, file size has a direct bearing on storage requirements. But it also affects the speed at which an image can be displayed or downloaded from the Internet. So, depending on your requirements and equipment, considerations of file size can be important. You can significantly affect file size by adjusting both resolution and color depth, and you can also utilize different image formats to compress an image into a smaller file.

As we have just explained, an image is defined in terms of its resolution, or the number of pixels it contains, and its color depth, or the number of bits needed for each pixel to represent colors. Clearly, then, file size increases directly with the number of pixels *and* the color depth. So, an 800 × 600 image has 480,000 pixels altogether. If it is a true black-and-white image, or 1-bit color, then the size of the image file will be about 480,000 bits (1 bit for each pixel), or approximately 60 kilobytes. If we increase the color depth to 24-bit color, then the size of the file jumps to 1.4 megabytes (mb), or 24 times greater.

An 8 × 10 photograph scanned at a resolution of 600 dpi in true color would require more than 86 mb! As you can see, image files become large rather quickly, which is the main reason you should limit the resolution and color depth to the minimum necessary to address your needs.

Compression

Another way to reduce the storage requirements of an image is through compression. *Compression* works, in effect, by calculating shorthand techniques for representing the information that is in an image. While there are a variety of compression techniques, they all fall into two basic categories: lossless and lossy.

Lossless compression uses techniques that exactly replicate the original content of the image without any loss of information. Imagine, for instance, an image 100 pixels wide and 100 pixels high consisting of the same white pixel. Rather than store this image as 10,000 individual white pixels (100 × 100), it can be stored with two pieces of information: 10,000 and the color white. Obviously the savings in space are huge. If it takes 1 byte to store the color white, then storing that same image without compression will require 10,000 bytes.

While most images are not one solid color and cannot be compressed with such effectiveness, you might be surprised how much information in an image is redundant and can be easily compressed using this simple technique. As the image is compressed, the computer looks for adjacent pixels with the exact same color and stores not the pixels themselves but the number of pixels with the same color and that color. Scanned text (black text on white pages) and 256-color images with large blocks of solid color are especially appropriate for this technique.

As the number of colors in the image increases, however, this technique gets harder to apply, since the odds of two adjacent pixels having the same color become lower and lower. If you try to capture an image of an apparently solid-color object or background, you will be surprised to find out that small variations in light and texture across the surface of the object result in pixels with slightly different colors.

For these kinds of images, lossy compression techniques, which do not try to exactly replicate the original image, usually work better. Lossy techniques break the image into regions that contain roughly similar-looking pixels. These regions are then summarized using, in effect, statistical techniques that re-create the look of each region without a pixel-by-pixel match with the original. How much a lossy technique actually compresses an image depends not only on the content of the original image, as it does with the lossless techniques, but also on how closely you want the compressed image to resemble the original. If you can tolerate a higher amount of graininess and a decrease in the sharpness of the image, then you can increase the compression level and thereby decrease the storage requirements quite a bit. Deterioration of the image quality can also be additive with lossy compression techniques, meaning that each time the image is altered and resaved, the sharpness will be diminished. Thus, it is a good idea to set aside an original copy of the image that can be called upon when repeated use of a lossy technique results in an unacceptable image.

The upside of compression is small files. This can be very important when you are collecting artifact images from a large collection or when you are working with very large high-resolution satellite images. One downside is the length of time it takes for the computer to compress and decompress the image. It takes time to analyze an image to calculate how to compress it, and it takes time to rebuild an image from a compressed image. While faster, more powerful computers make this less of an issue, it also seems that as computers become faster the images become larger and thus the savings in time disappear.

A more important consideration is whether you can use lossy compression techniques and, if so, how much. There are no rules for the latter. You will simply have to try various amounts of compression with a single image and compare the results. At some point the gains in terms of storage space will start to diminish and the loss of image quality will be too great.

In contrast, whether you can use lossy compression is quite clear. If the image consists of data, then you probably do not want to use a lossy technique. For instance, if the image is a digital elevation model (DEM) wherein each pixel stores the elevation of a particular point on the ground, then using a lossy technique will change the topography. Likewise, if the image is a satellite image wherein each pixel represents the vegetation of a particular point on the ground, then you also should not use a lossy technique. Images of things like artifacts, stratigraphy, and people, in which the contents of each pixel are not as important as the image created by all the pixels combined, are more suitable for lossy compression.

File Formats

Whether you use compression techniques at all, and whether you use a lossy versus a lossless compression technique, to a large extent determines the format or type of image file. There are dozens of, and possibly more than a hundred, different image file types, but Table 7.2 summarizes five of the more popular of these. If compression is not important but colors are, then BMP and TIFF are good choices. If you have only 256 colors (8-bit color), then you can use GIF format. You should experiment, however. Even though converting an 8-bit color image to 24 bits means increasing its size threefold, sometimes the lossy compression techniques are so effective that you can gain back that increased size and more.

TABLE 7.2   Popular image formats

Format	Colors	Compression Type	Comments
BMP	24-bit color	None	PC standard—images load quickly
GIF	8-bit color	Lossless	Good for graphics with solid colors—Mac and PC
JPG	24-bit color	Lossy	Good for images of artifacts—Mac and PC
TIFF or TIF	24-bit color	None or lossless	Widely used in publication—Mac and PC
PICT	32-bit color	None	Supports both images and vendor-based objects—Mac

ACQUIRING DIGITAL IMAGES

Methods of Acquiring Digital Images

There are two widely available methods for creating digital images: scanners and digital cameras. Each of these methods has its own advantages and disadvantages in comparison to the others. Flatbed scanners, for instance, work best with flat objects, such as artifact photographs, drawings and maps, but they are not as well suited for large, three-dimensional objects. Nevertheless, scanners are very affordable. Digital cameras work much better with three-dimensional objects and are quite fast, and they also offer the highest degree of portability and control. However, they produce fairly low-resolution images. As the technology improves, the resolution increases, but the costs are still high.

One issue in acquiring digital images involves distortion. While digital cameras offer certain distinct advantages for this type of work, the camera and lens can produce significant distortions in the digitized image. The effect of lens distortion is easily demonstrated by digitizing a section of square grid paper with a camera and superimposing the resulting image over the original grid pattern (see Figure 7.6). In each corner of the digitized image, lines that should remain parallel tend to bend either toward or away from the center of the image. The center of the image, however, remains largely unaffected by this type of distortion.

Lens distortion can be addressed in several ways. You can, for instance, mark a number of control points with known coordinates on the original image. By comparing the coordinates of the digitized control points with their true coordinates, you can derive formulas to shift each pixel in the digitized image to remove the distortion. In GIS this process is called rubber-sheeting, and it is used to remove distortion from aerial photographs. Despite faster computers,

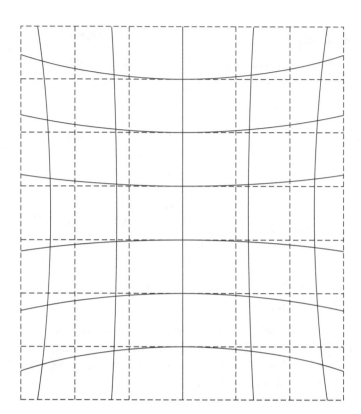

FIGURE 7.6 Lens distortion. The dashed lines represent a regularly spaced grid, and the solid lines represent the same grid as a result of lens distortion.

however, this remains a time-consuming and somewhat difficult process. It is possible to reduce the effect of lens distortion by placing the object being photographed as near as possible to the center of the image area.

A digital camera may also distort an image by changing its aspect ratio, which describes the width of each pixel in the image relative to its height. To make accurate measurements from an image, the width of each pixel should equal its height, for an aspect ratio of 1. Some cameras, however, produce pixels with heights considerably larger than their widths. As a result, 100 pixels might represent 10 millimeters along the horizontal axis and 14 millimeters along the vertical axis. Other digital cameras produce the same kinds of problems, though to different degrees and even in different directions. By way of comparison, flatbed scanners produce no noticeable bending distortion, and the aspect ratio is perfect. Thus, for two-dimensional objects, scanners are the best method for acquiring digital images.

Fortunately, unlike lens distortion, aspect ratio affects the entire image equally. As a result, once the aspect ratio error is known, it can be quickly and easily corrected by either compressing or expanding the image along one axis. The challenge, however, is to determine both the aspect ratio and the scale for each digitized image. One way to accomplish this is to digitize a circle of known diameter immediately before digitizing an artifact image. The software can then analyze the digitized image of the circle to determine its width and height, which, of course, should be an equal number of pixels. Based on this information, the program calculates the aspect ratio and the scale, represented as the number of pixels per centimeter.

Finally we should say a word about calculating the scale for a two-dimensional image taken from a three-dimensional object. With a three-dimensional object the region of the artifact nearest the camera lens has a different scale than the region farthest from the lens. Furthermore, with the circle scale technique described previously, the scale is easily recorded at either the top or the bottom of the artifact but not anywhere in between. On relatively flat artifacts, such as sherds and flakes, the differences in scale from the top to the bottom are not noticeable. To the contrary, on thicker objects, such as thick bifaces or whole ceramic vessels, the differences can be much more significant.

Tips for Acquiring Digital Images

If you are planning to take photographs of artifacts, there are a number of things you might experiment with to get the best results.

- *Depth of field.* Depth of field is another way of describing how much of the image is in focus. With a greater depth of field, objects in the foreground and background will be in focus. To increase the depth of field, set the aperture to the highest f-stop (i.e., stop it down to the smallest shutter opening). This helps to ensure that more of the image is in focus when there is more of a distance between the foreground and background of the object. Stopping down the aperture means, however, that you will need more light or need to increase the exposure time.

- *White balance.* Keep in mind that you have to adjust the camera to compensate for the color that is given off by different kinds of lighting. With a normal camera this is handled with different kinds of film or filters, but most digital cameras allow you either to set the white balance or to indicate explicitly the kind of lighting that you will be using. This helps to ensure that the colors in the image match the true colors of the object being photographed.

- *Lighting.* While overall lighting is important, you may also want to use a handheld source to provide extra lighting from the side or upper corner of the object. This is especially useful for stone tools to bring out scar patterns and retouch. Keep in mind that too much direct lighting tends to wash out those features.

- *Shadows.* To eliminate shadows, you can place the artifact on a sheet of frosted glass that is elevated a few inches from the table surface. On the table surface below the glass, place a sheet of colored paper to serve as the background color for the image. The shadows produced by the direct lighting will pass through the glass and become extremely diffuse before they reach the colored paper. This produces a very even background and makes it easier for graphics applications to differentiate between the object and the background in the digital image. The use of a lighter color for the background is often preferable to black simply because a black background tends to emphasize small specks and crumbs. Nonetheless, you should always try to keep the surface as clean as possible.

- *Flatbed scanners.* If you are using a flatbed scanner to photograph objects, put a sheet of thin glass on top of the scanner's glass in order to protect it against scratches—it is much easier and cheaper to replace this sheet than to replace the scanner's glass. Also, if you want to produce an even and diffused color background, elevate a sheet of frosted glass just above the objects and place the colored paper background on top of it.

- *Zoom.* Zoom in on the object as much as possible in order to maximize the pixel coverage of the object instead of the background. Afterward, you may want to crop the image again with your graphics application in order to minimize its file size. Keep in mind that with digital cameras optical zoom is better than digital zoom, since the latter is simply applying the same techniques of interpolating that we discussed earlier.

- *Labels.* It is a good idea to include in the image a small label indicating the number or other identifier for the object being photographed, even if you are recording the same information separately. This label can easily be removed digitally from the image at a later time, and it provides an almost foolproof method for ensuring that the object being photographed is correctly identified.

- *Scale.* Always include a scale in the photo, preferably one composed of alternating solid and open rectangles of the units (e.g., inches or centimeters) you are using. The use of the solid and open rectangles facilitates the reading of the scale (e.g., pixels per centimeter) by an image-processing application. Another good solution, when the scale is not going to be retained in the final image, is to use a solid circle of a fixed diameter. In any event you should avoid the use of rulers, coins, or other such objects that may be useful to a person who is viewing the photo but that provide little or no analytical capability within a graphic analysis application.

MORE ABOUT SCALE

If you plan on taking measurements from your images, then you probably want to know their scale. Scale in a digital image refers to the number of pixels per unit of measure (centimeters, inches, etc.). When you use a scanner, it is easy to calculate the scale since the scale equals the scanner's resolution. If the scanner is set to a resolution of 300 dpi, for instance, then 300 pixels in the scanned image are equal to 1 inch. When you use a camera, however, the scale is not fixed: zooming in on an artifact with a zoom lens or bringing the camera closer to the subject will change the scale because the number of pixels in the camera is constant, but the scene being recorded can expand or shrink. If a camera has 1000 pixels of horizontal resolution and the scene is 1 kilometer across, then each pixel represents 1 meter. If the same camera captures an artifact 10 centimeters across, then each pixel represents 0.1 millimeter. As we have just emphasized, and particularly when digitizing with a camera, it is important either to include a scale in the image or to capture first an image with the scale and then a second image without the scale and without readjusting the camera.

Regardless of whether you use a scanner or a camera, however, if you do not include a scale directly in the image, then it is important that you store the scale in an associated database. It is also imperative that the image not be resized unless you note the change in scale in your database. The possibility that images might get resized without the scale being updated is one reason you should strongly consider recording scale directly in the image. In this way, if the database information is lost or if the image is modified, the scale will not be lost.

DATABASING IMAGES

Acquiring digital images is one thing; keeping them organized afterward is another. Giving them informative file names is one way of handling the problem, but to make the most of your digital images, you will want to database them. There are two basic methods for databasing images. First, some database systems have a field type specially designed for images. So, rather than a text or numeric field for words and numbers, you have an image field that contains the image. One of the advantages of this method is that images are tightly associated with the rest of the information in the database. Imagine, for instance, an Image table with three fields: UNIT, ID, and IMAGE. Such a table is perfect for storing images of artifacts, each of which has its own unique ID composed of UNIT and ID. Any other information about these artifacts can be stored in other specialized tables that are then related to the Image table on the basis of UNIT-ID.

Database programs take different approaches to displaying the contents of image fields. Some contain all the tools you need in the program itself. While it differs from one database program to the next, generally to display an image you need only to create a database report or form that contains an image object linked to the contents of the image field in your database table. Other database programs use a secondary program, one you can typically specify yourself, to display the image. When you ask to see the image, the database program loads the other program and passes the contents of the image field to this program so that it can be displayed. While this approach is a little awkward, it offers some advantages. First, it is more flexible since you are not limited to the image types that your database program supports. Rather, you can display any kind of image as long as you have a separate program that recognizes it. Second, if the program used to display the image also has editing capabilities, then you can edit the image and save the results back to the database.

Image editing, however, leads to one of the more important downsides to this approach. When the images are bundled in the database, they are less accessible to image editing programs. While it is possible to work with images one at a time by linking an editor to the database table, it is difficult to act on the images as a group. Most image editors (like Adobe's PhotoShop or Corel's PhotoPaint) let you create a set of manipulations you want to apply to an image and then apply that set automatically to every image in a specified list or even an entire directory of images. This is sometimes called batch processing since it affects batches of files, and it can be difficult to do this if the images are stored in individual database records.

An alternative approach to databasing images is to store only the image file name in the database and to leave the images themselves on the computer's hard disk as separate files. The Image table mentioned previously becomes UNIT, ID, and IMAGE where IMAGE is a text field indicating the name of the file, or even a full path to the folder. A record from this table might look like this:

"A1","432","A1-432.JPG"

"A1-432.JPG" is an image file stored in a directory, or folder, on the computer's hard disk. Exactly which directory the image is stored in is not specified and must be included before the image can be displayed. One approach is to place the exact location, including the directory, in the database. Thus the record might read:

"A1","432","C:\SITE_50\IMAGES\A1-432.JPG"

This makes it possible to find the image, but it raises issues. What if the images are moved to another directory? What if they are burned onto a CD, for instance, and the name of your CD drive is E:\ rather than C:\? It is probably better, therefore, to separate the path from the image with a new text field called something like Imagepath. The record then looks like this:

"A1","432","C:\SITE_50\IMAGES\","A1-432.JPG"

Now, when the images are moved to a different place, it is easy to simply replace the contents of the Imagepath field with the name of the new folder or drive.

In this system the name of the image file becomes very important. In effect, a kind of relational link is established between the contents of the IMAGE field in the database and the file name. If either is changed then the link is broken. Worse yet, if a label is not written into the image itself, then if the name of the image file or the name stored in the database is inadvertently changed, it may be impossible to undo the mistake. As a result the association between the image and the data table will be lost. This is one of the downsides of not storing images directly in the database.

To display an image stored simply as a file name in a text field, the same options are typically available. That is, if the database has image display capabilities built in, then you can link those tools to the file name in the IMAGE field. Alternatively you may be able to launch external programs that will know to load the image from the file name given to them.

There is one last consideration. As we have already discussed, images are large. If you store them in your database, they will quickly make your database huge. For this reason alone we typically do not store images in our databases but instead keep them as separate files in various folders. Our database for the Paleolithic site of Pech de l'Azé is currently 140 megabytes of numeric and text data. The images we have, including scanned pages from notebooks and individual images of artifacts, require seven CDs of roughly 650 megabytes each. Had we included the images in our database, we would have needed nearly 6000 megabytes, or 6 gigabytes. Even with today's technology, a database file of this size will be difficult to work with, difficult to back up, and difficult to publish.

SUMMARY

In this chapter we have introduced topics related to acquiring, storing, and organizing artifact images. At one level the subject is rather basic. It is likely that you have already worked with images, just as you have undoubtedly worked with text in a word-processing program. At another level, however, images can be quite complex. This is especially true once you start to use them in an image analysis program or when you work with raster data sets in a GIS (see Chapter 9). We hope, however, that this chapter has given you a clear understanding of the fundamentals behind raster images so that you can make more informed decisions about how you work with them.

8 An Example of an Actual Archaeological Database

So far we have covered most of the fundamentals of organizing a database with simple examples that illustrate particular concepts or issues. In this chapter we present some more complex examples to show how to handle the many kinds of data generated during a field project. The examples presented here are based on our own data sets from various field and research projects.

To understand our database organization, it is necessary to understand a little bit of how we work in the field. We carry out excavations following the natural stratigraphy within each of the excavation units, usually meter squares. We measure all stone artifacts and bones with a maximum dimension greater than 2.5–3.0 centimeters in length and all unworked flint nodules larger than fist-sized in place according to a standard three-dimensional coordinate system. As we recover artifacts, we give them sequential numbers within each excavation unit. Thus, the identification number (the UNIT-ID) for each artifact consists of two parts: the excavation unit, or square, and a sequential number that continues to be incremented for as long as that square is excavated (e.g., A1-248 or N1015-47). Objects that have a clear linear axis are measured with two or more points at their ends, which gives not only the position of the piece relative to the site datum but also the vertical and horizontal orientation of the piece and a rough shape of the object for computer mapping. Objects smaller than the minimum size are put in a bucket with the sediment and later recovered during wet screening. Whenever samples are collected (sedimentological, geophysical, dating, etc.), we provenience each one in the same way, assign a UNIT-ID number, and so forth, just as with the objects.

We do all of our three-dimensional proveniencing with a total station. When we provenience an object and assign its identifying number, we enter any other observations concerning it directly into a field computer. These observations include the archaeological level in which the object was found, a code indicating the general nature of the object (e.g., flake, tool, core, bone) as determined by the excavator, the excavator's initials, and the date of excavation. During excavation we place all of the sediment and small finds from a restricted area of the square (normally about 0.1 m^2) and within the same level into a 7-liter bucket. When the bucket is full, we provenience the center of the area from which its contents were excavated with the total station, and we assign the bucket itself a two-part identifying number; we also record the level and other information, as with the numbered artifacts. The UNIT-ID number of the buckets is composed of the excavation unit followed by a random combination of letters (e.g., A2-SNVRE or K1015-UTIDX). We then wet-screen each bucket of sediment to recover smaller objects. Finally we bag all of the recovered worked flint and animal bone along with the corresponding computer-generated tag indicating the identifying number of the bucket. Thus, the site coordinates from where that portion of sediment was excavated are associated with each aggregate of small finds.

Our sites, which are all from the Lower and Middle Paleolithic, typically contain only two major classes of artifacts—stone artifacts and bones—each of which are analyzed by different specialists.

We have, therefore, two basic kinds of data that we collect: (1) field data, which consists of provenience and other information concerning how the object was found, and (2) analytical data that is generated during later analysis of the material. Each of these main data types is further subdivided into a number of different tables according to various needs. All relations between these tables are based on the UNIT-ID numbers of the individual artifacts, samples, or aggregated small finds, which are stored as two separate fields: UNIT and ID.

FIELD DATA

We separate the field data into two tables: the Context (see Table 8.1) and the XYZ (see Table 8.2). The Context table contains one record for each object, sample, or bucket and contains all of the field data except the X, Y, and Z coordinates, which are stored separately in the XYZ table. We do this because of the multiple provenience points that are taken for some objects, which means that the XYZ table contains one or more records per object.

For the most part these tables are straightforward in terms of the kinds of fields they contain, but we should touch on several issues. The first has to do with the fields used for the UNIT and ID number. Keep in mind that it is the UNIT-ID combination that uniquely identifies each excavated object, because many objects are recovered from the same unit, and ID numbers are repeated in each of the units. One option for us would have been to treat UNIT-ID as one field, but we did not do this because it makes it more difficult to find the objects from one square than if UNIT is a separate field. We defined ID as a character

TABLE 8.1   The Context table

Unit	ID	Level	Word Code	Excavator	Date
D27	1	X	COBBLE	HF	10/4/94
D27	4	X	COBBLE	HF	10/4/94
D27	5	1B	FLAKE	RN	10/5/94
D27	6	1B	FLAKE	RN	10/5/94
D27	7	1B	FLAKE	RN	10/5/94
D27	10	1B	MANDIBLE	RN	10/5/94
D27	FPXLF	X	BUCKET	RN	10/7/94
D27	WXDTN	1B	BUCKET	RN	10/5/94
D27	XIWOO	X	BUCKET	RN	10/8/94
D28	1	1A	FLAKE	RN	10/2/94
D28	2	1A	BONE	RN	10/2/94
D28	6	X0	TOOTH	KK	6/24/96
D28	8	X0	FLAKE	KK	6/24/96
D28	12	X0	COBBLE	KK	6/25/96
D28	13	X0	FLAKE	KK	6/25/96
D28	AFXJE	X0	BUCKET	KK	6/25/96
D28	IAKKX	1A	BUCKET	HIS	10/2/94
D28	ZZWHX	1A	BUCKET	KM	7/3/96

field because of the assignment of the random-letter character IDs for the buckets. This makes it necessary to pad the numeric ID with leading spaces in order to facilitate sorting by artifact ID number. Since each object or sample has a unique UNIT-ID combination, we build the primary index for this table on the two fields together.

So, it is on the basis of the UNIT-ID index that we can relate these two tables. But this relationship is not a straightforward one-to-one relation between the records of Context and the records of XYZ. The XYZ table may contain multiple records for a single object (when more than one provenience point is measured for it) whereas the Context table is always one record per object. Thus, the relationship between these two tables is a one-to-many relation (one record in Context may relate to many records in XYZ).

Because the XYZ table contains multiple records per object, we find it useful to number each of those records with the field SUFFIX. Thus, a value of 0 for SUFFIX indicates the first provenience point for an object, a value of 1 the second, and so on. Using such a field is not always necessary, but we include it for two reasons. First, the order of SUFFIX reflects the order that the provenience

TABLE 8.2 The XYZ table					
Unit	ID	Suffix	X	Y	Z
D27	1	0	3.926	27.935	−2.009
D27	1	1	3.873	28.1	−2.036
D27	1	2	3.874	28.096	−2.037
D27	4	0	3.995	27.786	−2.284
D27	5	0	3.378	27.966	−2.073
D27	6	0	3.26	27.873	−2.099
D27	7	0	3.132	27.906	−2.08
D27	10	0	5.218	28.032	−2.469
D27	10	1	5.224	28.101	−2.463
D27	FPXLF	0	3.649	27.7	−2.536
D27	WXDTN	0	3.488	27.793	−2.146
D27	XIWOO	0	3.67	27.385	−2.80
D28	1	0	3.941	28.112	−2.089
D28	2	0	3.886	28.035	−2.067
D28	6	0	3.963	28.956	−1.898
D28	8	0	3.74	28.941	−1.921
D28	8	1	3.888	28.968	−1.9
D28	12	0	3.741	28.833	−1.946
D28	12	1	3.711	28.996	−1.959
D28	13	0	3.757	28.855	−1.925
D28	13	1	3.689	28.999	−1.962
D28	AFXJE	0	3.339	28.346	−2.01
D28	IAKKX	0	3.92	28.108	−2.081
D28	ZZWHX	0	3.988	28.973	−1.931

points were taken with the total station. When we draw the object on the computer, we can follow the order of the SUFFIX field to re-create an approximate outline of the object as it was recorded in the field. Again, we would not need SUFFIX to do this as long as the records in the table remained in the proper order as they were recorded; that is, their physical location—one after the other—could just as well indicate their proper order. As we saw earlier, however, relying on physical location is dangerous, because if the table is ever resorted we will lose forever the proper ordering by provenience point. Thus, by including SUFFIX as a separate field and creating an index based on UNIT-ID-SUFFIX, we can always access this table in the proper sorted order we need for drawing artifacts.

The second reason for having a separate SUFFIX field is that it allows us to identify and access individual XYZ records. For example, suppose we would want to plot the artifacts from a single level in order to get an idea of the distribution of artifacts on a surface. If we include all of the provenience points taken for some objects, our view could be distorted by having objects with multiple points more heavily represented in the plot than they should be. By accessing only XYZ records with SUFFIX = 0, however, we get one and only one record per object, thus making all of the objects equally represented.

ANALYTICAL DATA

Let's now turn to some of the analytical tables that we have, beginning with the Lithics table, which is shown in Table 8.3. This table, which contains basic observations and measurements for each of the stone artifacts, has only one record per object. Thus, we define a one-to-one relation between this table and the Context table, and a one-to-many relation with the XYZ table. Note, however, that in this table we kept ID as a character field, with padded spaces to the left of the ID number. It is true that there are no random-letter IDs in the stone tool table, since all artifacts are given sequential numeric IDs. So, why do we keep this as a character field? The reason is that we have to use the combination of the Unit and ID fields to relate this table to the Context or XYZ tables, and building this relation requires that the fields are exactly the same in each table.

We like to photograph most of our stone artifacts and to illustrate as many of them as we can. As discussed in Chapter 7, our approach to storing the image files is to keep them as distinct files in a folder. Each file is named as the identifier of the object (UNIT-ID), joined with another number (essentially a suffix-like number) that keeps a record of how many images of that object we have. We do this because with some objects we take a photograph of each side of the object, and we also store scanned images of the hand-drawn illustrations of the object. In addition, we have an Images table in the database, as shown in Table 8.4, which has a field that records the kind of image it is (a photograph vs. an illustration), the path to the folder where the image file is stored, and the name of the image file.

The Small Finds table, as shown in Table 8.5, contains aggregated data—that is, one or more physical objects are represented in each of the records. Nevertheless, because there is only one record per UNIT-ID, we still build a one-to-one relation with the Context table and a one-to-many relation with the XYZ table.

As discussed in previous chapters, many times archaeological data are collected in aggregated lots, and for purposes of artifact recovery this can be a reasonably efficient method of excavation, as opposed to proveniencing each and every artifact. When data are aggregated, however, our ability to work with the

TABLE 8.3   The Lithics table

Unit	ID	Dataclass	Length	Weight
D27	1	COBBLE	58.55	136
D27	4	COBBLEFRAG	61.645	126
D27	5	PROXFLAKE	26.02	2
D27	6	COMPTOOL	42.5	8
D27	7	PROXFLAKE	40.225	6
D28	1	COMPTOOL	48.505	20
D28	8	PROXFLAKE	26.555	9
D28	12	COBBLE	56.42	75
D28	13	COMPFLAKE	34.54	8

TABLE 8.4   The Images table

Unit	ID	Suffix	Image Type	Path	File Name
D27	6	0	PHOTO	C:\IMAGES\	d27-6-0.jpg
D27	6	1	PHOTO	C:\IMAGES\	d27-6-1.jpg
D27	6	2	ILLUS	C:\IMAGES\	d27-6-2.jpg
D28	1	0	PHOTO	C:\IMAGES\	d28-1-0.jpg
D28	1	1	PHOTO	C:\IMAGES\	d28-1-1.jpg
D28	13	0	PHOTO	C:\IMAGES\	d28-13-0.jpg

TABLE 8.5   The Small Finds table

Unit	ID	N Flakes	F Weight	N Bones	B Weight
D27	FPXLF	3	1	1	1
D27	WXDTN	1	2	3	2
D27	XIWOO	3	5	2	1
D28	AFXJE	4	3	3	3
D28	IAKKX	1	4	5	6
D28	ZZWHK	2	4	6	8

individual artifacts within the aggregate is very limited. For example, in our Small Finds table we know the total number of flakes found in each of the screened buckets and their total weight, but we do not know the weights of the individual flakes from one sample. In fact, we really cannot record any observations that relate to specific objects, but rather must deal with the objects as a whole. This is the major drawback of aggregated data sets.

This can cause problems. For example, sometimes an excavator may miss a larger artifact or bone that should have been point provenienced and analyzed in more detail, but only later is it recovered, during screening. Or imagine that the field data are collected as aggregate lots and that in a subsequent stage of analysis we pick out the more diagnostic or otherwise more important artifacts for further analysis. Since we will want to refer to those artifacts individually, we have to somehow disaggregate them and give them unique identifying numbers that can then be related back to, in our case, the Context and XYZ tables.

This can be done in several ways. We separate the artifact found in the screen and assign it a new UNIT-ID number. The UNIT value is the same as the UNIT value in the Small Finds table, and the ID value is the next available ID number for that Unit. Then we create a new record in the Context table with those UNIT and ID values, copying the data from the other fields of the aggregated samples. We do the same thing for the XYZ table. From that point on, the artifact is treated as though it were point provenienced separately. This is a rather clumsy approach that can result in duplicate identifiers, but since this is only an occasional problem in our excavations, it is an effective method.

If this occurs on a larger scale, a more appropriate way of handling it might be to assign SUFFIX numbers to the diagnostic pieces recovered in the lots. For example, when sorting through the material of the lot, we might find, say, three stone objects that we want to reserve for further analysis. Retaining the same UNIT and ID information of the lot itself, we could assign suffixes of 1 through 3 to each of the artifacts and then simply add a SUFFIX field to the Lithics table, as shown in Table 8.6.

Each of the artifacts can now be analyzed separately in the Lithics table, with the remaining artifacts in the lot treated as an aggregate in the Small Finds table and the Context and XYZ tables left unchanged. Note, however, that now the Lithics table relates to the Context table in a one-to-many relation (where multiple Stone Tool records point back to one Context record) and to the XYZ table in a many-to-many relation (where both tables may contain multiple records for a given UNIT-ID). Such an organization allows for the faster recovery by lots while still retaining the ability to analyze artifacts separately.

Our Fauna table actually has this kind of approach built into it because of the need to analyze individual teeth that may be contained in a jaw fragment. Table 8.7 presents an excerpt from this table. Here object D27-10 is a mandible with three teeth present. In the field this mandible was provenienced as a single object, though two provenience measures were recorded for it. Thus, we assign 0 to SUFFIX for the overall object (in this case the mandible) and SUFFIX values greater than 0 for individual teeth still remaining in the jaw (numbering the

TABLE 8.6   The Lithics table modified to include suffix

Unit	ID	Suffix	Dataclass	Length	Weight
D27	1	0	COBBLE	58.55	136
D27	4	0	COBBLEFRAG	61.645	126
D27	5	0	PROXFLAKE	26.02	2
D27	6	0	COMPFLAKE	42.5	8
D27	7	0	PROXFLAKE	40.225	6
D28	1	0	COMPFLAKE	48.505	20
D28	8	0	PROXFLAKE	26.555	9
D28	12	0	COBBLE	56.42	75
D28	13	0	COMPFLAKE	34.54	8
D28	AIKKX	1	COMPFLAKE	47.5	9
D28	AIKKX	2	PROXFLAKE	30.225	3
D28	AIKKX	3	COMPFLAKE	42.505	23

TABLE 8.7   The Fauna table

Unit	ID	Suffix	Genus	Part	Side	Cut Marks
D27	10	0	PANTHERA	MANT	L	N
D27	10	1	PANTHERA	DLP2	L	
D27	10	2	PANTHERA	DLP3	L	
D27	10	3	PANTHERA	LM1	L	
D28	2	0	EQUUS	CER7		N
D28	6	0	CROCUTA	UP4	R	

TABLE 8.8   The Faunal Measurements table

Unit	ID	Suffix	Measure Name	Value
D27	10	1	Crown Height	2.45
D27	10	1	Crown Width	1.35
D27	10	2	Crown Height	2.89
D27	10	2	Crown Width	1.74
D27	10	3	Crown Height	2.9
D27	10	3	Crown Width	1.93
D28	6	0	Crown Height	3.21
D28	6	0	Crown Width	2.52

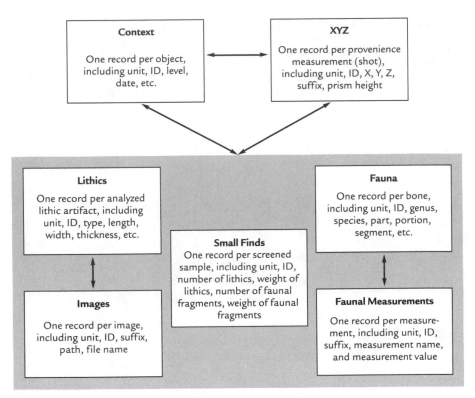

FIGURE 8.1   Schematic overview of the various tables

individual teeth sequentially from anterior to posterior). If an isolated tooth is found, as in the case of D28-6, the SUFFIX field is left as 0. Because we have multiple records per physical object, this leads us to define a one-to-many relation with the Context table and a many-to-many relation with the XYZ table.

With our Faunal Measurements table, we have to create an even more complicated relation. The problem here is that only certain measurements are taken on certain bones or teeth. In other words, while the total number of different kinds of measurements taken is quite high, the measurements taken on one kind of tooth or bone are limited, and very few bone remains will actually have any measurements taken on them. To handle this efficiently, we create a table that consists of one record per measurement. As shown in Table 8.8 on page 185, we define one field to store the name of the measurement, another to store the value of the measurement, and the fields UNIT, ID, and SUFFIX to relate the measurements back to specific bones stored in the Fauna table. Figure 8.1 provides a schematic overview of the various tables.

Summary

There are, of course, many other ways we can handle the data from our excavations. Our method is partly based on techniques that are particular to Paleolithic archaeology in France. Nevertheless, the example presented in this chapter touches on many of the basic principles that will be encountered in any archaeological excavation. It is not unusual, for instance, to have both point provenienced and aggregate data, and most excavations will have many more different kinds of artifact classes (aside from bones and stones in the Paleolithic) that need to be treated separately. The underlying theme throughout, however, is the creation of a database system that integrates all of the various kinds of data an excavation generates. The next chapter discusses a powerful tool for exploiting this integration: GIS.

9 Data Integration with Geographic Information Systems

In the previous chapters we introduced you to data collection and storage techniques in archaeology. First, you learned how to collect data in the field and to record the topography, the location of surface features, and the location of individual artifact finds or groups of artifacts. Next, you learned how to database the results of your laboratory analysis of the artifacts. And in the previous chapter we focused on how to collect and manage digital images of artifacts.

Throughout these chapters we have emphasized techniques that allow one set of data to be related to another, and the primary method we have discussed involves the use of unique artifact identifiers like Square-ID or Unit-ID. With unique identifiers you can easily link a database record containing an artifact's three-dimensional provenience to a record containing analysis information and to a file containing an image of the artifact. If you follow the steps outlined in these chapters, integrating the data will be a relatively straightforward task. This is one of the more important points we make in this book: if you take the right steps from the start, then some of the more difficult steps, like data integration, will come more easily later on.

The key question here involves what tool or tools to use to integrate the data. A relational database program can pull together records from separate tables, and a good database program can also display images. It is more difficult, however, to make a database program display maps or plans using the spatial data stored in the database tables. It can make lists of the artifact proveniences but not plot them.

Fortunately, there are lots of programs that work well with spatial information. Computer-aided design (CAD) programs, for instance, specialize in being able to display, edit, and organize two- and three-dimensional data. However, CAD programs, unlike relational database programs, typically are quite bad at integrating spatial information with database records and images. Thus, with a CAD program it is difficult if not impossible to click on a point representing an artifact and then automatically display all of its associated database information along with an image. To achieve this kind of data integration, the kind that archaeologists really want and need, we have to turn to Geographic Information Systems.

GEOGRAPHIC INFORMATION SYSTEMS

Essentially a *Geographic Information System (GIS)* integrates spatial information (maps) with nonspatial information (database records and images). GIS also provides a set of tools for working with spatial data that are analogous to the query tools in database programs and the statistical analysis tools in statistics packages. This means that you can ask questions about the map, and the results are displayed as another map or a chart or as a list of records or a set of images. You might ask, for instance, what the artifacts are in this corner of this room, and the GIS will return a list of database records identifying each. The real benefit of a GIS, thanks to the tight integration of spatial and nonspatial information, is that you can also turn the question around and ask the GIS to redraw the map of artifacts from the corner of the room using only those analyzed as, for instance, complete pots. In other words, not only does a GIS let you query your maps, but it also lets you query your data and view the results as a new map.

The concept is simple but very powerful, and even if you have never heard the term until now you certainly have seen GIS put to use. For instance, every four years we hold a presidential election, and people stay up late watching TV news reports featuring maps of the nation with the states color coded red or blue to indicate whether they went to the Republicans or the Democrats. That map is a GIS with spatial data (the outlines of the 50 states) and database information (the ballot counts for each state). The database information and the map are related on the field STATE. Thus, someone can ask the GIS to draw a map showing the counts by state appropriately color coded. As new records are entered into the database or as records are edited and updated, it is a simple matter for the GIS to redraw the map to reflect the changes.

As this example suggests, people have been using GIS since before there were computers to run GIS programs. Traditional maps have always included symbols that represent more information about the object being mapped than merely its location. The problem is that, before computers, changing how the symbols were defined meant hand-drawing a new map, obviously a time-consuming process. It is also quite clear that archaeologists have been doing GIS without realizing it. For instance, we wrote a three-dimensional GIS program for intrasite analysis of Paleolithic excavations in France years before either of us had heard the term "GIS." However, the advent of computer-driven GIS, especially in the 1990s as GIS programs were written for personal computers, has completely revolutionized the field of geography and is having a huge impact on archaeology.

The kinds of GIS analysis archaeologists are doing and the kinds of questions they are trying to answer are beyond the scope of this book. But just as Chapter 6 prepared you to collect data but did not explain how it can be analyzed, this chapter tackles some of the final steps in bringing your data into a GIS. We will leave it to you to decide what you do with the data.

Even if you do not use a GIS to analyze your data, because of its integration of different data sets it is a very important data management tool. If any of the information that links the various data sets is incorrect or if any of the spatial information has been incorrectly recorded, it will be immediately obvious in a GIS. In our own excavations, for instance, where we piece provenience every artifact, we have found a GIS to be extremely useful for simply visually inspecting the stratigraphy on a daily basis. We ask our GIS to make maps of the artifacts excavated that day or that season and to color code them by archaeological level. In this way, when we look at the points from the side, we can easily spot artifacts that have been given the wrong level designation or artifacts that have an incorrect Z because they were recorded with the wrong prism height. Elsewhere in this book we discussed techniques for preventing errors from entering into databases. A GIS is a powerful tool for quickly spotting and correcting errors in the database.

LAYERS

Whereas in a database information about a similar subject is grouped together in a table of records, a GIS has *layers*, or maps containing information about one particular subject or theme (see Figure 9.1). In fact, layers are sometimes called themes or coverages. Actually this multiplicity of terminology for similar or even identical concepts is common to GIS, and it can make entering the field the first time unnecessarily complicated.

To understand why a map is made up of layers, consider a typical road map. In a GIS a single road map can be divided into a set of layers. There might be one layer for the highways, another for main arteries, and still another for the secondary and rural roads. Towns might be on a separate layer, and streams, shorelines, rivers, parks, railroad tracks, hospitals, and government buildings might have their own layers as well.

There are no set rules on how maps are divided into layers, and one GIS might lump together things that another places in separate layers. Layers are also fluid in a GIS. That is, separate layers can be combined to make a new layer, and a single layer can be pulled apart into several layers using a GIS query. We will discuss this in more detail once we learn more about the types of layers, their contents, and their integration with other kinds of data. Table 9.1 lists the kinds of layers common in GIS and the terms that are applied to them.

FIGURE 9.1 A GIS
organizes spatial infor-
mation into layers, each
of which represent a
common theme. These
layers can be analyzed
separately or together,
and the results can be
saved on new layers.
Maps can then be made
by selecting which layers
to include.

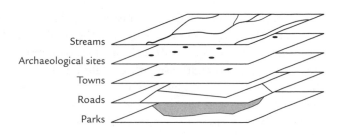

Streams
Archaeological sites
Towns
Roads
Parks

TABLE 9.1	GIS terms and layers
Terms	**Layers**
Topography or hypsography	Elevation
Hydrography	Streams, rivers, lakes, shorelines, etc.
Transportation	Railroads, roads, etc.
Bathymetry	Elevations under water

Raster Layers

There are two kinds of layers in a GIS: raster and vector. This is a very important and fundamental distinction that determines what kinds of things you will
be able to do with your GIS. Raster layers are basically the same as the raster
images that we discussed in the previous chapter: rectangular grids of pixels. The
primary difference between a raster image and a raster layer in a GIS, however,
is that in the latter each pixel corresponds to a specific geographic location, and
the contents of each pixel (i.e., its color) represents a specific kind of data rather
than its true color as would be recorded by a camera. In a GIS, pixels are a more
generalized concept; they store data that summarize a particular location.

The simplest raster layer might contain presence or absence data (the equivalent of a 1-bit, binary, black-and-white image). For instance, a hydrography raster
layer might have a 1 in each pixel that corresponds to a place on earth where the
surface is water and a 0 that corresponds to where the surface is land. Topography
can be represented with a raster layer by storing the elevation of each location in
the pixels and so representing different elevations with different colors. Storing
topography in this format is particularly useful in a GIS, and many other kinds of
layers can be derived from it. Thus, raster topographic layers are given their own
name: digital elevation model (DEM), or sometimes digital terrain model (DTM).

When we say that a pixel in a raster layer describes a particular location, this raises several issues. Suppose that, given the resolution of your raster layer, each pixel represents an area 1 mile on a side (1 square mile). If the topography of the area is varied, how can it have only one elevation in a raster layer? The answer is that the topography will have to be either represented by some arbitrary point (e.g., the center of the area covered by the pixel) or averaged. Similarly, what if there is a large pond in the center of the area covered by the pixel, but the pond does not cover the entire area (see Figure 9.2)? On a hydrography layer, does this pixel get a 1 to indicate the surface as water? You can decide to mark it as being water only when over 50 percent of the area is covered by water, but this means that small ponds will not be noted. It also means that a fairly large pond or lake that would have qualified had it fallen within the area covered by a single pixel will be missed if it is divided into quarters by four adjacent pixels.

The point here is that raster layers sample the underlying phenomenon they are measuring. The sampling rate is usually expressed in terms of the resolution of a single pixel. For instance, a raster layer might have 30-meter resolution, meaning that each pixel summarizes or samples an area that is 30×30 meters. Higher-resolution layers sample smaller areas with each pixel. The trade-off, of course, is image file size: covering the same area with a higher-resolution layer means a larger file size.

A satellite image of the world is also a raster layer, and in this case it corresponds most closely to a standard image as discussed in Chapter 7. Thus in this case the red, green, and blue components might require 24-bit pixels (8 bits each to store 256 shades). The colors or shades in a satellite image, however, need not correspond to colors as we see them. For instance, the cameras (or sensors) in satellite images are often set to record the reflection of the earth in the infrared portion of the color spectrum. This type of image is usually called a multi-spectral image since it combines data from several portions of the spectrum; in displaying the image, the shades of infrared have to be translated into shades of red, green, and blue. Thus, the image will appear in color, but the colors will not be "correct" in the sense that they do not really represent the true colors as we would see them. As a result, this kind of image is called a false-color image.

Because the colors of pixels in raster layers do not need to reflect actual colors, their contents are often called by the more generic term "bands" rather than colors. A raster layer containing a standard color photo has three bands corresponding to red, green, and blue. A black-and-white photo has only one band, corresponding to shades of gray. As discussed previously, a DEM is a single-band image.

To make matters even more complicated, raster layers vary in the way the bands are stored in the file. There are three basic methods. Consider a three-band image containing red, green, and blue bands, such as a color satellite image. In a standard image, as discussed in the previous chapter, the red, green,

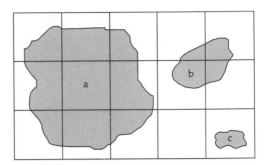

FIGURE 9.2 A vector layer representing water with a raster grid superimposed. The three different bodies of water represent some of the issues that are encountered when converting from vectors to raster. Pond a falls into nine separate grid cells, but it completely covers only one. A decision could be made to code a cell as water if more than 50 percent of the cell is water, but then pond b would not be represented despite the fact that it would cover more than 50 percent had it fallen completely within a grid cell. Likewise, pond c would not be represented. If, on the other hand, cells are coded for water if any part of them has water, then every cell but one in this example would show water, giving a false impression of a large body of water.

and blue information for each pixel is stored together in a single 24-bit number (8 bits each for the colors). The first 24-bit number in the file corresponds to the first pixel, the next 24-bit number corresponds to the second pixel, and so forth. This is one way to store the bands in a file, pixel by pixel, in what is sometimes called a BIP (band interleaved by pixel) file (see Figure 9.3a). Another possibility is to store each band in the image line by line instead of pixel by pixel. The first line of 8-bit numbers in the file represents the first line of pixels for the first band, the second line of 8-bit numbers the second band for the first line, and the third line of 8-bit numbers the third band for the first line. Put it all together and you have a 24-bit number for each pixel of the first line in the image. This is called a BIL (band interleaved by line) file (see Figure 9.3b). There is a third possibility. Rather than store the bands line by line, an entire band can be written to the file, followed by the entire second band, followed by the entire third band. Once all the bands are read, they can be combined to produce a set of 24-bit pixels ready to be displayed. This is called a BSQ (band sequential) file (see Figure 9.3c).

Why so many methods and why does it matter? Why not simply store raster layers in a GIS in the same way as for digital images? The simple answer is that in a multiband or multispectral image it is sometimes preferable to keep the bands separated (row interleave or band sequential) so that they can be accessed and analyzed separately more easily. Think of a three-band, multispectral image

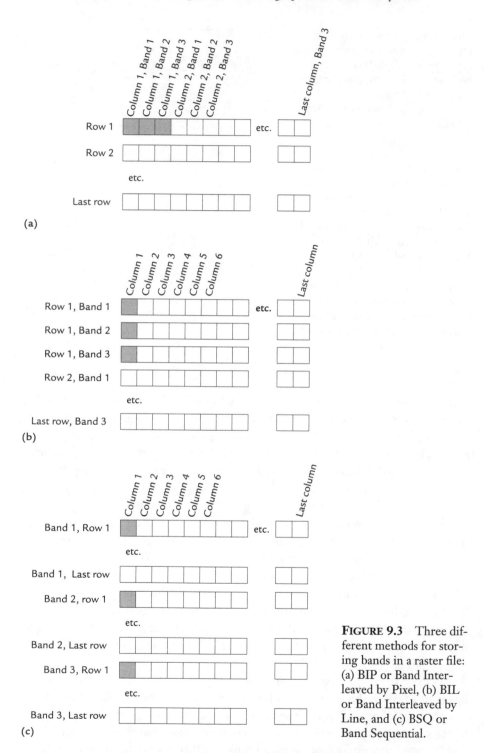

FIGURE 9.3   Three different methods for storing bands in a raster file: (a) BIP or Band Interleaved by Pixel, (b) BIL or Band Interleaved by Line, and (c) BSQ or Band Sequential.

as a set of three distinct GIS layers rather than a single layer. In fact, most GIS systems provide you with tools for separating a multiband image into discrete layers, each representing a band in the original image. You might want to do this, for instance, if you are only interested in the infrared component and the way it correlates with other features in your GIS.

Raster layers can be a very powerful way to represent spatial information in a GIS, but they have a number of disadvantages as well. Perhaps the most basic of these is the difficulty involved in changing the scale. Recall that raster images have a fixed level of detail that cannot be increased. For instance, a good satellite image of the earth might have a pixel resolution of 30 meters. This means that, when a map of archaeological sites in an area 1 kilometer (1000 meters) square is superimposed on this raster layer, the resulting image will have only 33 pixels on a side. This will produce a fairly unsatisfactory visual result, and there is little that can be done about it. Perhaps more importantly from the perspective of GIS analysis, raster layers do not provide discrete entities or objects that can be easily isolated and manipulated.

Vector Layers

Vector layers are completely different. The most basic unit in a vector layer is a point as represented by its two- or three-dimensional coordinates. In some ways a point is roughly the same as a pixel in a raster layer. For instance, both correspond to some location in the world. However, whereas a pixel represents an area, a point in a vector layer does not. Furthermore, a raster layer always contains a fixed number of pixels, regardless of whether any useful information is stored in each. A vector layer, in contrast, contains any number of points, and each is there only because it represents useful information. As a result, under certain circumstances a vector layer is a much more efficient means of storing information. We will return to this topic later. (See the box on page 196 for a discussion of popular vector image formats.)

Points in a vector layer can be linked together to form two other basic units: lines and polygons (see Figure 9.4). Obviously a line is defined by a pair of points, and a polygon is a series of connected points. Polygons are the only way to describe an area in a vector layer since points and lines, in themselves, have no area. In a vector layer points, lines, and polygons are all associated with an attribute, which is the equivalent of the value stored in a raster layer's pixels. It is typically a number that stands for something else or a number that links it to database information, but it can be most anything. Consider a couple of examples.

Previously we discussed how elevation can be represented in a raster layer in which each pixel stores the average elevation of the corresponding location. Alternatively elevation can be represented using contour lines in a vector layer. Though

VECTOR IMAGE FORMATS

There are not nearly as many issues surrounding vector images as there are with raster images. Because vector files essentially contain only the commands for drawing various shapes, scaling is less of an issue. And while the number of shapes to be drawn will affect file size, vector files are almost always much smaller than raster files. There are, however, a number of different formats for vector images, and almost all of them can be read by most graphics applications. Popular vector formats include the following:

- CGM (Computer Graphics Metafile): a format developed by several standards organizations. CGM is supported by many PC software products.
- DXF (Data Exchange File): a format created by AutoDesk, the makers of AutoCAD. Almost all PC-based CAD and GIS systems support DXF.
- HPGL (Hewlett-Packard Graphics Language): one of the oldest file formats. Although it is not very sophisticated, it is supported by many PC-based graphics products.
- WMF (Windows Metafile Format): a file format for exchanging graphics between Microsoft Windows applications. WMF files can also hold bit-mapped images.

they may look like smooth curves, contours can really be thought of and represented by a series of short, connected lines. The contour for a particular elevation is one line element in a vector file, and its associated attribute is the elevation.

Another example comes from intrasite mapping of artifacts as discussed in Chapter 5. Figure 9.5 shows a vector representation of artifacts we recovered from one square and one level of Combe-Capelle Bas. In this case, points (shown here as small circles) represent instances when only one location was recorded for an artifact. Artifacts that were relatively elongated were recorded with lines so that their orientation could be calculated. Finally, artifacts that were large but not obviously elongated were recorded with a polygon to delineate the area they occupy. In this case the attribute associated with each artifact is its unique ID number.

Vector layers have several advantages over raster layers. For one thing, they easily represent discrete entities. For another, they are much more easily scaled. A point representing the location of a site is just as easily represented on a map of the United States as it is on a map of one small river valley. This does not mean, however, that a vector layer can be represented at any scale. The scale depends on the precision of the underlying data. If a site's location is known to within 100 meters, it may look fine on a map whose scale encompasses, say, 50 kilometers. On a map of only 1 kilometer, however, the site's actual location could vary from its recorded location by as much as 10 percent. This issue of

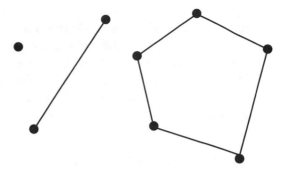

FIGURE 9.4   The basic unit of a vector layer is the point. Points can then be combined into lines and polygons.

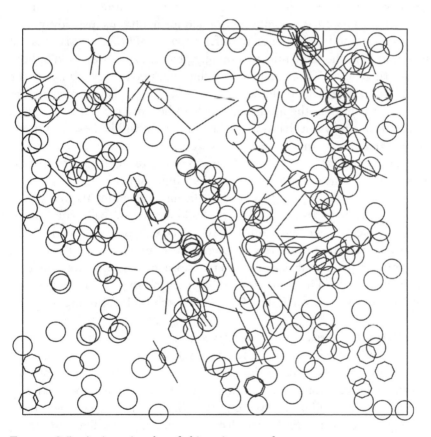

FIGURE 9.5   An intrasite plot of objects in vector format

scale is one of the most difficult and most complex in GIS. What happens, for instance, when you combine two separate vector layers recorded with different levels of precision? If a vector layer of site locations recorded with a total station is combined with a layer of stream locations obtained from the U.S. Geological

Survey (USGS), a site might appear on the wrong side of a stream if the stream locations are recorded less precisely than the site locations. It is also quite common to have sites recorded along the edge of a body of water appear in the water. The only solutions are (1) to show the map with a less detailed scale so that the size of the dot representing the location of the site effectively represents the precision of the least accurate layer in the map or (2) to obtain more precise maps for your study area.

More on Vector vs. Raster Layers

The question then arises of when one format should be used over the other. There are no set answers to this question. Each format has its own advantages and disadvantages, and each is open to different kinds of GIS analysis. It is not uncommon to have the same information (e.g., elevation) represented in both formats in a single GIS. To understand why this might be the case, consider the representation in a GIS of a mountain. If you want to associate particular sites with this mountain, then the mountain needs to be a discrete entity. Thus, a vector layer with a polygon that outlines the mountain will be best. But if you want to look at where on the mountain sites are located—at what elevation, facing in what direction, on what kind of slope—then a raster representation of the mountain that shows its changes in topography will be best.

This example leads us to a general rule of thumb: phenomena that can be thought of as discrete entities (e.g., artifacts, buildings, walls, roads, sites, rivers, streams) are typically best represented as vector layers; phenomena that vary continuously across the surface (e.g., topography, rainfall, solar radiation) are typically better represented as raster layers. Nevertheless, it is often the case that one format needs to be converted to the other in order to conduct certain kinds of GIS analysis. Fortunately a GIS comes with tools for doing just that.

Vector-to-Raster Conversion   In general, vector layers are analyzed with other vector layers, and raster layers are analyzed with other raster layers. Thus, if you want to look for a correspondence between site locations, stored as points in a vector layer, and vegetation, stored as the infrared band in a multispectral raster layer, one or the other will have to be converted. Since an infrared image is more logically represented in a raster format than as a series of points, lines, and areas, it is best in this case to convert the vector site locations to a raster layer. To do this, you (1) create a blank raster layer the same size as the infrared layer, (2) locate the pixels corresponding to each site location in this new raster layer, and (3) give these pixels a value indicating the presence of a site. In this case the raster layer could be binary with a 0 pixel value indicating no sites and a 1 value indicating the presence of a site. Alternatively, since more than one site might fall within the area covered by a pixel, each pixel could store the number of sites in that location. Once this conversion is complete, it becomes a simple matter for the GIS to compare infrared values for each location with the presence or absence of sites.

We discussed another kind of vector-to-raster conversion in Chapter 5 when we looked at how topographic programs convert irregularly spaced survey points into a regular grid of elevations using various methods of interpolation. In the previous example, the raster image was left blank when sites or points were not present. In the case of survey points, however, the topographic software attempts to fill in the blanks by estimating the elevation from nearby grid cells that have known elevations. The end result is exactly equivalent to a raster layer and, as noted previously, is called a digital elevation model (DEM).

Raster-to-Vector Conversion   Likewise, topographic programs can convert a DEM or raster image back into vectors in order to draw a contour map, but this is more complicated. Take, for instance, the grid of elevations shown in Figure 9.6a. A glance at the numbers reveals the pattern. There is a high point in the middle of the map, and the topography falls off equally around this point until it reaches the edges. If you ask for contours every meter, then the program can draw a circle around the highest point and then connect the dots by drawing lines that link grid points with equal elevations (see Figure 9.6b).

It gets more complicated when you ask for contour intervals that are not actually present in the data. This time refer to Figure 9.7 on pages 202–203. This map has a similar topography with a high point in the center, but this time the slope is irregular and not every meter is represented. Now, when you ask for meter contours, the program is forced to estimate where the meter contours should fall. This process of estimation, known as interpolation, involves identifying trends in the data and using those trends to fill in missing values. In effect, the program is obliged to increase the number of grid cells in the image until it gets the contour interval values it needs. Of course, it does not actually increase the size or resolution of the grid; rather, this is all done mathematically.

Is interpolation merely a fancy way of saying that the computer is making up new data? In a way it is, and the computer will make up as much data as you like. In other words, you can ask for contour intervals of, say, 1 millimeter and the computer will do it. Clearly, however, the millimeter contours will be meaningless in the sense that they do not necessarily accurately reflect the underlying data. It's helpful if you know something about the precision of each grid cell value in the raster layer. If, for instance, the elevation of each grid cell has an error of ± 5 meters, then contour intervals of less than 10 meters are suspect. The size of each grid cell also has to be factored in.

Topographic data are not the only kinds of data amenable to conversion from a raster to a vector format as contours, since contours can be used to

	1	2	3	4	5	6	7	8	9	10	11
11	0	0	0	0	0	0	0	0	0	0	0
10	0	0	0	0	0	1	0	0	0	0	0
9	0	0	0	0	1	2	1	0	0	0	0
8	0	0	0	1	2	3	2	1	0	0	0
7	0	0	1	2	3	4	3	2	1	0	0
6	0	1	2	3	4	5	4	3	2	1	0
5	0	0	1	2	3	4	3	2	1	0	0
4	0	0	0	1	2	3	2	1	0	0	0
3	0	0	0	0	1	2	1	0	0	0	0
2	0	0	0	0	0	1	0	0	0	0	0
1	0	0	0	0	0	0	0	0	0	0	0

(a)

FIGURE 9.6   (a) A grid of elevations. There is a high point in the center and the elevations fall off toward the edges. (b) A contour map made from these elevations.

represent other kinds of data as well. Rainfall, for instance, is well represented as a series of contours. In general, data sets that vary relatively smoothly and that have large patches or strips of similar values are amenable to contours.

Using contours is not the only way of converting a raster layer to a vector layer. Another common task is to convert a raster layer into a series of points, lines and polygons. Figure 9.8 on page 204 is an example of this. Figure 9.8a shows a scanned, digital image of a map; Figure 9.8b shows the same features, but they are represented using vectors. As we have already discussed, vector layers offer the important advantage of being able to represent discrete entities, so you will often want to convert a digital image or paper map into this kind of vector representation. Unlike topographic contours, however, the process can be extremely time consuming.

There are two ways to convert a raster representation of a line into a vector line. First, you can form the line yourself by marking, on screen with a mouse or on a digitizing tablet with a stylus, the end points of the line. Second, a computer program can scan the raster image, attempt to identify the line, and automatically create the end points of the line as a vector. There are pros and cons to each method, so let's consider each.

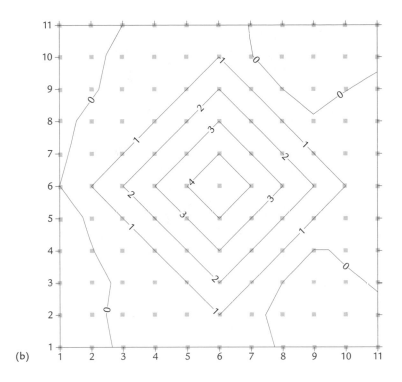

(b)

Initially, by far the fastest way to convert raster to vector is to have the computer automatically scan the image looking for points, lines, and polygons. In essence, this is what *optical character recognition (OCR)* is about. The computer scans a page of printed text, and then a program works through the scanned page, looking at each pixel, to identify patterns in clusters of pixels that represent characters. These days the software to do this is fast and generally quite effective. There is an important difference, however, between OCR and map conversion. In OCR the computer has a very good idea of what to expect. But with a map the computer has no idea what the pixels mean or how they might be related to one another. Unless the map is quite good, the computer does not even know the difference between text and figures on the map. It can only make guesses, and usually these are far from perfect (see Figure 9.9 on page 206). Moreover, in our experience images that are not simple black-and-white (1-bit) representations can completely confuse a program. As a result, while using a program to automatically convert a raster map to vector is initially quite fast, you spend a great deal of time afterward editing the results. For instance, you will have to delete many lines, attach short line segments together to form a single, longer line, and link together lines that belong to a single polygon. Moreover, you will have to add attributes to each line afterward, which is, again, a time-consuming process.

11	0	0	0	0	0	0	0	0	0	0	0
10	0	0	0	0	0	10	0	0	0	0	0
9	0	0	0	0	10	20	10	0	0	0	0
8	0	0	0	10	20	50	20	10	0	0	0
7	0	0	10	20	50	100	50	20	10	0	0
6	0	10	20	50	100	200	100	50	20	10	0
5	0	0	10	20	50	100	50	20	10	0	0
4	0	0	0	10	20	50	20	10	0	0	0
3	0	0	0	0	10	20	10	0	0	0	0
2	0	0	0	0	0	10	0	0	0	0	0
1	0	0	0	0	0	0	0	0	0	0	0
	1	2	3	4	5	6	7	8	9	10	11

(a)

FIGURE 9.7 (a) Another grid of elevations, but in this grid the slope falls off toward the edges exponentially. (b) A contour map made from these elevations.

On-screen digitizing and digitizing tablets have the advantage that the only vectors added to the images are the ones you desire, and the lines that belong together are digitized together as a single entity. The amount of editing that you have to do afterward is greatly reduced. In addition, it becomes a simple matter to attach attribute codes to each vector as you digitize. On-screen digitizing with a mouse also offers a number of advantages over using a digitizing tablet. Foremost among these is the fact that you can enlarge the image to any scale. This means that when you are digitizing a particular point, rather than try to position the tablet's stylus over a tiny dot on a piece of paper, you can enlarge the dot to fill the screen before you click in the center of it.

This does not mean that on-screen digitizing is more precise. Though you may be able to click exactly in the center of a dot, the precision of that location is still limited by the precision with which it was placed on the original paper map. In other words, the best that on-screen digitizing can do is to equal the precision of the original. Related to this, of great importance in on-screen digitizing is the fact that you can see the vector representation overlaid on the raster image and

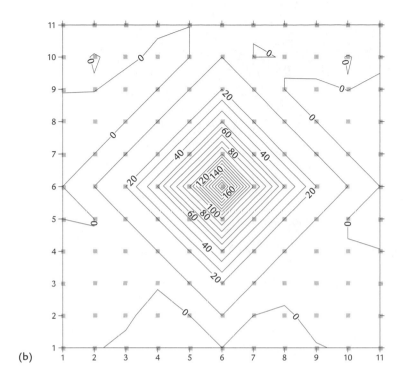

(b)

thereby verify its accuracy. Then you can edit the vector points to make them correspond to the underlying raster image.

The automatic program scanning method and the on-screen digitizing method share one drawback: file size. Suppose you have a map that is 30 inches on a side and you want to scan it at 300 dots per inch. That means creating an image that is 9000 pixels across by 9000 pixels high, or 81 million pixels. If the image is scanned in black and white (1 bit per pixel), then the file size will be approximately 10 megabytes. If you want to retain 256 colors or shades of gray from the map, then you will need 77 megabytes. It can be quite cumbersome to work with images of this size, thus you may have to divide the image into a series of small portions.

ATTACHING A LOCATION TO DATA

Geocoding

Thus far we have talked about layers, both raster and vector, but not about how these layers are linked to databases. The process of linking map elements to records in a database is called *geocoding*. At the most basic level each object in the

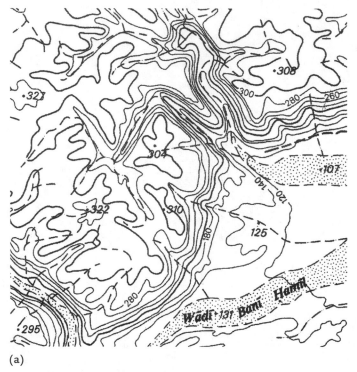

(a)

FIGURE 9.8   (a) A portion of a scanned topographic map that was then converted to a 1-bit black-and-white raster image, and (b) a vector representation of the same raster image created automatically by a program specifically designed for this purpose. While the overall effect is quite good, look closely and you can see where the program confused and merged contour lines with text or lines indicating streams (see Figure 9.9).

map must have an identifier that is also contained in a table field in the database, or each record in the database must contain explicit spatial information.

Imagine, for instance, a table containing a record for each object found in a site, as well as the X, Y, and Z coordinates. These data are said to be geocoded because the spatial information is encoded into each object's record. With this information a GIS can draw a map showing the locations of all the objects, and in doing so it will establish a link between the dots on the map and the corresponding record in the table. This means that you can point to a dot on the map, and the GIS can quickly find the corresponding record and display its data. Alternatively you can query a set of records from the database and have the corresponding artifacts highlighted on the map.

Often, however, the geocode is more indirect. The example often given in GIS literature involves street addresses. Imagine a supermarket with a database containing the purchases of each customer. In adding spatial information to

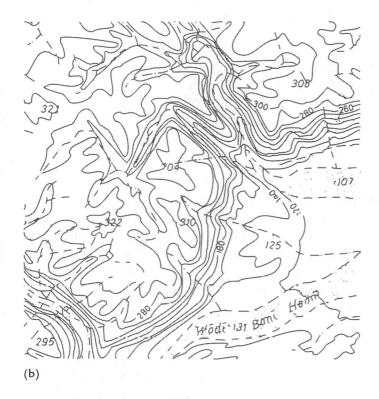

(b)

each of these records—that is, to geocode them—the supermarket adds, not an X, Y, and Z coordinate representing the exact location of the customer's home, but rather a street address or possibly just a zip code. Zip codes and street addresses are spatial data, but they cannot be placed on a map without more information. Another file is needed that contains the XYZ coordinates of each street address, or at least a way of estimating them.

Street addresses and zip codes, however, are not typically useful to archaeologists, so let's consider a second example—a database of sites from throughout the world. Unfortunately the exact coordinates of each site are unknown. Instead, the table contains a field called COUNTRY. This is clearly not enough information to draw a map showing the location of sites in the database. A GIS layer is needed with the outline (vector) of each country in the world, and each outline needs an attribute that corresponds to the country name. In this way the GIS can link the country layer to the database table using the COUNTRY field, and the archaeological site map can be drawn. With this link established, the GIS can then do things like shade the interior of each country based on another field derived from the database (e.g., the number of sites from each country).

Another common geocoding problem in archaeology involves linking archaeological finds with test units or architectural features. A database table

FIGURE 9.9   Close-up of one section of vector map from Figure 9.8b. Notice how the elevation text "322" has become incorporated into a contour line. The dashed lines represent dry stream beds and belong on a layer separate from the contours, but they, too, have become entangled with contour lines.

may contain a record-by-record listing of the finds from the site organized by level and unit. To create a GIS layer representing this information, you first need to create a layer containing the coordinates of the corners of each excavation unit. You then give each unit an attribute corresponding to the unit name exactly as it is written in the database table with the site finds. Linking the two sets of information on the basis of the unit name effectively geocodes the data.

In the case of finds from architectural features, the situation is a bit more complex. First, as with the units example, you need to create a vector layer with polygons representing all of the architectural features (e.g., rooms from excavated houses). You can assign each room a name or number to provide a link to the artifact database. In this example, however, the linking process is a bit more complicated because the room number likely is not a field in the main database table. Instead, artifacts are probably organized by layer or lot within each excavation unit. Thus, you need to create a separate table created with at least two fields: room number and layer or lot number. Now, the layer containing the map of the rooms can be linked to the contents via this intermediate table.

If geocoding sounds a lot like building relational databases, as discussed in Chapter 1, it is because it should. In many cases all a GIS is doing is adding a new relational table that contains specific spatial information. As such, all of the issues we discussed in Chapter 1 are relevant here. For instance, in the example just presented, the relationship between the table containing the room and level/lot numbers and the table containing the finds from each level/lot is probably a one-to-many relationship. In other words, there will be many records of information for each level/lot. This is one reason that creating a separate table for room numbers makes more sense than adding room numbers to the table of finds. It is much easier to maintain, add, or remove lots from a simple room number table than to update each record in a finds table. As with other relational databases, GIS also makes use of indexes, though in this case you have to create a new type of spatial index so that the GIS can quickly find records by location criteria.

Thus far we have discussed location as if it were a simple matter. As the next section illustrates, however, location in a GIS is far from straightforward.

Datums and Coordinates

As simple as it might sound at first, recording the location of an archaeological feature can actually be quite complicated. When you use a total station to create your own grid system to record artifacts, features, or sites, as we described in Chapter 3, you have a standard Cartesian grid that treats the earth as if it were flat. This works for large-scale maps that show only a small portion of the earth (e.g., a site map). Thus, the curvature of the earth does not affect large-scale maps. In fact, we suggest that you ignore the curvature of the earth when considering error correction in total station measurements. Unfortunately, when placing your recorded points onto smaller-scale maps that show entire regions, counties, states, or countries, you can no longer ignore it. As discussed previously, what really complicates things is the fact that there are many approaches to dealing with the difference between our round planet and the flat maps that represent portions of it.

As we touched on in Chapter 2, the basic problem is that the earth is spherical and maps are flat. In addition, the earth is not perfectly spherical for a number of reasons, including gravity, centrifugal force, differences in its geological makeup, and tectonic forces. On large-scale maps the difference between a perfect sphere and the actual shape of the earth is not perceptible, but on small-scale maps, the difference is large enough that it cannot be ignored.

Over the years surveyors have developed mathematical models for estimating the spheroid (or ellipsoid) that best describes the shape and size of the earth. As you might imagine, particularly with the advent of satellites that allow us to measure the size and shape of the earth from space, estimations of the spheroid have varied over the years and are constantly being revised. Some of the more common models that you will encounter in working with GIS data sets are listed in Table 9.2. Each time the spheroid is recalculated, it shifts coordinate grids like latitude and longitude. This is why, for instance, a latitude/longitude point on an old map may have coordinates that differ from the same point on a newer map. Fortunately GIS programs automatically convert from one spheroid to another, but this does not mean that you can ignore the spheroid. When you digitize a map, for instance, you have to note the spheroid used in creating that map so that the GIS can make the appropriate transformations as needed.

A concept closely related to the spheroid is the datum. In previous chapters we used the term "datum" to refer to a survey point or benchmark in the ground with known coordinates. In a GIS a datum is not only a set of survey points but also the specific spheroid used to establish the grid on which the datum points are measured. In other words, a GIS datum bundles known survey points, their coordinates, and a particular spheroid into one package.

Two of the more popular datums that you might encounter in working with spatial data from North America are the North American Datum of 1927

TABLE 9.2   Common mathematical models for estimating the earth's spheroid in working with GIS data sets

Model	Comments
Clarke 1866	First widely used description of the shape of the earth; works particularly well in North America
WGS72 (World Geodetic System)	Developed by the Department of Defense using terrestrial and, most importantly, satellite measurements
GRS80 (Geodetic Reference System)	Improved version of WGS72 using more satellite measurements and providing a greater coverage of the earth
WGS84 (World Geodetic System)	Improved version of WGS72 and GRS80

(NAD27) and the North American Datum of 1983 (NAD83). The former is based on the Clarke 1866 spheroid, and the latter on the GRS80. The base point or primary datum for the NAD27 was located at Meades Ranch in Kansas, and a series of datums were distributed throughout North America based on this reference point. When the datum was recalculated in 1983, the base point became a hypothetical point at the center of the earth. The use of a more accurate spheroid based on satellite measurements meant that the location of datums previously recorded using the NAD27 had to be recalculated. In some cases the datums moved by as much as 350 feet, or 106 meters. Thus, when you survey across the countryside in order to relate your site to a national survey benchmark, you need to note its coordinates in a datum that is compatible with other data you might be using. Here, again, a GIS will take care of the conversion for you, but you need to be aware of the issue so that it can be properly done.

To this point we have talked about coordinates without really defining them. Clearly coordinates are a set of two (X and Y) or three (X, Y, and Z) numbers that describe a point's location. However, just as there are different ways to express length measurements (e.g., feet, meters), there are several coordinate systems. They can be divided into two categories: (1) spherical (or radial) coordinate systems, which work with the earth as it is, and (2) Cartesian (or plane) coordinate systems, which require that the earth be mathematically flattened into a set of orthogonal (at right angles to one another) axes.

By far the most familiar coordinate system is latitude/longitude, which is a spherical coordinate system (see Figure 9.10). Locations on the earth's surface are described by their angle above or below the equator (latitude) and their angle around the world from an arbitrary starting point (Greenwich, England) (longitude). Latitude angles vary from 0 to 90 degrees, with 0 equal to the equa-

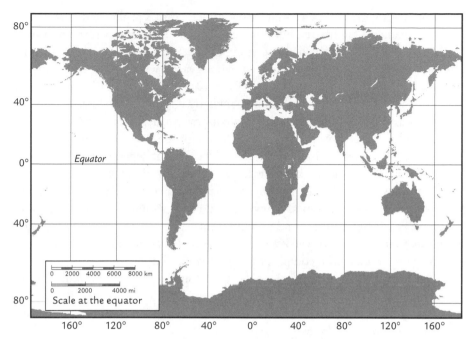

FIGURE 9.10 Map of the world showing latitude and longitude markings, with 0 degrees longitude a line running through Greenwich, England, and 0 degrees latitude the equator

tor and 90 equal to either the South or North Pole. To distinguish a point 20 degrees above the equator from a point 20 degrees below the equator, it is necessary to add south or north. Alternatively, since the number 20N does not work well in a numeric database field, it is standard practice to denote northern points as positive angles and southern points as negative angles. Likewise, longitude begins at Greenwich with an angle of 0 degrees and increases to the east and west until these points meet again on the opposite side of the globe, at 180 degrees. Again, rather than express angles as 120W, it is standard database practice to express eastern longitudes as positive numbers and western longitudes as negative numbers.

Angles are subdivided into smaller units according to the rules discussed in Chapter 2 for horizontal and vertical angles used in survey. Typically, however, while latitude/longitude are expressed on maps in degrees, minutes, and seconds, they are stored in a GIS in decimal degrees. Decimal degrees are more suitable to storage in a numeric database field and are easier to work with when performing calculations. Since most people are more familiar with degrees, minutes, and seconds, you might want to convert the decimal degrees of the GIS back into this format when making a final map.

Latitude/longitude has a certain attractiveness that is probably due at least in part to its general familiarity, but it is a cumbersome system for some purposes. For one thing, it is very difficult to compute distances and areas with latitude/longitude since the spacing of the degree lines varies with their location on the earth. For example, the distance between 0 and 10 degrees longitude is much greater near the equator than it is near the poles. Similarly it is difficult to look at a latitude or longitude number and understand from it how precisely it records a location. For example, exactly how precise is 23.3406 longitude, and is 23.3407 longitude 10 meters, 100 meters, or 1 kilometer away? Of course, it depends on what latitude we are talking about, and it takes some trigonometric calculations to find out.

Latitude/longitude can also be problematic because elevations are not expressed in these same units. Thus, a three-dimensional coordinate in a GIS will have two different units and two different scales, one for the XY (latitude/longitude) and another for the Z (meters or feet). This can make certain kinds of mapping operations more complex than they would otherwise be.

Despite all these disadvantages, latitude/longitude remain popular, especially in relation to systems that are global in scale. This is because, in contrast to other systems, it provides a single coordinate system that results in a unique value for each spot on the earth.

Systems based on *Cartesian coordinates* avoid some of the problems inherent in latitude/longitude, but they introduce some of their own. Foremost among these problems is the fact that Cartesian coordinate systems require that the earth be mathematically transformed into a flat surface, in a process called a projection. As with spheroids, datums, and coordinate systems, there are also a number of projection methods for converting the earth into a flat map. The reason for this is that all projections distort shapes, areas, distances, and directions in varying ways. Depending on which of these is most important, you will use a different projection. Also, as with modeling the earth as a spheroid rather than a perfect sphere, the significance of this error depends on your scale. On large-scale maps, such as a map showing the location of sites in a small area, the effect probably is not great. But on small-scale maps, such as a map of the Old World showing the location of Paleolithic sites, the effect will be much greater.

Cartesian coordinate systems minimize the problem by dividing the world into a series of smaller grid cells, each with its own coordinate system. One of the more popular of these systems is the universal transverse Mercator (UTM), which is based on the projection of the same name. This grid system divides the world into two sets of grid cells 6 degrees of longitude wide (see Figure 9.11). One set is above the equator, and the other is below. Since the world is 360 degrees around, this means that there are 60 grid cells in each hemisphere. Grid cell 4N, for instance, represents the area of the world between 18 and 24 degrees latitude from the equator to the North Pole.

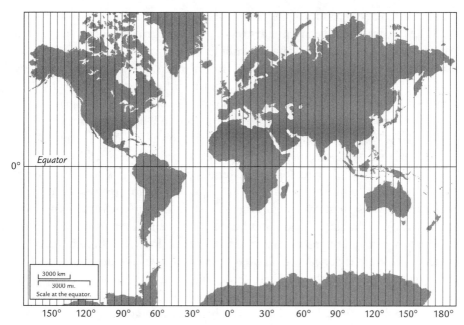

FIGURE 9.11   Map of the world showing the UTM grid

Within each cell, locations are measured as XY coordinates in meters. The Y coordinate measures the distance from the equator. The X coordinate, however, is measured from an arbitrary point that falls to the west of the western limit of the grid cell. This point is designed to make the middle point of the grid cell equal to 500,000 and to ensure that no point in the grid cell will be negative. Note that with this system a point such as (560000, 230000) could be any number of locations on the earth unless the grid cell is also specified. This makes it more difficult and somewhat confusing to create a map that includes several grid cells; in fact, the UTM projection is not designed to represent large areas well. However, the UTM is well suited to handling maps that reside entirely within a grid cell. In addition, since the coordinates are in meters, you can more easily understand locations and their precision, you can more easily calculate distances and areas, and you can represent three-dimensional coordinates in a single system with a single scale. Naturally your particular area of interest will often cross over into an adjacent grid cell. In these instances, however, you can simply extend the coordinate system of one cell into the other so that the entire map can, in effect, stay in a single grid cell. This is done in Hawaii, for instance, to keep the major islands in one cell, which enables all agencies doing GIS work there to share their data.

Another popular grid or coordinate system is the State Plane Coordinate System (SPCS). In the United States each state has created its own grid cell or set of cells to encompass the state. This system differs in a number of ways from the UTM. First, the cells are not arranged in a neat grid across the world, but rather are arranged state by state depending on the size and shape of the state. If the state is long from south to north, for instance, then it may have several grid cells in this direction. If it is long east to west, then the grid cells will be arranged accordingly. Here, again, the point of creating multiple grid cells is simply to keep errors associated with the projection below a certain threshold (1 part in 10,000). The second difference between the UTM and the SPCS is that in the latter, system coordinates within each grid are specified in feet rather than meters. While archaeologists generally prefer to work in meters, state agencies generally prefer feet. Thus, it is quite common to have to convert between the two systems when working with state agencies or when using maps generated for or by state agencies. The third difference is that the SPCS does not imply a particular projection as the UTM does. Rather, different states use different projections depending on their shape. For example, states that are long east to west tend to use the Lambert conformal conic projection, whereas states that are long north to south use the same transverse Mercator projection as the UTM. For the panhandle of Alaska, which stretches diagonally both south to north and east to west, the oblique Mercator projection is used.

This discussion of projections and their relationship to plane or Cartesian coordinate systems does not imply that spherical systems like latitude/longitude do not need a projection. While projection is not inherent to these systems, meaning that coordinates can be recorded without reference to a projection, displaying features recorded with latitude/longitude on a flat map will still require a projection. Here, again, which projection you use will depend on the scale of your map.

What all of this means is that when you enter spatial data into your GIS you have to consider how the coordinates are defined. It also means that when you publish your GIS you have to fully document the coordinates. It is not enough simply to specify that two fields contain the latitude and longitude of sites in your study area. Rather, in order for the data to be truly useful, you need to publish the spheroid and the datum as well. This supporting information is called metadata, and we address this topic more fully in the next chapter.

BUILDING A GIS

Now that we have introduced some of the basic concepts of a GIS, how do you actually build one? We cannot go into the specifics because these will vary depending on which GIS software you use. There are some general guidelines, however.

If you have a database with XY or XYZ coordinates, then you already have all you need to get started. Any GIS program should be able to work with these data to create and analyze layers showing particular patterns in your data. Suppose that you have, not coordinates in your database, but rather spatial information like excavation unit, site name, county, state, or country. You need to either add the specific coordinate information or, if you are lucky, find a layer already in existence that contains this information and that can be linked to your data by some common field.

If the layers you need do not exist, this stage can be by far the most time-consuming task in creating a GIS. Unfortunately we are in a period of transition. Most maps in existence are on paper and so are of no use to a GIS. Thus, mapping agencies across the world are currently in the process of converting their paper maps to electronic forms suitable for inclusion in a GIS. The USGS, for instance, is systematically converting its paper maps and aerial photos to digital formats that can be downloaded from the Internet or purchased from its data centers. This means that if you work in the United States or some other advanced nations, you might be able to populate your GIS with important layers such as topography, hydrography, and even soils. It is also likely that aerial or especially satellite imagery is already available for inclusion in a GIS.

A lot of archaeology, however, is done in areas of the world where finding a good map can be difficult and finding an electronic version of this map is impossible. Furthermore, even if you are working in the United States, doing archaeology means generating data that others will not yet have digitized. For instance, you might have a series of regional survey publications that show the location of sites encountered on a portion of a standard USGS topographic map, but the coordinates of each site are not included in the report. Thus, you will have to digitize the locations from the map using either a digitizing tablet or on-screen digitizing. Even if the coordinates are listed, you have to enter them into a database and note the coordinate system and datums.

Digitizing site locations or even a map of the features in a site, however, is relatively easy compared to digitizing layers like topography. When conducting a GIS analysis on a regional scale, the topography is one of the most basic layers needed. Here, you have to decide on the level of topographic detail that will be digitized. The topographic map may have 20-foot contour intervals, but including this kind of detail might take too long, so you might digitize only 100-foot intervals. Once you digitize the contours and assign elevations to each, you will have a vector layer ready for analysis. You will likely want to use the vector-to-raster conversion tools in the GIS to convert this layer into a raster layer. Fortunately the recent global surveyor project probably will produce topographic data of sufficient detail for the entire planet, so you will not have to digitize topographic maps.

If aerial photos are available but not yet digitized, you can scan them and include them in your GIS. However, aerial photos typically require a lot of processing before they can be added. The problem is that photographs are not a perfect representation of the surface of the planet; rather, they are distorted, so that the scale is not the same across the entire photograph. Sometimes this is because the photograph is recorded at an angle such that items in the foreground have a different scale from items in the background. Even if the photo is recorded looking straight down, the scale will vary from the center to the edges. In addition, a scanned photograph does not have any spatial information attached to it. For the photograph to be useful, the GIS needs to know exactly where the photograph was taken so that it can calculate the exact coordinates of each pixel in the image. Thus, before these images can be included in a GIS, they have to be rectified and georegistered (i.e., given spatial coordinates, as in geocoding). This is typically done with a technique called rubber-sheeting, in which the program places a number of control points on the image with known coordinates and then stretches and shrinks the image to make the control points move into their correct locations.

This discussion has glossed over much detail. Rubber-sheeting and georegistering aerial images is difficult and time consuming, as is converting paper maps into vector layers by digitizing the map elements. If you only need to assign locations to things like sites, then the process can go quickly. In fact, depending on where in the world your sites are located and on what level of precision you need, you might be able to build your spatial database by assigning the coordinates of nearby towns or geographic features. A number of Web-based spatial databases can provide this information.

Finally, in pulling your GIS together, you should avoid placing your data into proprietary formats that do not provide a reliable method for extracting the data at a later time. With some GIS systems it is fairly easy to enter your data but much more difficult to extract it should you decide to move to another system. In addition, as always, we recommend that you keep your data in the most popular formats. For vector maps, for instance, AutoCAD DXF files are still the most widely used standard. For databases, format is perhaps less of an issue since most programs today provide methods of accessing data stored in a number of database formats. We will consider this topic a bit more in the next chapter when we discuss publication of data and archival issues.

SUMMARY

Geographic Information Systems are a powerful extension of relational database systems that include spatial information and tools for working with spatial information. In the past, creating and using a GIS meant having to work with complex software that was difficult for nonspecialists in the field to use. Although many systems are still structured in this way, the future of GIS is identical to that of relational database systems. At one time the systems were operated only by specialists and required very powerful computers. Eventually basic GIS functionality will be available to archaeologists just as database programs, spreadsheets, and word processors are available today.

Like relational database systems, geographic information systems can become quite complex. Like statistical analysis, some of the basic tools in GIS analysis are difficult to understand. And, like statistics, the challenge is to understand not only how the analyses are conducted but also when they are appropriate to use and which types of analyses can address a particular problem.

10 Digital Publication of Archaeological Data

Thus far we have covered a number of areas in which computer technology changed the way we do archaeology, from excavation to analysis. Most of these developments have occurred over the past 30 years. Now, with the development of technologies like CD/DVD and the growth of the Internet, we are faced with yet another potential application, namely, publishing archaeological reports in digital format.

Clearly we are entering a new age of digital publication, but the role that digital publication will play and the forms it will take are unknown. Many approaches are now being tried for the first time. There are traditional print journals with Internet versions that exactly replicate the print version, and there are journals that are available only on the Internet. Archaeological data are being published in media such as digital compact disc (CD) both as raw data and as site reports with accompanying text. Sometimes these CDs supplement information found in standard print formats; other times the CD is a stand-alone publication meant to address the full picture. There are also many examples of Internet sites with archaeological data sets. Sometimes these are accompanied by text descriptions approaching a full site report, but more often they rely on standard print publications to provide the background to the data.

Undoubtedly, as the technology changes and improves, other alternatives will develop that are difficult even to imagine at this time. For example, in 1988, when we started digitizing images of artifacts at the Paleolithic site of Combe-Capelle Bas, computer hard disks were not large enough to store all our images. We had to use a large, external CD-ROM burner with a nonstandard CD format. The storage capacity of each of these discs was a mere 100 megabytes, but at the time that seemed huge. Once we were ready to publish the Combe-Capelle Bas data 7 years later, the technology had improved enough that we were able to place the entire set of images on a single CD that is currently standard in all PC systems.

We are doing the same thing with our current site, but improvements in digital capture technology (primarily digital cameras) mean that we now have over seven CDs of digital information, databases, artifact images, and scanned field notes—and the project is only half over. We anticipate that by the time we are ready to publish this information CD storage capacities will have reached the point at which a single DVD replaces several CDs. Alternatively the Internet may make it no longer necessary to place the data on a physical medium such as a CD.

Our experience illustrates a couple points. First, constant and rapid changes in technology combined with the relatively slow pace of archaeological analysis and reporting make it very difficult to anticipate exactly what the possibilities will be when the day finally arrives to release the results. As a consequence, we simply ignore technological constraints to the extent possible and let the needs of our archaeological research design dictate what we actually do. In all likelihood technology will catch up by the time we need it.

Second, in order to continue reading those 100-megabyte CD-ROMs today, we have had to retain a very old and slow PC (faster PCs are incompatible with the external CD-ROM burner) that uses an old version of DOS (Windows is incompatible with the device). Moreover, the images on the discs are stored in a format that was very popular at the time and supported by a large corporation that is still in business today. The format, however, is no longer widely known or supported, and this corporation has long since left the business of making computer hardware or software. Thus, to read these old images, we also have to retain copies of the software that understands this format. Without these efforts, the data would have been effectively lost forever. However, it seems fairly clear that despite our best efforts the original CD-ROMs will be unreadable fairly soon, as our ability to keep the old system around and running diminishes. The solution is to move the data from the old format to a new format, but that solves the problem only temporarily. If we place the data on CDs and put those on a shelf, how long will it be before they can no longer be read? If we are not constantly vigilant, we might forget to move old data onto new formats, and they will be lost.

Thus, in this chapter we need to discuss not only techniques for publishing digital data but also strategies for making sure those data are physically available and comprehensible in the future.

COMPATIBILITY ISSUES

There are currently a number of specific ways in which to publish digital data. But for the purposes of this discussion of technical issues we can divide them into two basic categories: (1) on some physical medium (e.g., floppy disk, CD, DVD), or (2) on a computer accessible through the Internet. Many of the technical issues in digital publication affect both of these methods equally, and there are also advantages and disadvantages specific to each. Also, some of the technical issues discussed here may be solved fairly soon, whereas others are simply inherent problems and will likely remain so for a while. Our focus is on the latter.

Platforms

Perhaps one of the most difficult issues in digital publication, and one not likely to be solved any time soon, is compatibility between different platforms. By platform we mean a particular type of computer and its operating system. For instance, the two most popular desktop platforms today are Macintosh and PC, the latter running some version of Microsoft's Windows operating system. Note that each version of the operating system, and not merely just different operating systems, is in effect a different platform. Thus, Unix and Windows are obviously two different PC platforms, but so are Windows 95 and Windows XP, since software written for one may not be compatible with the other. If one of the goals of digital publication is to make the data widely available, then it has to be published in a format that can be accessed by as many different platforms as possible.

Platform compatibility is currently a larger issue for digital publication on a physical medium such as a CD than it is for the Internet. Macintosh and Windows PCs, for instance, have completely different file systems, which makes exchanging discs between the two sometimes difficult. Moreover, the difficulty is not symmetrical. That is, Macintosh computers typically read PC discs, but not vice versa. Fortunately CDs, currently the most popular medium for digital publication, can be written in a standard format that allows both Macintosh and PC computers to view their contents. Presumably, given their popularity, new platforms will continue to support CDs. It is certain, however, that a day will come when CDs are no longer popular, and finding a computer that can read a CD will be as difficult as finding one that can read a stack of computer punch cards or 5.25-inch floppies.

Fortunately the Internet is largely designed to tackle just this problem of platform compatibility. The Internet is based on a set of standards that describe how data will be formatted as it is passed from one computer to another and on how computers will recognize and communicate with one another. Based on these standards, programs like Web browsers and file-sharing programs that use a standard like FTP (File Transfer Protocol) can be written for each platform. Thus, Macintosh and Windows both have Web browsers that work on their respective platforms. Without these specific programs, cross-platform compatibility is only theoretically possible. In other words, if a new computer system is invented tomorrow with a completely new operating system, until a Web browser is written for this new platform, data published on the Internet will not be accessible.

Still, the Internet has a huge advantage in terms of its long-term utility, namely, that it is based on a set of standards rather than a particular piece of hardware. Hardware is constantly being improved, and thus hardware quickly becomes obsolete. Successful standards, however, have a longer life. Furthermore, standards are typically added to and improved in a way that keeps them compatible with the old standards, in what is called backwards compatibility. Note, however, that eventually most computer standards go the way of computer hardware, because it becomes too difficult to add to them while retaining support for the old ones. Thus, they are eventually replaced.

Being able to physically read a CD or download a file from the Internet and being able to work with them are two different things. To understand why, we need to introduce another distinction in digital publication. There are two basic types of files on a computer: (1) program files, which do something (i.e., take action), and (2) data files, which do not. Operating systems affect these two kinds of file differently. By and large, any operating system (e.g., Macintosh, Windows) can access data in data files if it can physically read the medium on which they are stored. Program files, however, are typically specific to particular operating systems. Without the help of special software, for instance, Windows computers do not recognize Macintosh programs. Thus, as with Web browsers, if gaining access to the archaeological data requires a particular program published with the data, then platform compatibility becomes a much larger issue.

That said, there are still serious issues with data files that need to be addressed. Simply being able to read a data file does not necessarily mean that what is read will be comprehensible. Thus, the next issue to consider is the data format. Some data formats are compatible on a great number of platforms, whereas others are basically platform specific, meaning that they work on only one particular kind of computer and operating system. Clearly, since one of the primary goals of digital publication is to make the data widely available, a standardized, cross-platform format is desirable. Moreover, and perhaps most importantly, the format should be accessible not only now but in the future.

File Formats

Data formats can be divided into two basic categories: binary and ASCII. We have already discussed these two formats elsewhere, particularly in Chapter 1, but let's look at them again here in the context of publication. Ultimately all computer data are stored in binary format as a series of 1s and 0s, and computers have the capacity to understand and manipulate data easily and quickly in this format. The human brain, however, does not. Thus, while a computer instantly recognizes the binary number 1000001 as the decimal number 65, we do not. If you want to include in your binary data file the fact that 65 fragments of bone were recovered from a particular level, then somewhere in your file the binary number 1000001 will appear. Alternatively the ASCII format represents data as they appear to us, as a string of characters. Thus, each character in the alphabet, including numbers and many special symbols, is given a code number (see the box in Chapter 1 for a complete listing), which itself is stored in binary. For instance, the capital letter A is given ASCII code 65. Thus, in an ASCII file the binary number 1000001 means A, and not the decimal number 65. In an ASCII file the "number" 65 is stored as two separate characters, 6 and 5, each with its own ASCII code.

What does this mean? While binary files are very efficient for storing data, they also add another layer of complexity because of the way they are coded. To understand the contents of a binary file, you have to be able to understand the binary code in which they are written. You cannot simply view the contents of a binary file on the computer screen or a printer and start interpreting it as you can with an ASCII file. Rather, to understand a binary file, you need to know the exact format used to write it. A 65, for instance, might mean, not 65 fragments of bone, but the color of a pixel if the file is an image.

The key to knowing the format of a binary file without having to peer inside the file is its extension (usually the three-letter code that follows the file's name). In Chapter 7, for instance, we listed several image file formats including JPG, BMP, and GIF. Thus, an image stored in one of these file formats might appear as Image1.bmp, Image1.jpg, or Image1.gif. To actually view the image stored in these files requires a program that understands these formats so that it can properly decode the binary data. Similarly a DBF extension indicates a database file created for the database program dBase, and an MDB extension indicates a database file created for the database program Access. For the information in these various binary file formats to be accessible today and in the future, we will need computer programs that understand the format. Sometimes a wide variety of programs understand a particular format; other times only a single program understands it. The latter are called *proprietary formats*, and they should definitely be avoided if long-term access to a data file is the goal.

So, given this situation, it is very important when publishing data in a binary format to chose a common, popular, cross-platform standard format. For images the most common today are JPG, GIF, and TIFF. For data the situation is much less clear. DBF, the format created by the now extinct program dBase, remains very popular. It is a fairly simple format, and so it is easy to support. MDB, the Microsoft Access format, is also popular, but it comes in a number of different versions and has not remained consistent. Furthermore, to fully exploit the format requires the Microsoft program Access. In other words, while some programs can read portions of MDB files, they may not be able to fully work with MDB files. For vector-based images the closest we have to a standard is Auto-CAD's DXF format, but DXF is an ASCII format, and not a binary. This means that their contents can be easily read without a special program. However, DXF is quite difficult to understand.

METADATA

In considering file formats and long-term storage, it is important to consider not only readability but also interpretability. Consider the following excerpt from a DXF file:

```
6E
100
AcDbEntity
8
GridLayer
6
DOT
48
0.2
100
AcDbLine
10
4
20
-10.57559
30
0
11
4
21
-3.55775
31
0
0
LINE
5
```

Because this file is written in ASCII format, it is easily read. The words and numbers are clear, and this segment seems to be describing a vector object (probably a line). Beyond that, however, little is clear. If this example seems extreme, consider a seemingly straightforward listing of data in ASCII format:

```
"UNIT","ID","DATE","HANGLE","VANGLE","SLOPED"
"PARK",734,"01-02-10",324.2745,96.455,4.321
"PARK",735,"01-02-10",320.011,92.35,13.772
```

The first line of this file contains the names of the fields that follow, a standard practice in ASCII data files. Each value is separated by a comma, and text values are enclosed in quotes—again, standard practice. This format, known as comma-quote delimited, is a good way to publish data tables.

The meaning of the first three fields is fairly clear, but the last three fields are abbreviated. If you have worked with survey data, you might recognize that they stand for horizontal angle, vertical angle, and slope distance. Thus, this file seems to list a series of measurements recorded with a survey instrument. There are, however, many more ambiguities in these data that hamper their utility. For instance, what format was used to record the angle measurements? Are they decimal degrees? Are they degrees, minutes, seconds? Is the slope distance in meters or feet? Is the date January 2, 1910, or February 10, 2001, or October 2, 2001? What is the accuracy of the distance measurement? Was it made with a laser on a total station or with a tape measure? What is the precision of the angle measurement? Does the instrument round to the nearest 5 seconds or 10 seconds or 1 second?

Despite the clear text format they are written in, to truly understand these data we need more information; we need data about the data, or metadata. Metadata is an extremely important concept for the publication and dissemination of data. While we have illustrated this point with ASCII data, it is no less true of binary data, and it affects every kind of data: images, databases, maps, and so on. This topic is huge, and while there is simply no way we can provide a definitive list of the kinds of things that should be included in the metadata, we can offer some guidelines.

What to Include in Metadata

In considering spatial data, as the previous chapter emphasized, the most important things to document are the coordinate system, projection, and datum. If the map is of a site and not linked to a national or global datum, it is nevertheless necessary to indicate the location of the datums on the map and to provide their coordinates, reference angles as necessary, and a good description of where these points are located on the site so that future archaeologists can reestablish the grid. We have, for instance, worked on a number of sites excavated between 50 and 20 years ago for which good maps were available to show where specific archaeological features had been encountered during excavation. Unfortunately we could not link those maps to the present-day site because we could not locate the original datums.

The metadata for spatial data should also include a description of the equipment and methods used to collect the data. If multiple methods were used—for instance, string line levels and folding meter sticks to record artifact locations and a total station to record the unit boundaries and the topography—this needs to be noted. An indication of the accuracy and precision of each method should also be given. While it may seem sufficient simply to note the brand and model number of the mapping instrument, this information might be meaningless in the very near future. If the instrument is a GPS unit, information about the accuracy of the measurement is going to change with each measurement, and if the measurements are differentially corrected, this needs to be mentioned. As with nearly any data set, it is also good to indicate who took the measurements and when. Of course, it is also difficult to know where to draw the line. As we discussed in Chapter 2, total station measurements are affected by the temperature and atmospheric pressure. Some surveyors record these data and include them as part of the survey record, but in most archaeological instances it is not necessary.

Metadata should also include specifics that help decode the format of the file containing the data and the codes attached to each measurement. In our example from the DXF file, the metadata should include a detailed description of the DXF file format so that all the code words and numbers can be understood. Fortunately AutoCAD publishes the format of DXF files so that other people can write programs that read and write this format. Thus, this document, published in ASCII, should also become part of the metadata if you use the DXF format. Assuming that there are no copyright issues, it is best to include the document side by side with the DXF files rather than depending on it always being available elsewhere. It is possible, and indeed likely, that the DXF file format will change, and so the documents that describe it will change as well. Therefore, it is best to describe the format as it is at that moment.

In addition to the codes inherent to the file format, the metadata should include a description of the codes assigned to the points. In the old days when nearly all computer data were coded to save storage space, the need for a description of the codes was obvious. Now, when we can in essence spell everything out, the need to provide even more detail is less obvious. However, if an object is recorded as a core or a flake or a tool, somewhere in the metadata—perhaps in the metadata for the stone tool analysis file—there should be a definition of these terms. It is also important to document what is *not* in the file, as well as what is—in other words, what were the criteria for recording a measurement. Perhaps only flakes larger than 25 millimeters were given specific spatial coordinates, and all flakes smaller than this were lumped together by level.

Images also require metadata, and here, too, it is difficult to know where to draw the line. Metadata for images taken with a digital camera can include the brand and model of the camera, the image resolution, the file format, and the level of compression (if any). Metadata for photos from a film camera can include the type of film and its speed. All camera pictures, whether digital or not, can include information about the shutter speed and exposure. Metadata for scenery or excavation photos typically include the date and time of the photo, the name of the photographer, the place the photo was taken, and the direction the camera was facing. As we discussed in Chapter 7, one of the most important issues with artifact images is the scale. Thus, the metadata can include the scale.

Clearly some of this information will change on a photograph-by-photograph basis, so it has to be included in a database along with the name of each image, rather than in a single metadata file. Recording all of this information is also tedious and time consuming. Fortunately some digital cameras provide much of this information automatically.

The metadata for observations made on objects primarily amounts to definitions of terms. A great many observations are based on a set of categories or a typology, each of which needs to be clearly defined. Measurements should be documented in terms of their scale (meters or centimeters or millimeters), units (meters or feet), and precision (number of significant digits). The type of instrument used to make the measurement should be mentioned, and the way the measurements were taken should be described as well. Even seemingly simple measurements can be difficult to document. There are, for instance, several ways to measure the length of a stone flake. Some kinds of stone tools use a different measure of length than flakes, and length measurements may differ on broken pieces. Presumably much of this information was gathered before the analysis even started, so creating the metadata might mean merely making this information available with the data.

Above all, the metadata should be easy to read itself. Thus, it should always be written in ASCII rather than a word processor's own format because those formats are typically binary and are impossible to decode without the word processing program itself. Fortunately all word processing programs provide either an export feature or some other way of specifying the format of the saved file, and ASCII or text (txt) files are always a supported format. Likewise, most database, spreadsheet, and statistics programs provide a means for exporting data as ASCII. Finding a way to save raster images as ASCII is more difficult. For vector images there are several ASCII formats that can be exported from most programs.

Back to ASCII vs. Binary

So which is better, ASCII or binary? ASCII is the single best standard we have in computing. It has been around for decades, it is recognized by most if not all computers, it is easy to describe and easy to read, and it seems to be our best bet for a format that will be understood in the future. However, ASCII has a number of limitations, and so certain kinds of data lend themselves more easily to this format than others. For example, tabular data, data from spreadsheets, and database tables are typically easily represented in ASCII format. In this regard, the comma-quote delimited file format discussed previously is a standard method for representing tabular data in an ASCII format. One common variant of this format is to substitute tabs for commas. This is especially useful in parts of Europe where commas are used to separate the decimal and whole portions of a number (e.g., 123.45 vs. 123,45).

A database, however, is more than merely a collection of tabular data sets. Queries, relationships between tables, indexes, report formats, data entry screens, and lots of other features related to database applications are more difficult or impossible to translate into ASCII. Some of these things, especially the relationships between tables, are best represented in the metadata.

As we just discussed, spatial data represented as vectors are also easily written as ASCII. DXF is one way to do this, but it is fairly complicated. A much simpler approach is represented by the following Idrisi (a GIS program) vector file:

```
200        1
5.99857687500000E+0005 2.36131300000000E+0006
300        2
6.18933312500000E+0005 2.37687700000000E+0006
6.18968000000000E+0005 2.37699925000000E+0006
400        5
5.93256375000000E+0005 2.35529725000000E+0006
5.93444437500000E+0005 2.35528550000000E+0006
5.93609500000000E+0005 2.35528650000000E+0006
5.94028250000000E+0005 2.35535225000000E+0006
5.94289875000000E+0005 2.35534875000000E+0006
500        8
6.04372687500000E+0005 2.40087000000000E+0006
6.04397812500000E+0005 2.40090325000000E+0006
6.04448312500000E+0005 2.40094175000000E+0006
6.04635062500000E+0005 2.40111075000000E+0006
6.04690500000000E+0005 2.40117200000000E+0006
6.04715812500000E+0005 2.40118500000000E+0006
6.04758750000000E+0005 2.40122575000000E+0006
6.04771125000000E+0005 2.40126400000000E+0006
0 0
```

This file contains four vector objects. The first line of the file tells us that the first object is represented by a single point and has an attribute of 200. The second object is a line with an attribute code of 300. The next two objects are either open or closed polygons with 5 and 8 points, respectively. The last line of the file, 0 0, marks the end of the file. Note, too, that the numbers are expressed in scientific notation. This means that the portion of the number before the E should be multiplied by 10 to the power of the number after the E. To know more about this file—what the attributes mean, whether the polygons should be closed (by connecting the last point back to the first), what the projection and the datum are, and so on—clearly requires some metadata. In fact, Idrisi vector files come with a matching metadata file also stored in ASCII that provides some of the missing information. Idrisi metadata files, however, do not describe what the attributes mean. This has to be added separately.

Images and spatial data in raster format do not lend themselves to ASCII. The main problem is the size of the file. For instance, consider a black-and-white image wherein each pixel of the image is either a 1 or a 0, for black or white. In a binary format each pixel takes only 1 bit. In an ASCII format, in which 1s are written as ASCII 49 and 0s are written as ASCII 58, each pixel takes 8 bits because 8 bits is the minimum size for an ASCII code. Thus, the file size will necessarily be eight times larger than it would otherwise be. Since file size is already a problem with images, storing them as ASCII can be an issue. In addition, larger files take longer to load and display.

That said, there is no reason that you cannot store image data in ASCII. What follows is a small raster data set (a DEM from Surfer) written as an ASCII file:

```
DSAA
2 2
962.657 1033.57
994.127 1018.31
-9.48642 -5.74141

-8.30478 -9.48642
-6.33292 -5.74141
```

The first line in this file is a Surfer-specific code indicating that the file is written in ASCII format. This is needed because Surfer can write the same data in a binary format as well. In fact, particular file formats often have a binary and an ASCII representation to exploit the advantages of each. The second line indicates the size of the image: 2×2 (we said that it was small). The following three lines place the DEM in three-dimensional space by providing the minimum and maximum X, Y, and Z coordinates for its edges. The last two lines give the value (Z in this case) of each cell or pixel in the raster data set ($2 \times 2 = 4$ cells). We need some additional metadata to know in which order to fill the cells (from the bottom up, from the top down, left to right, right to left, etc.). While this is an example of a very small raster data set, it is easy to see how this could be expanded to describe an image of any size.

Finally it is worth noting that there is no reason not to store the data in more than one format. Preferably at least one of the formats will be ASCII, but multiple binary formats are also possible. For instance, images can be stored in several different binary formats for easy access on particular platforms and in ASCII format for long-term accessibility and greater cross-platform compatibility.

THE INTERNET

Given our discussion on cross-platform compatibility and file formats, it is worth looking again at the Internet and its potential for archaeological publishing. There are two ways to use the Internet to publish. First, you can use the Internet simply as a way to transfer files. By this we mean that you can post your data files, in whatever format—ASCII or binary, MDB or DBF—on a server that is easily accessible via Internet protocols. In doing so, you avoid a number of problems involved in publishing data on a medium like CDs. First, the size and number of the files is for all practical purposes limitless, whereas today's CDs store approximately 650 megabytes of data. Improvements in CD technology and the development of other kinds of storage technologies will push this number steadily upward, but the Internet will remain limitless. Second, as we discussed earlier, the Internet virtually eliminates platform issues related to access to files. In other words, regardless of the platform, the files posted on your server will be accessible. If a new platform is created tomorrow, one of the first applications written for it will be a Web browser. Third, it seems likely that the Internet is here to stay, but the same cannot be said about CDs. In fact, it is quite likely that CDs, or any other physical medium, will not be here in the future. How near that future is, of course, is hard to say. Furthermore, it is not clear that all platforms will support all media. Early Linux systems, for instance, did not support DVD movies.

At the same time, while using the Internet to transfer files solves some problems, it introduces others and fails to address still others. Although the storage space of the Internet is for all practical purposes unlimited, the time it takes to transfer files can be a limiting factor. This is an area of very rapid change, and eventually this will cease to be an issue, but as of this writing it remains an issue. More importantly, perhaps, using the Internet to share files does not address the problem of file format incompatibilities. For example, it would be a simple matter for us to share all of the original digital maps (not the raw data but the finished maps) from our Combe-Capelle Bas report on the Internet, but they are all in a file format that is no longer supported by any of today's software. Thus, merely sharing files on the Internet does not address the long-term usability of those files.

This brings us to the second way in which the Internet can be used to publish data. Rather than share the data in its original format, the data can be converted to the standard format used for the Web: Hypertext Markup Language (HTML). This is a bit like converting all of your data to ASCII. In fact, HTML files are stored in ASCII format, and plain ASCII files can be displayed by any Web browser. Basically HTML is a set of instructions that tell a Web browser how to arrange and present the data included in the HTML file. In this regard HTML blurs the line between programs and data. That is, HTML files are not programs, but they contain program instructions that are acted upon by Web browsers. Thus, for instance, there are instructions for setting text in boldface (<bold>) or italics (<italics>) and more complicated instructions for formatting the page, creating tables, and establishing links to other pages or other pieces of data.

Two image formats are supported on the Web: JPG and GIF. The former handles images with 16 million colors and uses a lossy compression technique; the latter is lossless and is better for graphics since it supports only 256 colors (see Chapter 7 for more details). Currently the Web does not have a vector image format though there are numerous add-ons to standard HTML that do support vector formats. Add-ons, however tempting, remove one of the main benefits of HTML: cross-platform compatibility.

Thus, if your data can be reformatted into HTML with JPG or GIF images, they can be easily accessed over the Internet with a Web browser. The downside is that they are less useful in this form. Tabular data displayed as HTML tables or as a simple ASCII comma-quote delimited file cannot be analyzed until they are somehow imported into a database. This is a relatively minor issue, and the same is true if the data are stored in this format on something like a CD.

Of course, even here the situation is likely to change over the next few years. In fact, HTML is slowly being replaced by either XML (Extensible Markup Language) or XHTML (Extensible Hypertext Markup Language), and many other specialized markup languages are in use today. Whether HTML will remain the standard, or for how long, is unknown.

ARCHAEOLOGICAL SITE REPORTS

Given the focus of this book, the emphasis of this chapter has been on publishing data rather than text. Excavations produce a tremendous amount of data that, until the advent of digital publishing, could not be published. Text, in contrast, is easily published in a standard printed book. Thus, one approach to publishing a site report is to combine the traditional monograph with digital publication of the raw data, an approach that taps the strengths of each medium. The monograph can contain, for instance, chapters written by various specialists connected with the overall research design of the project, descriptions of the archaeological levels and their associated artifacts (with illustrations), geological descriptions and interpretations, discussions of site formation, and interpretations of the behaviors of the site's inhabitants. Like all traditional site reports a monograph is designed to stand alone, painting a comprehensive picture of how and why the site was excavated, what the results of the excavations were, and how the behaviors were interpreted.

In this approach the digital publication of the data is a bit like an extended appendix to the monograph. As such, it does not stand on its own. It presents neither background information about the site nor any interpretations. Rather, it contains only material that would be virtually impossible to include in the monograph itself. It is still prohibitively expensive, for instance, to print a large number of full-color photographs. As we have discussed, the large storage capacity of CDs and the effectively infinite storage capacity of the Internet make it possible to publish many more photographs than could be accommodated in a book and that would otherwise not be published. In other words, one approach to publication today is to play to the strengths of each medium, placing the text in a printed monograph and the data in a digital format.

Digital Publication vs. Printed Monograph

Besides the large amount of information that can be published, one of the principal advantages of digital publication relates to the kinds of access to both data and images that are possible in this format. Artifact images are a good example of this. In a monograph basic artifact descriptions are typically presented by level, since stratigraphy represents the primary organization for the excavation, description, and analysis of a site. Accompanying the description of each level might be several illustrations of typical artifacts from the level. In this format readers can easily see examples of particular artifact types from a given level. It is more difficult, however, for the reader to assemble all of one artifact type from all levels. In contrast, with a relational database and access to all of the artifact images, readers can group artifact images as they like. They can write queries to find just the desired records and their associated images.

However, when the only access to a collection of images is through a relational database with essentially random access to the data, it is almost impossible to develop and communicate themes thought to be important to the author or authors of the site report. A random-access format is not particularly useful, for example, in communicating a specific interpretation. Interpretations are, after all, based on arguments, and arguments are essentially linear in form. You simply cannot make a coherent argument by presenting all of its necessary premises, steps, and relations in a random order. It is not a question of the kind of medium used (digital or printed), but rather the kind of access that is made available to readers.

This discussion, therefore, has created an artificial distinction between the random access available with CDs and other digital media and the sequential access typical of books. While it is very difficult to make a printed book work as a random-access document, there is no reason that the contents of a CD cannot be accessed in a sequential manner like a book. This brings us to an alternative model for publication. Rather than combine a traditional monograph with a digital publication of the supporting data, the entire report can be published in digital form to create a kind of archive.

Once the text is in digital form, a number of things become possible. First, despite the fact that the text is meant to be read in a sequential fashion from start to finish, it becomes a simple matter to automatically search through the text to find pieces of text that match key words of interest. In other words, once the text becomes a digital document, it can be accessed randomly as well as sequentially. Second, the author can link the text to other parts of the text or to other kinds of data. These links, typically called *hyperlinks*, in effect provide alternative paths through the text. Thus, the original sequential path is still retained, but at predefined places readers can follow new paths that are impossible to construct when the text is in a traditional printed form. A figure in the text, for instance, can be hyperlinked to a query that shows the data used to create the figure. An image in the text can be linked to several more of the same object or to higher-resolution images. And a two-dimensional image of an object can be linked to a three-dimensional model of the same object.

While the possibilities are endless, they come at a cost. First, it takes a lot longer to create, edit, and produce a document written in this way than a traditional printed monograph. This, of course, translates to monetary costs. Second, implementing some of the more creative and interesting hyperlinks or relations between data and text means straying from the goals of platform compatibility and long-term access. HTML is good at linking text and images in various ways, but it is not good at including data. Efforts have been made to improve the ability of HTML to incorporate different kinds of data, but the results have yet to be incorporated into the standards. Furthermore, in order to achieve compatibility, standards like HTML tend to be quite simple. Thus, publishers have generally found HTML to be lacking even for the basic presentation of text. It is quite difficult, for instance, to represent characters with accents in HTML. Instead, the emerging standard, created by Adobe Corporation, is called PDF (Portable Document Format). The PDF file format is excellent at representing printed pages, complete with figures and graphics. It is, however, an add-on, and it is a proprietary, binary format. A Web browser cannot view a PDF document unless it has a PDF viewer, and while PDF viewers exist for Macintosh and PC platforms, they do not exist for all platforms.

Ultimately full digital publication of text and data may be where we are going, but this raises several issues. First, it is important to remember that not all archaeologists or members of the public have access to computers, particularly in some parts of the world where the sites being reported on are located. Thus, a solely digital publication could significantly limit the potential readership of reports. However, once digital access becomes widely available, digital publication will make these reports much more accessible than printed volumes.

Second, as discussed here, there are still issues with hardware and software compatibility. Raw data and image files are easier to share across platforms unless special programs are required to fully access these data since the programs themselves are likely platform specific. In effect, if the programs are platform specific, the data become platform specific as well. Third, at a rather practical level, even for those who have the necessary hardware, it is still not as comfortable to read a 350-page report on a computer screen as it is to read it in printed format. Note that the production costs of producing a digital version are somewhat less than for a printed book, though surprisingly the difference is not as great as you might think since most of the costs of a book are in the production rather than the printing.

CURATION

The most significant reason, however, to consider publishing a traditional printed monograph is future accessibility. Archaeology, of course, involves destruction of the archaeological record. As a result, we have an ethical obligation to recover as much information as possible and to make as much of this information as possible available to the public. The question arises, however, whether our digital publications, which allow us to achieve so much in terms of quantity of material published, reduce long-term accessibility. Will our digital publications still be accessible in 10 years? In 20 years? In a century? Nearly all archaeologists have at some time consulted archaeological publications from the early part of the 1900s, and many have relied on publications from the 1800s. Indeed, some of the most important works in the field come from the first century of our discipline, and these volumes typically are in excellent condition. Many archaeologists also consult written records that are thousands of years old.

At the beginning of this chapter, we related a story about our trying to maintain access to our own data stored in a format that is no longer supported—data that were little more than a decade old. And many, if not most, of the early digital records from our fieldwork are in a similarly precarious state. The problem is not just hardware, either. Recently a colleague of ours tried to access data collected in the 1970s and stored "permanently" on computer tape. The tape itself was fine, but there was only one remaining person in the university computer center who still knew how to read it! Similarly we pity the people who have all of their data stored on 8-inch floppy disks or on punch cards. Surprisingly some of the first CDs printed in the mid-1980s are no longer readable—not because the medium failed, but because of changing software and hardware standards. Given these concerns, it is simply unrealistic to assume that the digital media of today will be readable in a decade, let alone a century.

At first glance the Internet seems to offer a solution to some of these problems, and even more so if you are a consumer rather than a producer of digital information. From the consumer's point of view, data on the Internet are easily accessible despite constant changing platforms as long as the address of the data remains constant. From the producer's point of view, however, we have glossed over numerous technical issues here. The computers that host or serve the information have to be constantly upgraded and maintained, and the software they run is constantly changing. You cannot simply place a site report on a computer, connect it to the Internet, and expect that 100 years from now the site report will still be accessible.

The problem is that nothing is permanent in the digital realm. Regardless of whether you publish on digital media such as CD or on the Internet, you must maintain that publication, and good efforts notwithstanding, no organization can guarantee the long-term preservation of digital publications. Contrast this situation with that for printed publications, where the mechanics of producing archival-quality publications on acid-free paper are well understood and where a network of thousands of libraries exists whose sole mission is to protect and ensure future access to those printed works.

In short, the future remains hazy. Everything is moving toward digital publication, but many issues remain to be solved. We can make the following summary statements and suggestions.

Publication on digital media such as CD or DVD offers a number of advantages over Internet publication. For one, the publication is final; that is, once the author produces the finished product there are no continuing costs or maintenance or support issues. This assumes, however, that the author is not personally responsible for preserving long-term access to the media. If it is not the author, then is it the publisher? And if it is not the publisher, then is it the libraries that purchase the product? None of these options seems likely. Publishers are not a long-term solution since they are motivated by profit margins and not curation in perpetuity. Libraries have the motivation but currently lack the technology and skills. Publication on the Internet requires constant maintenance, which in turn costs money. Exactly who will take on this burden and how costs will be covered is unclear. Currently, however, libraries do not seem to be the institutions that will do this job, and they do not appear to be moving in that direction. Rather, private enterprises likely will take on this role since providing continued access to large stores of information can be profitable for them.

Digital publications of data and text should be based on ASCII to ensure the broadest possible cross-platform compatibility today and in the future. All data sets must be accompanied by metadata files that describe the full content of the data. Metadata files should describe not only how the data were recorded but also how they are structured in the file. This is particularly important when the data are written in binary format because the structure of the data becomes virtually impenetrable in this format. Since binary formats are typically more useful than ASCII format to programs that manipulate the data, one solution is to provide the data in both formats: binary for easy access today and ASCII for long-term access.

Given that an ASCII copy will be provided, it is also advisable to print the ASCII files on acid-free paper and to provide them to an archive facility along with the other documents that are normally turned over to an archive at the completion of the project. A printed version of the data is still the best long-term solution to data curation issues. Since printing the data will also produce far more paper than an archive can typically handle, decisions will have to be made about what gets printed and what does not. Printing an ASCII version of every artifact image, for instance, is not practical. It's important to consider which kinds of information can be recaptured from the physical remains of the excavation. For instance, digital images that are lost can be recaptured if the original artifacts themselves are permanently curated. The find location of each artifact, however, is information that might be impossible to recapture if lost. And if the artifacts are to be reburied, it places an even greater burden on archaeologists in terms of the curation of the information obtained from them.

SUMMARY

The digital techniques discussed in this book make the collection and analysis of archaeological data faster and easier than ever before. Now, with the advent of digital publication, we can, and should, share the primary data on which our work is based as never before. As this chapter has shown, however, digital publication involves a number of challenges for which there are no easy answers. Fortunately as archaeologists we are not alone in this regard. Every field faces these same challenges, and so a great many institutions are working on solutions. In the meantime we can continue to exploit the existing technologies to their fullest while working hard to ensure that our own data sets remain accessible to future generations.

11 Preparing for a Field Project

A practical guide to computer use in archaeological fieldwork would not be complete without some discussion about how to prepare for a field project. In this chapter we discuss two important topics. The first is power, which is an essential component to a computerized project. Each electrical component has its own power requirements, and it is important to understand what these requirements are. Moreover, archaeological fieldwork usually takes place some distance from normal power outlets, so you have to consider ways of getting power to a remote setup. Finally, projects in other countries may face problems such as different voltages and different outlet shapes.

Second, we discuss some of the things you should consider to protect yourself from equipment failures and data loss. These all involve backup issues, but in two senses: replacements of essential pieces of equipment and copies of your data. Failure to consider these can ruin an entire field season's worth of work.

UNDERSTANDING POWER REQUIREMENTS

Every electronic device is powered in a standard way, through either batteries or connection to a power receptacle, or perhaps both. At home you do not have any problems in providing electrical current for your devices. In the field, however, all sorts of problems can arise. One basic problem is how to get power to the devices in the first place, because not many archaeological sites are equipped with electrical outlets. A second problem has to do with voltage: the standard voltage in the United States is 110–115 volts, whereas in many other areas of the world it is 220–240 volts. If you use devices that work from batteries, you avoid these problems, but you still have to keep a supply of batteries. Before we discuss practical solutions to such problems, however, we should provide some background on how electricity works.

One concept that is fundamental to an understanding of how to power electronic devices is the direction of the current, which is either one-way (direct current, or DC, which has both negative and positive poles) or two-way (alternating current, or AC). For our purposes we can say that DC power is the type provided by batteries and most power adapters, and AC current is what is provided by electrical receptacles. Most devices that consume a relatively larger amount of electricity, such as computers and printers, work with AC; smaller devices often expect DC current.

Other important concepts related to electrical power include volts, amperes (amps), and watts, which work together. To understand these concepts, think of electricity as water running through a hose. In this analogy volts represent the force or pressure with which the water flows, amps represent the speed or rate of the flow, and watts represent how much water is used, or the actual power consumption. Thus, these measures are directly related to one another. For instance, multiplying amps by volts gives the number of watts, so a device that uses 10 amps and runs on 115 volts consumes 1150 watts of power. Electrical devices expect current with a specific voltage and amps, and it is important to make sure that the power you supply conforms to the device's expectations.

Finally, with AC current each change from one direction to the other and back again represents a cycle. Most alternating current is generated at 50 or 60 cycles per second or hertz (Hz).

International and Other Issues with AC Current

One of the most common problems you will face is the need to transform the voltage of your AC current. Transforming voltage means changing the output from, say, 110 volts AC to 220 volts AC, or vice versa. The device that does this is a transformer. You can get transformers in all different sizes, and the most significant aspect that differentiates one from another is usually the wattage output. For example, you can buy small transformers for small appliances, designed with travelers in mind, that output up to 1600 watts. Using either of these with small devices usually works fine. However, and this is especially true of the 1600-watt transformers, we recommend that you not use them for long periods of time and that you never plug more than one device into them.

Unfortunately not all equipment is compatible with these small transformers. In general, equipment that draws a lot of power (indicated in either watts or amps) and equipment that is sensitive to cycles (50 vs. 60 Hz) will not operate or will operate poorly with small, portable power converters. Computer monitors, desktop computers, laser printers, and popcorn makers are all examples of devices that will *not* operate with them. Total station battery chargers, digital camera battery chargers, laptop computers, and electronic scales are all examples of equipment that will.

For more serious transforming needs you might consider buying a large transformer from an electrical supply company. To determine the size you need, simply total the wattage of all the devices you intend to connect, and get a transformer with at least that much output. You can then connect it to a power strip and plug in several devices at the same time. Be aware, however, that as each device plugged into the transformer is turned on it may draw an initial surge of power that exceeds the limits of the transformer (this is especially true of laser printers and monitors). Therefore, try to get a transformer that exceeds your combined wattage needs by at least 10–20 percent.

Today many devices have transformers built into them, in what is called an auto-sensing or auto-switching power supply, in which case you can simply plug them into existing wall outlets. If you are unsure whether your device has this feature, look at the bottom of the machine or the bottom of the power supply. If it can switch, then a range of voltages will be indicated. Typically it will look something like this:

100-240V ~ 15A 50/60Hz

What this means is that this power supply accepts voltages in the range of 100 to 240 volts, pulls 15 amps maximum, and operates with either 50 or 60 cycles.

However, still another problem is that outlet shapes vary in different countries. The easiest way to get around this problem is simply to buy an appropriate plug adapter, which is a small device that slips over the prongs of your plug. You should obtain these devices before you leave the country, as it is often difficult to find them abroad. Since it is very easy to pull the plug and leave the plug converter behind, it is also a very good idea to (1) tape the converter to your power cord and (2) buy several more of these than you think you could possibly use. Alternatively, if the power cord is detachable from the power supply or device, you might purchase a power cord made locally for the given country's outlets. Although this is a bit more expensive, it may be the best solution. It is also possible, in a pinch, to cut the plug from the power cord and to wire a new one from a local hardware store. If you do this, remember that how you connect the hot (usually black) wire and neutral (usually white) wire to the prongs of the plug is not important. You must, however, be sure to connect the ground (usually green) wire to the proper grounding prong. Again, bear in mind that plug adapters and different cables do nothing to change the voltage.

Another problem you may face has to do with the dependability of the local current. Many parts of the world experience frequent outages and/or power surges. To protect yourself against the latter, be sure to use a power filter that has some sort of surge protection. This device will automatically switch off the current to your equipment if the voltage suddenly rises. Of course, any surge in or loss of power can result in a loss of data, and so you might want to purchase an uninterrupted power supply (UPS). This is, in effect, a battery that is connected between your AC power supply and your equipment. The battery is continuously being charged by the AC current, and when the AC power is interrupted, the battery continues to send power to your equipment. Some UPSs can supply power for several hours, but the more inexpensive models supply power only long enough for you to save your work and shut down normally. If you are using a laptop with an internal battery, the battery functions like a UPS.

What if power is simply not available? In this case you have to generate your own, with the two most common options being gasoline and solar generators. With either type you should use the generator to charge an array of batteries; you should not run your devices directly off of them. If you must run directly off of something like a generator, be sure to use a UPS to protect your computer when it runs out of gas and a surge protector to protect against power fluctuations.

Power Adapters

In spite of the fact that most electronic devices can be plugged directly into an AC outlet, the power that actually goes into them is most often DC current. Converting AC to DC is done with a device called a rectifier, which is built into the small, boxlike power adapter that serves as the plug. Typically the cable has a round male plug at the other end that is inserted into the device by being fit over a small pin.

Although superficially most power adapters look the same, they differ in many important respects. On almost all of them is written what they expect in the way of input and output, as well as a small graphic (see Figure 11.1) indicating the polarity of the plug that attaches to the device. So, in this example the power supply is able to auto-switch between 120 and 240 volts AC, and it transforms the current to 9 volts DC, with a maximum draw of 200 milliamps (or 0.2 amp). The figure also shows the polarity of the plug. The line going to the outside ring indicates the polarity of the outside contact, and the line going to the inner circle indicates the polarity of the inner contact that fits over the pin. Not only can the polarity differ (i.e., the positive pole can be on the outside or the inside), but the overall size of the plug can vary as well. If you do not use the power adapter that originally came with the device, be sure that the adapter you do use matches the specifications required. It is possible to buy "universal" power adapters that come with a series of different-sized plugs and that can be switched to various output specifications and polarity.

Batteries

Today most equipment you will use in the field can run off of batteries—which is both a blessing and a curse. Take, for instance, the total station system that we use to point provenience artifacts. Our first model had batteries that lasted 4 hours or less under normal usage, which meant that we could not even survey until lunch

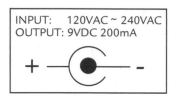

FIGURE 11.1   AC/DC power adapter

without having extra batteries with us. Fortunately the batteries in today's models are much better. Most can be counted on to last an entire day, though it is still necessary to have a backup just in case. Two batteries are required so that one can charge while the other is in use, but three are even better—one battery is charging at the lab and the main and backup batteries in the field.

Next, the portable computer used as a data collector for the total station requires batteries. Here, the trend is the opposite that of the total station. In the past a single set of AA batteries might have powered our data collector for days, weeks, or even the entire field season. However, as computers have become more powerful, as screens have become larger, and as color screens have become standard, battery life has plummeted. Our current system, which is no longer available, runs for something less than a day or two on a set of AA batteries.

Finally, our data collector is connected to a small label printer that creates the tickets for each provenienced artifact. These printers will not last more than 3 or 4 hours on four AA batteries under normal conditions.

There are three options regarding batteries. For devices that use standard sizes (AAA, AA, 9 volt, etc.), you can purchase new batteries as needed, but this can be extremely expensive. The second option is to use rechargeable batteries, which cost more initially but which can be reused many times. Depending on your situation you may want to buy several sets so that you can use some while others are charging. Keep in mind that, depending on your recharger, the batteries may discharge faster than they charge, and they almost always discharge faster than a nonrechargeable type. Also, with most batteries (especially the nickel-cadmium type), it is important that they be fully discharged and fully charged with each cycle. Otherwise, the amount of time that they can hold a charge rapidly decreases.

The third option regarding batteries is to use one large battery to power all of your various devices. The standard here is easy: use a 12-volt battery. Twelve-volt motorcycle, car, and truck batteries and their chargers are readily available throughout the world, and they are quite inexpensive. In addition, an increasing number of devices can accept 12-volt power, usually through a power adapter that is shaped to fit into a car's cigarette lighter. In fact, the cigarette lighter adapter is fast becoming a global standard, available not only in cars but also on airplanes. The array of products that can operate this way ranges from computers and refrigerators to coffee pots and fans.

Switching over to 12 volts is a straightforward process. The key is to purchase a battery with enough power to run all of your equipment for at least a day and probably longer (allowing you to recharge it at night). You determine your power needs by adding up the total amperage of the equipment. Twelve-volt batteries come with an amp-hour rating, which indicates how much power they can output over a certain period. A battery with a 20-amp-hour rating, for instance, can provide 20 amps of power for 1 hour or, more importantly for our purposes, 1 amp of power for 20 hours. How many amp-hours a battery provides is one of the more important factors in its cost. An inexpensive motorcycle battery might not even have enough power to run a total station, data collector, and printer for a minute, much less a day. Unfortunately amp-hours are also related to the size of the battery: larger, heavier, and less portable batteries will last substantially longer than the smaller ones. As a result, the 12-volt system might not be suitable if you are moving around on foot.

There are other downsides to car batteries. First, the less expensive ones are all wet-cell, meaning that they contain acid. This acid is highly corrosive, so you need to be careful not to spill it on your skin, clothes, or other equipment. Second, you need to take special care when recharging wet-cell batteries. The charging process produces gases in the cells that if not vented may cause the battery to explode. Thus, when recharging a wet-cell battery be sure to remove the caps on the cells. Third, car batteries are not designed to be slowly drained and recharged; rather, they are designed to produce a great deal of power over a very short period as the vehicle is being started. Once the vehicle is started, the battery is quickly brought back up to full charge and kept that way until it is needed to start the vehicle again. In contrast, using a car battery to power a total station produces a completely different pattern—one that resembles what happens when you leave your car lights on overnight. As this happens repeatedly, the time between charges decreases, and eventually the battery stops taking a charge. Nevertheless, it is our experience that a battery designed for a small to medium-sized car will power a total station, data collector, and printer for an entire week without a charge and will last for several 6- to 8-week field seasons before it needs to be replaced.

There are also many advantages to the 12-volt system. First, rather than having to charge many sets of batteries each night with several different rechargers, you only have to charge one battery once a week (or even less frequently) with one recharger. This eliminates the clutter of different battery sizes and different rechargers. Second, you can purchase the battery locally rather than having to haul it into the field with the rest of your equipment. And third, you can purchase the battery charger itself locally, which means that there are no power conversion issues surrounding it.

Getting the power from the 12-volt battery to your equipment usually involves some conversion issues, however. All batteries output DC current, which is why they have positive and negative poles. As we explained previously, most of your equipment works with DC current, which is why most power adapters have a rectifier to convert the AC current in the wall outlet to DC. When connecting directly to a battery, you eliminate the need for the rectifier, but you still need to adjust the voltage to the proper level. There are two ways to do this.

The first method is to purchase special power adapters that do the conversion automatically. As mentioned previously, these usually have a male plug designed to go into a cigarette lighter, though some may have alligator clips that you attach directly to the battery. The second method is to convert the 12-volt DC current back to 110 or 220 AC current, with a device known as an inverter. Then you simply plug in your devices with their original AC power adapters. While a little inefficient, this is the best solution when you generate your own power. For example, before electric lines were strung into the desert at Abydos, Egypt, the excavation there used a solar panel attached to a series of large truck batteries. These batteries provided power during the day for one desktop computer, several laptop computers, and many lights. At night they were supplemented with a gasoline generator.

When connecting either a power adapter or an inverter to the battery with alligator clips, you must be sure to match the polarity—that is, to attach the positive clip (usually marked in red or with a + sign) to the positive pole of the battery and the negative clip (usually marked in black or with a – sign) to the negative pole. Reversing these can destroy the equipment. If your power adapters have the cigarette lighter plug, you should buy a simple adapter, which consists of a pair of alligator clips at one end and a female cigarette lighter fitting at the other. These can be purchased at most automotive, camping, or truck supply stores.

PACKING FOR THE FIELD

Whether the field is a 30-minute drive away or a plane flight halfway around the world, it is extremely important to plan appropriately when packing computer gear. It is surprisingly easy to leave behind a $15 cable or cable adapter whose absence brings the whole system to a crashing halt. A common mistake, for instance, is to arrive in the field only to discover that the cable that links the data collector and the total station is still connected to the back of the desktop computer back in the laboratory where it was used to transfer data from the data collector to the desktop. Thus, checklists are an excellent idea. List *every* piece of equipment, all the way down to cable connectors and spare AA batteries.

Also, when the successful completion of a project depends on the hardware and software working correctly, take at least one backup of every piece of equipment and program possible. It is, of course, extremely frustrating to lose time and to put the project at risk due to a blown fuse in a total station or to a fried battery charger. Cables are particularly vulnerable in the field, so two backups may be a good idea. Take the original disks for all of your software including the operating system for each computer. You can pack software CDs into travel packs typically used for music CDs, but do not forget to make a note of the serial numbers that are often pasted on the outside of the original CD case. Also take recovery floppy disks, and be sure you know how to use them. And install the latest virus protection software on all of your machines.

On overnight trips, plan for backups of your data in the field. Sometimes this is as easy as taking a box of floppy disks to save raw data files each evening. Remember, however, that floppy disks have a high failure rate, particularly under typical field conditions, so you should never trust your data to a single floppy disk. Always make backups on two separate disks each night. Backing up large databases and digital images that will not fit on a floppy disk is more problematic. One solution that can buy some time is compression. There are a number of compression programs that can make files substantially smaller. Databases are particularly easy to compress, and it is not unusual to compress a database to one-tenth its original size. Another solution is to take two laptop computers and to transfer files from one to the other over a cable each night. Software exists that makes this process fairly quick and painless. Using a laptop simply for backups may sound expensive and inefficient, but remember that if a laptop is required for the project then having a backup laptop is a good idea anyway. In fact, we have found that having two identical laptops means that, as parts fail in one, they can be swapped into the other to keep at least one laptop running at all times. Finally there are a number of mass storage devices that can be attached to a computer. These include CD-ROM burners, tape drives, and large-capacity external floppy/hard disks such as Zip drives. These units are not very expensive and are typically quite portable (though power can be an issue).

When making backups, remember to periodically test them by trying to recover a file. It is easy to lull yourself into thinking that you have a safe backup system, only to discover that it was not working when you most needed it to work—that is, when you have actually lost a file and are trying to recover it. Try recovering files before you need them, and if your backup software has an automatic verify option, use it.

Here are some other things to think about regarding the security of your data in the field. Never pack the computers and the backups in the same suitcase, carry-on, or even vehicle if at all possible. Having two laptops with backup copies and a stack of CDs with more backups is not sufficient protection if all these items are packed into the trunk of the same car. Sometimes it can be difficult to physically separate copies of your data, particularly if you are traveling in a group. If you are on a long-term project overseas and have a local contact, leave behind a backup copy of the data. If you are worried about leaving your data with someone, simply mail a copy of the data to yourself.

All of this advice applies as well to the paper notes and data produced during an excavation. It is amazing how often, on excavations costing ten or even hundreds of thousands of dollars to conduct and producing priceless, irreplaceable data, teams still have only a single copy of the field notebooks even decades after the excavations were completed. Given the low cost of photocopying and its pervasiveness even in some of the most remote parts of the world, there is seldom a good reason to leave the field with only one copy of the notes. Photocopies have the added benefit of being immediately amenable to simple document scanning.

While all of this talk of backups might seem excessive, it really is not when you consider how much the data cost to produce in the first place. Of course, cost and the extra bulk can be limiting factors in creating backups. It is difficult to have a replacement total station, for instance, but if having a total station is essential to the project, it is worth considering purchasing even an older, second-hand machine.

SUMMARY

Supplying power to the array of electronic devices used in modern excavations can be a significant problem. The fact is that most excavations take place far from the nearest wall outlet, and for international projects even the local power that is available must be converted. While most of us never worry about such things as AC vs. DC, amps, and volts and watts, or rectifiers and inverters, these are important considerations in planning a successful field season.

Equally important to your planning is anticipating having to replace certain pieces of equipment, because of either loss or failure. The more remote your project location, the more important it is to have backups of every essential item. Of course, this adds costs to your initial project budget, but it will save you a considerable amount in downtime.

Finally, always remember to be overly cautious in terms of backing up your data.

Glossary

accuracy A measure of how closely a piece of data represents the true, standard, or actual value. Accuracy will be measured differently depending on the type of data (e.g., length of an object, image of an artifact, map of a site). See also *precision*.

aggregate provenience Artifacts from an excavation area or stratigraphic level that are grouped together and assigned a single provenience.

ASCII American Standard Code of Information Interchange, a standard list for representing characters with numeric codes. An ASCII file is also sometimes called a text file or is said to be written in plain text. ASCII codes are used for sorting databases as well. For a complete listing of the ASCII codes, see the table in Chapter 1.

azimuth The horizontal direction of a point, measured clockwise in degrees of rotation from the positive Y-axis (north)—for example, degrees on a compass.

backsight The angle from a survey point back to the survey instrument (total station). Trigonometrically, it is the complement of the foresight. This term is also sometimes used to refer to a sighting from the total station back to a known point or datum.

bit Short for binary integer, the smallest unit of information a computer records. A bit is a binary unit that stores either a 0 or a 1. There are 8 bits in a byte.

bitmap Synomym for raster image. Also a specific raster image file type called BMP that is supported by Windows systems.

byte 8 bits. A single character from the ASCII chart or an integer between 0 and 255 can be stored in a byte. Bytes are the basic unit used when describing storage capacities on computers.

CAD and CADD Computer-aided design and computer-aided design and drafting. Typically used in archaeology to work with maps of archaeological features or landscapes.

Cartesian coordinate or grid system An XYZ grid system. In a Cartesian grid, the X-, Y-, and Z-axes are perpendicular to one another. Typically an angle of 0.0000 degrees is given to the positive Y-axis, 90.0000 degrees to the positive X-axis, 180.0000 degrees to the negative Y-axis, and −270.0000 to the negative X-axis. The Cartesian system is planar in contrast to radial systems such as latitude/longitude.

closing A survey term for the process of surveying back to an original datum after having traversed an area with other newly established datums.

Surveying back to an original datum allows survey errors to be identified.

CMYK   Cyan, magenta, yellow, and black, one of many models for representing colors. This model is most commonly used for printing images since printers use inks of these varieties to produce the full spectrum of colors.

color depth   The number of distinct colors that can be represented by a particular piece of computer hardware or software. Color depth is also sometimes called bit depth since the number of colors is directly related to the number of bits used to store the color value.

complement   The angle 180 degrees opposite the original angle. You can calculate the complement by either adding or subtracting 180 degrees from an angle. Whether you add or subtract matters only to obtain a result between 0 and 360 degrees.

compression   Generally, techniques used to reduce the amount of space (bytes) required to store information. Compression techniques fall into two broad categories: lossless and lossy. The former reduce the storage space without altering the information being stored; the latter alter the information in order to achieve greater levels of compression.

contour   A line across a map that shows a constant elevation.

coordinate system   A system for expressing the location of a point. Generally there are planar coordinate systems (such as the Cartesian system) and radial systems (such as latitude/longitude).

database   Either a single table containing a collection of records or a collection of tables, indexes, reports, and so on.

datum   In survey and mapping, a point on the ground with known X, Y, and Z coordinates. In GIS, the term is synonymous with geodetic datum, a three-dimensional (ellipsoidal) model used to represent the shape of the earth and associated with a particular coordinate system.

DBMS   Database Management System.

DEM   A digital elevation model, a data exchange format developed by the United States Geological Survey for geographical and topographical data. Basically a DEM is a raster image wherein each pixel contains not a color but an elevation. A DEM is normally georeferenced, meaning that the spatial coordinates of each pixel are also known.

differential   correction   A method whereby more accurate GPS measurements can be made. This method involves a base station positioned over a known point that measures the error in each GPS reading. This error factor is then used to correct GPS readings taken by mobile receivers in the vicinity of the base station.

digitize   The process of converting information into a computer or digital format. For instance, scanning an image is digitizing, as is tracing a line on a map with a digitizing tablet.

DLG   A digital line graph, a vector type of digital map developed by the United States Geological Survey.

DOP   Dilution of precision, a measure of the configuration of GPS satellites that quantifies the accuracy of an associated GPS measurement.

DPI   Dots per inch, a common way to measure the resolution or quality of a scanned or printed image.

DTM   Digital terrain model, a method of transforming elevation data into a contoured surface or a three-dimensional display.

easting The X-axis in a Cartesian coordinate system. Though east is the positive X-axis, an easting describes both negative and positive values on the X-axis. See also *northing* and *elevation*.

EDM Electronic distance meter, the laser component of a total station that measures the distance from the total station to a reflective prism. Some older-model total stations have an EDM mounted on them as a separate component, but on most new total stations the EDM is built into the instrument.

elevation The Z value in an XYZ coordinate system. On a global scale, elevation usually is measured relative to mean average sea level. On the local scale (e.g., at a site), elevations are usually recorded from some fixed, arbitrarily assigned point.

field A database record in which each field stores information. In most databases, fields have a specified length that cannot change from record to record. All records in particular databases or tables contain the same set of fields.

flat-file database A database that contains only one table that holds all observations. A flat-file database is the opposite of a relational database wherein data are divided into multiple tables and then linked back together.

foresight The angle from the total station to a point. The foresight is the complement of the backsight.

geocoding The process of assigning map coordinates to database records or of otherwise linking map features to database records. Geocoding is integral to GIS analysis.

gigabyte 1024 megabytes.

GIS Geographic Information System, which relates and integrates spatial and nonspatial information. A GIS includes tools to enter, manipulate, query, analyze, and display spatial information.

GPS Global Positioning System, based on a set of 24 satellites that constantly send signals toward the earth that can be used by a GPS unit to calculate its position.

hydrography A GIS layer showing water-related features such as streams, rivers, and lakes.

hyperlink An element in a computer file or display that links to another location in that file or to a completely different file.

hypsography A GIS layer showing elevations as contour lines.

index A component of a database system. Index files contain sorted lists of particular fields in a database table. Information in the table can be located much more quickly using a sorted list. Indexes are also important for linking two tables together in a relational database system.

keyboard wedge A device that translates input from an instrument (such as calipers or scales) into keystrokes so that they can be fed into the keyboard port.

kilobyte 1024 bytes.

layer A common term in GIS to describe a map of a single feature like topography, water resources, or archaeological sites. Synonyms for this term include coverage and theme.

line At least two connected points or nodes on a vector map. Nodes, lines, and polygons are the three elements that make up vector maps. See also *node* and *polygon*.

look-up table   A table containing a list of unique and valid entries for a particular variable or field. A list of valid zip codes in the United States, for instance, might serve as a look-up table for a data entry form that includes addresses.

mask angle   The angle from the horizon below which the signal sent from GPS satellites becomes unreliable. All satellites below the mask angle are ignored by GPS receivers when calculating a position. The mask angle can be modified, but a value between 15 and 20 degrees is normal.

master index   See *primary key*.

megabyte   1024 kilobytes.

NEZ   Northing, easting, and elevation.

node   A single point in a vector map. Nodes, lines, and polygons are the three elements that make up vector maps. See also *line* and *polygon*.

northing   The Y-axis in a Cartesian coordinate system. Though north is the positive Y-axis, a northing describes both negative and positive values on the Y-axis.

null   Null values in a database field indicate that no value has ever been set for that field.

null modem   Sometimes used when connecting cables to one another. Null modems work by reversing or flipping the receiving and sending wires, which aligns the receiving wires of one cable to the sending wires of another, and vice versa.

OCR   Optical character recognition, the process of converting a raster image of a text document into actual text that can then be edited in a word processor.

parallel communications   The transfer of several bits simultaneously (as opposed to serial communications).

pixel   Short for picture element, the smallest unit in a computer screen, digital image, or bit-mapped graphic. A digital raster image, for instance, might have a size or resolution of 800×600 pixels.

platform   A combination of an operating system and a type of computer. A PC running Windows 98, for instance, is a platform. All versions of Windows can also be lumped together and referred to collectively as the Windows platform.

point provenience   The process of assigning a specific provenience to each excavated object. See also *aggregate provenience*.

polygon   A series of connected points or nodes that are closed (the first point and the last point are the same point). Nodes, lines, and polygons are the three elements that make up vector maps. See also *node* and *line*.

precision   Generally, refers to the exactness of a measurement or observation. In computer terminology, precision refers to the number of significant digits that can be stored for a number. A single-precision number, for instance, is not as precise as a double-precision number, meaning that the latter can hold more significant digits.

primary key   A key is a field or set of fields in an index used to find and sort records in a database table. The primary key differs from other keys in that each record must have a unique value. In an archaeological database, the primary key is usually the artifact's ID number. The primary key is also sometimes called the master key, and it is typically the key used in a relational database system to link one table to another.

prism offset   The distance between the point as measured by the total station and the actual location of the prism.

Different prisms and prism mounts will have different prism offsets.

projection   A geometric model that transforms the locations of features on the earth's curved surface to corresponding locations on a two-dimensional surface.

PSD   Primary site datum.

query   A database term for finding a set of records that match a particular set of criteria.

radian   A way of expressing angles. In this system, a circle has 2*Pi radians (or 360 degrees). A degree is equal to approximately 0.017453292 radian (or 2*Pi/360).

raster or raster image   In a raster representation of data, a rectangular grid of pixels or cells each of which contains a value. In a raster photographic image, each pixel contains a representation of the color of the photograph at that location. In a DEM raster image, each cell contains an elevation.

raster to vector   The process of converting a raster image, consisting of pixels each with its own value, to a vector image, consisting of points, lines, and polygons or of mathematical formulas.

record   In a database system, a set of fields each of which contains information about a particular item. A database table is composed of records.

relational database   Refers to the method of linking database tables to one another using common fields such as artifact ID. There are several different ways in which tables can be linked to one another: one-to-one, one-to-many, and many-to-one. These different ways specify, in effect, how many records of one table can be linked to how many records of another.

relations   In a database system, specifies the manner in which records for a particular item from one table can be linked to records in another table for that same item. See also *relational database.*

resolution   Generally, used to describe the quality of images from graphics output devices (e.g., computer monitors, video cards, and printers), and graphics input devices (e.g., scanners). On printers and scanners, resolution is typically represented as dots per inch (DPI). Otherwise, resolution is expressed as the number of horizontal and vertical pixels. Thus, a computer monitor might have a resolution of 1024 × 768 (horizontal by vertical) pixels.

RGB   Red, green, blue, one of several models used to represent colors. Combinations of red, green, and blue are used to produce the full range of colors. Computer monitors use RGB, so it is a common format for displaying images. For printing images, CMYK is more common.

serial communcations   At its most basic level, any method that transmits data one bit at a time (as opposed to parallel communications).

SPCS   State Plane Coordinate System, a planar coordinate system (e.g., UTM) that is typically based on either the universal Mercator or Lambert conformal conic projections. SPCS locations are typically listed in feet.

SQL   Structured Query Language, a set of rules and terms used to write database queries. SQL is increasingly the standard format for database queries; however, there are some differences in (or dialects of) SQL.

strings   A term most often used in computer programming to mean a collection or string of characters.

table   A collection of records that all share the same set of fields. Table is sometimes synonymous with database. Other times multiple tables can be grouped together into one database.

terabyte   1024 gigabytes.

thematic maps   Another word for a map built of layers in a GIS. See also *layer.*

theodolite   A survey instrument that can record horizontal and vertical angles. See also *total station.*

total station   A theodolite with an EDM that can automatically measure and compute the three-dimensional, Cartesian coordinates of a measured point.

tribrach   The portion at the base of a theodolite or total station that supports the instrument. Typically the tribrach will contain the leveling screws, a leveling bubble, and an optical plumb. The instrument can be separated from the tribrach as well.

UPS   Uninterruptible power supply. A UPS contains a battery that can continue providing power to a device even after the main power source has failed.

USB   Universal serial bus, one of several recently developed systems for transferring information between computer devices. These systems address a number of the limitations in standard serial communications.

USGS   United States Geological Survey, the principal U.S. mapping agency.

UTM   Universal transverse Mercator, a coordinate system based on the transverse Mercator projection. UTM divides the world into a set of metric grid cells.

vector   A line segment. Vector files use points, lines, and polygons to represent features.

Index